LIFE AND TRAVEL IN INDIA

LIFE AND TRAVEL IN INDIA

BEING RECOLLECTIONS OF A JOURNEY
BEFORE THE DAYS OF RAILROADS

ANNA HARRIETTE LEONOWENS

GYAN

Published by

GYAN

Gyan Publishing House
5, Ansari Road
Daryaganj, New Delhi-110002
Phone: 011-47034999, 9811692060
E-mail: books@gyanbooks.com

Distribution Network
gyanbooks.com
India, USA, Canada, UK, Australia, France

ISBN: 978-81-212-8580-3 (PB)
First Published, 1884

2nd Impression 2023

Printed at: Gyan Press, Delhi.

LIFE AND TRAVEL IN INDIA
Author: Anna Harriette Leonowens

THE GATE AND GARDEN OF SECUNDRA—TAJ.

LIFE AND TRAVEL

IN

INDIA:

BEING

RECOLLECTIONS OF A JOURNEY BEFORE THE DAYS OF RAILROADS.

BY

ANNA HARRIETTE LEONOWENS,

AUTHOR OF "THE ENGLISH GOVERNESS AT THE SIAMESE COURT"
AND "THE ROMANCE OF THE HAREEM."

PHILADELPHIA:
PORTER & COATES.
LONDON:
TRÜBNER & CO.

THIS LITTLE VOLUME OF TRAVELS

Is Inscribed to

MR. AND MRS. WILLIAM W. JUSTICE,

IN

GRATEFUL APPRECIATION OF THEIR FRIENDSHIP,

BY

THE AUTHOR.

CONTENTS.

CHAPTER VI.

CHAPTER VII.

CHAPTER VIII.

CHAPTER IX.

CHAPTER X.

CHAPTER XI.

CHAPTER XII.

CHAPTER XIII.

CHAPTER XIV.

PREFACE.

In the following pages, gathered from voluminous notes of early travel, I have tried to give a faithful account of life in India, as well as of the sights and scenes visited by me, with my husband, before the days of railroad travel.

It is well known that the introduction of the railroad into India has in no sense affected the life of the people, and has only very slightly modified the general appearance of the country. India is still what it was in the Vèdic period, a land of peasant classes; she still invokes, as did the ancient Aryans in the Rig Vèda, the "Khetra-pati," or the divinity of the soil, for blessings on the land. The Hindoo to-day lives, as did his forefathers, close to the heart of Nature, deifying the mountains, streams, woods, and lakes, while the sun, moon, stars, fire, water, earth, air, sky, and corn are his highest deities. The most beautiful personification in the Ramâyânâ of womanly grace and virtue is called *Sita*, "a furrow," showing how deep was the national reverence paid to the plough; and to this day at the *Rathsaptimi*, the day on which the new sun is supposed to mount his heavenly chariot, a feast is observed in honor of the sun, and the ryots on this occasion decorate with flowers and paint their ploughs, and worship them as the saviors of the land.

I do not, however, mean to say that India has made no progress whatever in all these years—her imaginative and glorious youth has no doubt been succeeded by the calm reason of mature age—but this transition has been gradual and progressive rather than fitful and sudden.

The transfer of India by the East India Company to the British Crown, and the recent laws for the protection of the ryot—or more properly the *raiyat*, a leaser of land held in perpetuity—against the oppressions of the zemindars, or governmental landlords, with the right of underletting the land, have to an extraordinary degree awakened the inborn desire of the Hindoo to become possessor of the soil and to return to his hereditary occupation of agriculture. To these may be added the security which England has conferred upon India, now that she is no longer disturbed by frequent wars, which desolated the land, and every now and then forced the people to abandon their villages and fly to the jungles and mountains for safety, under the Afghans, Mohguls, Mahrattas, and other predatory chiefs. Among the lasting benefits to India it may be mentioned that sutteeism, infanticide, self-immolation to the idols, Thuggism, and slavery have all been partially, if not quite, abolished by the strong arm of the law. Railroads have been built, the country has been opened, schools established, civil service appointments thrown open to the natives and Europeans alike, good roads made, canals and huge reservoirs for water excavated, ancient water-courses reopened, giving an impetus to private enterprise and industry in every direction. All these happy changes have been the result of the more liberal policy of England toward India since the days of the terrible mutiny of 1857; and it may fairly be hoped that British India has before her as glorious a future as her brilliant youth and maturity have foreshadowed for her.

A. H. L.

SUNNYSIDE, Halifax, Nova Scotia,
August 7, 1884.

LIFE AND TRAVEL IN INDIA.

CHAPTER I.

The Island of Bambâ Dèvi.—Sights and Scenes round about Bombay.

IN that most delightful of all Indian months, the cool month of November, with the distant booming of a great gun that announced its arrival, the steamer from Aden came to anchor in the harbor of Bombay, bringing me among its many passengers. Here I was in this strange land, a young girl fresh from school, now entering upon a life so different, one which I was to lead through a long term of years.

The sun shone through the mists and haze of the early dawn, and I could see from my cabin window, with a sense of mingled wonder and curiosity, the great stone quays and the long flights of stone steps which led to the beautiful island of Bombay, lying there like a gem in the water, and of which I knew nothing whatever, save that it was once the marriage-dowry of a queen of England.

According to some authorities, it takes its name from two Portuguese words, "Buon Bahia," Good Bay; but in reality it has a still more ancient origin, being called after a very beautiful Hindoo queen, afterward deified as Bambâ Dèvi, who long before the days of Alexander the Great was the presiding genius of the land. She was worshipped as "Mahimâ Dèvi," or the Great Mother, in one of the oldest and largest Hindoo temples which formerly stood in the great plain now called the Esplanade. It was pulled down about a hundred years ago, and rebuilt near the Bhendee Bazaar, and is to this day called by her name and set apart to her peculiar service.

The longer I looked on that bay, and on those ancient islands with their towers and spires, both pagan and Christian, gleaming in the pure morning sunlight, the more I felt that it was one of the loveliest scenes in the world and one of the best worth admiring.

The harbor is not only one of the safest known to navigators from all parts of the world, affording in its hollow rock-bound cup entire shelter from sudden storms to vessels of all burthens, large and small crafts of every imaginable size and color, but it is in itself a bit of landlocked water unrivalled in picturesqueness, furnishing a variety of beautiful views at every point, and, one might almost say, at every passing moment.

Its peculiar interest, however, depends much on the season of the year, the brightness of the lights, the softness of the shadows, and the picturesque character of the numberless native boats, which, with their well-filled lateen sails, skim like white sea-birds on the surface of the waters.

The islands of Salsette, Elephanta, and Versovah, abounding in luxuriant vegetation, rise like huge green temples out of the bay. A great part of its beauty, however, is derived from the singularly shaped hills that are found in its vicinity. Old as the world, they appear to have gone through the hands of some gigantic architect—some so exquisitely rounded, some regularly terraced, and others, again, sharply pointed, not unlike spires. Lifting themselves proudly above the broad glittering sea that bathes their palm-fringed base, they help to make the scenery distinct from that of any other bay in the world. Then, beyond question, there is nothing to equal in grace and beauty the palm forest. The cocoanut, the sago, the betel, the date, the wild plantain, and the palmyra, all cluster in such profusion here and there along the seashore that the whole seems too beautiful to be real, and you half expect to see the island melt away like a dream before you.

While I look on from the cabin window things take clearer shape and form. Far away is the dim outline of the mighty Ghauts, towering amid soft fleecy-white clouds, and extending farther than the eye can reach in the purple distance. The striking views of the adjoining mainland, with ruins innumerable of chapels, convents, and monasteries erected by the Portuguese conquerors, all covered with a rich tangle of tropical foliage; the strange shapes of pagan temples, each in its own peculiar style of architecture, Hindoo, Parsee, Jain, and Mohammedan; the noble remains of the old Mahratta* forts and castles, which in former days were the habitations of the famous Rajpoots, with a long line of native and European palaces, —gradually unfold themselves under the golden haze of an Indian atmosphere.

One sees in no other part of the world just such an assemblage as the passengers on an Indian-bound steamer. In the vessel that took me to Bombay the most touching object to my mind was a young married woman, who was looking anxiously out for her husband, a missionary in whose labors she was now about to share for the first time. He was weak, haggard, and spiritless, worn out, no doubt,

* The name Mahratta is applied to all the Indo-European races who dwell in that portion of India extending from the Arabian Sea on the west to the Satpura Mountains in the north, to which in ancient times was given the Sanskrit name of Maharashtra, or "the good country." The Mahrattas are Hindoos, divided like them into four castes—the Brahmans, priests and professors; the Kumbis, cultivators of the soil; the Rajpoots, or warriors; and the Sudras, or menials. The Mahratta Brahmans are remarkable for the high physical, intellectual, and moral qualities of that caste. Their language, a fine sonorous and flexible tongue, is a dialect of the Sanskrit, called Mahratti.

by his combined efforts to acquire a foreign language, convince an obstinate people, and bear the enervating influence of a hot, muggy climate; all of which was enough to break down the stoutest of frames and the most hopeful of spirits that England has ever produced. A number of officers, civil and military, some in light-brown coats of China silk and wide-brimmed straw hats, others in frogged blue frocks and military caps, were seen pressing through the crowd. A young cadet just out rushed into the open arms of a handsome officer, like himself, but older by twenty or thirty years. The deck was being fast cleared of its eager crowd. Everywhere the passengers were separating amid almost sad adieux, enlivened only by the oft-repeated promises to write to each other regularly—promises which are never fulfilled. On the great continent of Asia all nations meet and hail each other as friends, only to part, perhaps never to meet again, as vessels do at sea. But we were all sincere enough at the moment, which is all that can be expected from travellers scattering over the vast unknown land of India. I remember I was very greatly troubled because I was about to part from a gentle, blue-eyed young friend, a frank, bright, innocent young Scotch girl, who had become very dear to me during the most tedious and sultry part of our voyage from Aden to Bombay.

We were thrown a good deal together, and were almost of the same age. One day, while passing through the Red Sea, we exchanged vows of eternal friendship. There was on board a sprightly young officer, Ensign W——, to whom she was already secretly betrothed. Why secretly she would not confide to me, or perhaps explain even to herself, for every one on the vessel knew it, and of her naturally tender and loving disposition, as well as of her peculiarly lonely position on board, being sent out under the charge of the captain. I only know that I shared her happiness and her anxiety, for she would have to break the news almost immediately to her father, whom she was expecting momentarily on board. She informed me that her father was a widower—that she had come out to India expressly to keep house for him in some remote inland province somewhere in Guzerat.

At last her father appeared on board, a fat, sun-burnt, frowzy-looking man, and inquired from the captain as to which was his daughter, in order to assert his ownership over her. Instead of rushing to greet a father, she shrank back and nervously clutched my arm; and it was not strange. She had not seen him for many years; in the mean time her mother had died, her little brothers and sisters had all died in their infancy; she alone had survived, and had been sent home to Scotland, where she had been educated by an aunt. Here, then, she was alone in the presence of an almost entire stranger, although he was her father; and this is not an isolated case, but the fate of the thousands of European children who are born in India.

No blood-relationship avails anything in such cases. The mysterious sanctities of a young girl's nature, be they more or less profound, interpose themselves as barriers between father and daughter at the best of times and under the happiest of circumstances. Those dim nooks and corners of her budding sentiment can only be reached by a mother, so justly called the mediator in the most ancient language of the heart.

Years after I learned that my young Scotch friend had married Ensign W——, the young officer to whom she had engaged herself on her voyage out to India. But in one short year after her sweet blue eyes were closed for ever on this world. She died in giving birth to a daughter, who sleeps side by side with her young mother in the quiet little European burial-ground at Deesa, a British station on the confines of the great province of Guzerat.

Very little was known about India until Alexander the Great led his conquering army across the Punjaub (or, more properly, "Panch jeeb," or five tongues, from the five rivers that water this portion of Northern India) to the banks of the Hydaspes and the Hyphasis. The armies of Alexander had hitherto visited no country which was so fertile, populous, and abounding in the most valuable productions of nature and art as that portion of India through which they marched. Fortunately for the Greeks, Alexander had with him a few men who were admirably qualified to observe and describe the country. At the mouth of the Indus the army and fleet of Alexander parted company. The troops proceeded by land. Nearchus took charge of the ships, sailed down the Indus, and from its mouth, round the southern coast of Asia, to the mouth of the Euphrates. The results of his observations during the voyage were taken down and preserved. This expedition, undertaken 325 B. C., furnished a vast amount of information in regard to India, its extent and wonderful resources. Rome and most of her prosperous and civilized provinces were also very familiar with the silks, brocades, fine muslins, gems of great value, spices, and many other manufactures and products of the remote East. The Latin name of rice, *Oryza sativa*, is derived from the country, Orissa, whence the Romans first obtained it. During the so-called Dark Ages which followed the subversion of their Western Empire the trade with India was greatly diminished, though it never entirely ceased in parts of Europe, especially as some of the productions of the East had been consecrated to the services of the Roman Catholic ritual, and have ever since continued in request with the Christian churches of Greece and Rome. Even in the remote island of Great Britain, and in the semi-barbaric Saxon period, some of the precious spices and scented woods of India had been carefully treasured by the Venerable Bede and his co-laborers in their bleak northern monastery at Jarrow. In fact, at the very dawn of European civilization, under the good and wise Alfred the Great, English missionaries are said to have found their way to the coast of Malabar.

The great seat of Eastern trade was, down to the eleventh century, the city of Constantine the Great. Amalfi, Venice, and many other enterprising Italian republics acquired about this time great commercial importance, owing to their Eastern trade, which they extended to Egypt and the Persian Gulf.

In the twelfth and thirteenth centuries some of the more adventurous Italians found their way to various parts of Hindostan. One of these, the famous Marco Paulo, has given to the world much curious information about the regions which lie between the Himalaya Mountains, the Indian Ocean, and the numerous islands bordering on the Celestial Empire and on India proper.

The first European traveller who has given us an account of the country near the island of Bombay was an Italian friar named Odoricus, who passed nearly a month at Tana—or more properly Thanah—where four of his family fell victims to the intolerant spirit of the natives, and suffered martyrdom. His narrative was published in Latin in 1330 A. D. by William de Solanga. The first Englishman who visited the western coast of India was Thomas Stephens, of New College, Oxford. He reached Goa in October, 1579, and in the year 1608 Pryard de Laval mentions him at the time as rector of a college at Salsette.

It was during the early career of the famous Zehir-ed

Deen Mohammed, a descendant of the renowned Genghis-khân, and the founder of the so-called Mohgul dynasty, better known by his common name of Bâber, or "the Tiger," that the Portuguese, whose maritime discoveries were beginning to produce an important revolution in the commercial world, succeeded in accomplishing their long-desired object of finding a passage by the Cape of Good Hope to India. In the year 1498, just ten months and two days after leaving the port of Lisbon, Vasco da Gama landed on the coast of Malabar at Calicut, or more properly Kale Khoda, "City of the Black Goddess." Calicut was at that period not only a very ancient seaport, but an extensive territory, which, stretching along the western coast of Southern India, reached from Bombay and the adjacent islands to Cape Comorin. It was, at an early period, so famous for its weaving and dyeing of cotton cloth that its name became identified with the manufactured fabric, whence the name *calico*. The dyeing of cotton cloths seems to have been in practice in India in very remote ages. Pliny as early as the first century mentions in his *Natural History* that there existed in Egypt a wonderful method of dyeing white cloth. It is now generally admitted that this ingenious art originated in India, and from that country found its way into Egypt. It was not till toward the middle of the seventeenth century that calico-printing was introduced into Europe. A knowledge of the art was acquired by some of the servants in the service of the Dutch East India Company, and carried to Holland, whence it was introduced in London in the year 1676.

The town of Calicut, though repeatedly burnt and destroyed by Portuguese and Mohammedan conquerors, still stands, as it has done for many hundreds of years, on the seashore, in a somewhat low and exposed position, possessing neither a river nor any harbor within several miles of it, so that ships are compelled to cast anchor five or six miles from the landing-place, almost in mid-ocean. Its want of a convenient harbor does not seem to have detracted from its commercial importance. At the very beginning of the Eastern trade, when Constantinople was attracting to itself all the commerce of the East, Calicut was visited by vessels from Asia Minor, Egypt, and Arabia. It was so well known to the Arabians that in the seventeenth century a fanatical sect of Mohammedans named Moplahs immigrated to Calicut, and entered with great success into the commercial life of the city, and occupy in it, even to this day, a most important place, carrying on a very profitable trade between Calicut, the Red Sea, the Persian Gulf, and various parts of India, its chief exports being rice, cocoanut, ginger, cardamoms, and sandal- and teak-wood. At the time of the landing of the Portuguese, Calicut is described as a fine city, with numerous magnificent buildings, among which a Brahmanical temple and college are especially mentioned, so remarkable were they for their size and architectural adornments.

It would be out of place to enter into particulars of the long struggle that ensued, or the disgraceful acts of treachery and cruelty that attended the conquests of the Portuguese. It will suffice to say that in a very few years they were firmly established in the south of India. Having possessed themselves of the large maritime city of Goa, they formed a regular government, headed by a viceroy appointed by the king of Portugal. They soon turned the trade of Hindostan and the Deccan into new and more profitable channels, thus depriving the Venetians, Genoese, and many other nations of all the advantages derived from their long-established European commerce between the Persian Gulf, the Red Sea, Egypt, and the Mediterranean

Sea. From that time the Italians began to decline in wealth, influence, and prosperity until the close of the sixteenth and in the beginning of the seventeenth century, when the English, Dutch, and French, sailing round by the Cape of Good Hope, began to appear upon the scene. No sooner was this accomplished than the Portuguese, who had monopolized the commerce with Europe during the sixteenth century, lost (almost as rapidly as they had acquired it) their immense influence in the East.

In 1585, Thomas Cavendish, one of the boldest and most adventurous navigators in the reign of Queen Elizabeth, had accomplished successfully a two years' voyage round the world. Among other places, he had visited and explored the spice islands called the Moluccas, but his discoveries resulted in no permanent benefit to the British traders. In the year following an English expedition consisting of three vessels, under the command of Captain Raymond, was sent out to India, but its object was rather more warlike than commercial, as it was intended to cruise against the Portuguese. Sickness, shipwreck, and other disasters overtook the vessels; Captain Raymond, one of the most spirited men of his time, was lost without even having seen the Eldorado of his dreams, and Captain Lancaster, his second in command, returned home a sad and almost ruined man. Francis Drake, afterward knighted by Queen Elizabeth for his many remarkable exploits at sea, succeeded in capturing five Portuguese vessels laden with the rich products of India. These, with the successes of the Levant Company and the accumulating information obtained from private sources, contributed to keep alive the excitement and to increase to an inordinate degree the desire of English traders and merchants for a more immediate participation in the Eastern commerce. Nevertheless, the ambition and jealousy of the British merchants were not fully aroused until they heard that the Dutch in 1595 had fitted out and despatched four ships to trade with India.

Then the British merchants immediately set to work. A fund was raised by subscriptions of a number of individuals amounting to £30,133 6*s.* 8*d.*, a company was formed, and a committee of fifteen able men was elected to manage it, which was the origin of the "East India Company." On the 31st of December, 1600, just two hundred and eighty-four years ago, a royal charter of privileges was granted, conditionally for fifteen years, to the company. By means of this charter, and furnished with letters from Queen Elizabeth to various Eastern rajahs, who were probably unconscious of her existence, a squadron of five ships sailed on the 2d of May, 1601, from Torbay. It was placed under the command of Captain Lancaster, the companion of the unfortunate Raymond. Fortune now appeared to favor the brave Lancaster. The very first place which he and his crews visited was Acheen in the island of Sumatra. Owing to the fact that Northern Sumatra had already been repeatedly visited by European travellers, among whom were Marco Paulo, Friar Odoricus, and Nicolo Conti, Captain Lancaster was remarkably well received by Aladin Shah, the then reigning sovereign; and, to add to his good fortune, while cruising in the Straits of Malacca he succeeded in capturing a large and heavily-laden Portuguese vessel having on board a cargo of fine calicoes, spices, and some of the fine gold for which Acheen was then celebrated. Thus unexpectedly enriched, he sailed away, and, entering the Straits of Angeer, landed at Bantam in the island of Java, where he established an agency—the first germ of the great East India Company's factories—and returned in safety to England in the autumn of the year 1603. For many years following the trading vessels of the East India Company made successful voyages to many of the best-known islands in the Indian Ocean, realizing immense profits, and returning home to enrich the company to such an extent as to excite the jealousy of the British government, which vainly attempted to limit the privileges of the royal charter granted to it by Queen Elizabeth. Not many years after the success of the company was assured by a firman of the great Mohgul emperor, confirming to them certain privileges, and, above all, authorizing their establishment of factories at some of the most important ports of Hindostan.

The Dutch, who had dispossessed the Portuguese of their factory in Amboyna, one of the largest of the spice islands in the Molucca group, now began to regard the English traders with much jealousy. These, only eighteen in number, had established themselves in a defenceless house in town, trusting to the agreements and treaties they had made with the Dutch traders. The Dutch invited them in a friendly manner to pay a visit to their castle, fortified and garrisoned by two hundred men. The unsuspecting English had no sooner entered the castle than they were seized, put to the rack and torture, and ten of the number, holding out firmly to the last, were put to death.

During the memorable conflict between Charles I. and the Parliament nearly all foreign enterprise flagged. Distracted by the great civil war that followed, the East India Company sank into comparative inaction. But no sooner was the great Oliver Cromwell at the head of affairs than he reconfirmed the privileges of the company, and gave every encouragement to its trade; he also compelled the Dutch government to pay the sum of £300,000, together with a grant of one of the smaller spice islands, as some compensation to the descendants of those who suffered in the "Amboyna massacre."

A new charter was granted to the company by Charles II. in 1661, in which, in addition to the old privileges, new and important ones were given to them. They were vested with the right of full civil jurisdiction and military authority over all Europeans in their employment, as well as with the power of making war and concluding peace with the "infidels of India." In 1662, Charles II. married Catharine, princess of Portugal, who brought him a million pounds sterling and gifts of the island of Bombay and the fortress of Tangiers. In 1668, at the request of the company, Charles sold to them for a trifling sum of money the island of Bombay, granting to them shortly after the island of St. Helena, an equally convenient station for their merchantmen; and at length, induced by the defensible character of the island and its convenient and most commodious harbor, the company transferred from Surat to Bombay the seat of their government. Thus the island of Bombay became the presidency over all their settlements, and from that moment numerous Oriental nations were attracted to the island, commerce rapidly increased, the native town began to spread, and the foundation of a great empire in India was securely laid.

In no other part of the world are found so many races and peoples living side by side as in the island of Bombay. In the spacious streets and bazaars one meets Buddhists, Jains, Brahmans, Hindoos, Chinese, Musulmans (both Persians and Arabs), Seedees or Africans, Indo-Portuguese, Indo-Britons, Jews, Armenians, Afghans, Caucasians, Parsees, Americans, and Europeans of all nationalities. The most important of all these are undoubtedly the Parsees. They are as a class the richest, most industrious, and most honorable of all the native populations. They are the most extensive merchants and land-owners in the island; they share largely in foreign speculation both in the European and mercantile houses. They hold to two principles as indispensable to their permanent success and efficiency in trade: First, that every Parsee in any part of the Indian empire shall be subject to the established government, whatever it may be. By this means they diffuse a spirit of obedience and promptitude among their co-religionists, whether in India, Persia, China, or Egypt, and are at once able to secure the co-operation of one and every member of the faith in any emergency that may demand the combined efforts of the entire sect. Secondly, that every Parsee, no matter what the accident of his birth, is the equal of his more prosperous fellow-laborers.

The island of Bombay is separated from the mainland by an arm of the sea, and forms, in conjunction with the adjacent islands of Salsette on the north, Colabah and Old Woman's Island on the south, a magnificent and well-sheltered harbor. Handsome causeways raised above the sea at high water span the narrow channels on the south, and connect Bombay with two of the most picturesque islands I have ever seen. To the north, Bombay is again connected with Salsette by a causeway with a fine arched stone bridge, and yet another causeway has been thrown over the strait, so as to connect the great India Peninsular Railway with the mainland. Thus Bombay and the islands which surround it form a continuous breakwater extending from north to south for several miles. Toward the east lies the celebrated island of Elephanta; just opposite to the mouth of the harbor lies a thickly-wooded island of little elevation, with the exception of two remarkable projections which are shot upward almost perpendicularly from the level of the land, called Great and Little Caranja Hills.

One of our first drives was to the fort and town of Bombay. The latter is situated within the fort, and is almost a mile in length from the Apollo Gate to that of the bazaar, but hardly a quarter of a mile in its broadest part, from the Custom-house across the great Green to what is called Church gate. It is now called Fort George, and with its moats, drawbridges, and gateways is still in tolerably good repair. There are two gateways facing the beautiful harbor, having commodious wharfs and cranes built out from each, with a fine broad stone quay or landing-place for passengers. Passing through these gates, we visited the famous Bombay Castle, a regular quadrangle built of hard stone. In one of the bastions we saw a spacious reservoir for water. The fortifications are sufficiently formidable, and are frequently repaired, if not improved. Dungarree Hill, which commands the town, has now been included within the fort, by which accession the seaward points of the island are rendered extremely strong, the harbor being completely commanded by successive ranges of batteries placed one above the other. The Government House, a showy but a most inconvenient building, the old church, and a spacious Maidan, or Common, are also situated within the fort.

The rise of the tides has been found such as to admit of the construction of docks on a truly magnificent scale. Indeed, the dry-dock of Bombay is said to be unequalled in the East for its immense size and convenience. It has been built with three divisions, each of which is furnished with a pair of strong gates, so that it is capable of receiving three ships-of-the-line at a time. This operation is generally entrusted to Parsees, and executed with great rapidity and skill. These docks have sprung up here since the days when the island passed into the possession of the East India Company. Another remarkable feature of this part of Bombay is the so-called ropewalk, which is said to be equal to any in England (with the single exception of the king's yard at Portsmouth). Here rope cables and every variety of lesser cordage are manufactured in great abundance. The workmen can be seen seated under covered awnings diligently plying their respective occupations—some cleaning the caiah, or cocoanut-husks, others plaiting, and yet again others twisting heavy ropes and cords.

The Bombay dockyard is also worth visiting; it is admirably contrived, and abounds in fine stone warehouses well stocked with timber for building and repairing vessels and ships of all kinds and sizes, with forges, and well-instructed Parsees, who, among other qualifications, are counted the best ship-carpenters to be found in the East. Many of the merchantmen and ships-of-the-line in the service of the late East India Company have been built here from time to time, and are still built, of Malabar and Mylonghee teak-wood, which is much esteemed throughout India. One of the most magnificent teak forests, from which supplies of wood are obtained, lies on the north-western boundaries of the kingdom of Siam; the other on the western side of the Ghauts and all along the mountains lying north and east of the old Portuguese town of Bassein. They are floated down to Bombay by means of the numerous streams which descend from these mountain-ridges.

Another curious feature is the celebrated cotton-press, of which there are a great many in use here—marvellous in themselves, but more striking amid the mountains of cotton piled up waiting to be pressed before transportation to Europe, China, and other parts of the world. Not very far from these one comes upon a square around which cluster most of the European warehouses and the banks, huge blocks of masonry, dark and dismal as the tomb, impregnated with the odors of tea, coffee, spices, and every other known Indian commodity or manufacture.

It was my first initiation to the commerce of the world to visit this spot. Previous to this day I had hardly so much as purchased a ribbon for myself, and could not conceive what trade really meant. But, driving here about ten o'clock one morning, the whole scene dawned upon me with peculiar force. The great square was thronged with a motley crowd of dark- and white-faced foreigners, all eager, jostling, and contending with each amid the confused hubbub of all languages and all manner of dialects. Here were strange specimens of every nationality and every phase of life, from the lordly English and Scotch merchants, the skilful and assiduous Parsees, to the half-nude, wretched-looking fakeers and beggars who haunt this spot in the hope of getting a few pice.*

For six hours these masses of humanity struggle, work, barter, buy and sell, load and unload, and carry on the strangely-exciting warfare, not of flesh and blood, but of pounds, shillings, and pence, straining every nerve each to outdo his neighbor, to enrich himself, at great sacrifice of life, health, and at times even of honor, in the hope of returning to his native land to enjoy the spoils—a hope which, alas! is realized only in rare instances.

But at four o'clock, as if by magic, the eager, bustling, jostling crowd suddenly vanishes; the din and confusion cease. Long lines of carriages and handsome equipages drive up to the great stone warehouses, and dash away with their white-faced occupants. Where is now the commerce of the world? Gone with the powerful, all-grasping white man. A silence profound as the grave succeeds to the rush, noise, and turmoil of the day. In less than half an hour not a human being is to be seen anywhere, save the solitary begrimed watchmen seated here and there in dim nooks and corners, and the armed

* Pieces of money each of the value of one-fourth of a penny.

white-faced sentinels standing grim and silent at their posts.

On this first visit we were the last to quit the scene. Nothing ever made so deep and, I might truly say, so depressing an impression on my mind as the fierce and unnatural activity which pervaded this spot.

A day or two after we drove through the markets or bazaars of the Parsees, or Fire-worshippers, and another and peculiar class of native traders called the Borahs—the two most enterprising of the many different peoples who occupy this island. These markets, nearly three miles in extent, are perhaps the most picturesque in the world, composed entirely of lofty, handsome Oriental houses, with projecting lattice windows and wooden balconies elaborately carved and hung in many places with rich tapestries. The upper stories of the houses are the dwellings of the merchants and their families; the lower portions are given up to stalls, shops, and alcoves where the most delicate fabrics and the most exquisite work of all kinds are manufactured by native artisans—boxes, fans, drinking-cups carved out of cocoanut-shells, with stools, tables, chairs, and other articles of furniture for the homes of European residents, as well as for exportation. Here are made kinkaubs, or cloths of gold; mulmuls, or muslins, of such transparent texture as to be called "running waters;" and many other articles are wrought out here by half-nude, savage-looking men and women with tools of the rudest and most primitive kind. Nearly all the Oriental work done here, though very beautiful and delicate of its kind, is imitative, and it lacks that freedom and diversity so peculiar to European manufacture.

The street that Europeans most visit in this quarter, and the best worth seeing for its unmixed and purely Oriental character, is called the "Bhendee Bazaar." It abounds in the queerest and most picturesque sights—solemn merchants, turbaned and with long flowing robes, seated cross-legged in their dens smoking long hookas; native women, handsomely dressed, in a variety of costumes, and half-nude beggars, who seem to beg for fun or for a wager; cripples, vagabonds; coolies with great heavy burdens on their backs, beneath which head and shoulders have disappeared, and only two bare legs can be seen struggling along amid the crowd; peddlers yelling like fiends; turbaned Mohammedans; Hindoo and Parsee ladies closely veiled, either on foot or in draped carriages drawn by milk-white bullocks instead of horses; indolent loungers sleeping in the shade; dogs yelping and native soldiers crushing through this great crowded aisle of the Bhendee Bazaar. It is not only full of everything Oriental, but everything Occidental, even to the idols so largely manufactured in Europe for the Indian markets—from the costliest gems from the mines of Punnah and Golconda to the commonest English prints; and since the introduction of free trade one can absolutely purchase English goods cheaper in this market than in the cities where they are manufactured.

After visiting Bhendee we came one day upon a most interesting portion of the bazaar, the Arabian horse-markets. Long lines of stables stretch along for some distance, making a noble display of goodly Arabian steeds. These splendid high-bred creatures are greatly esteemed by the native traders, nawabs, and princes, as well as by the rich English merchants, and often bring fabulous prices. It was very pleasant to go through these stables and see the care and attention bestowed upon the horses by the native grooms, who, while washing, feeding, and rubbing them down, talk to them as if they were children. Our Hindoo *scyce*, or groom, while grooming his horse always told him everything that had happened to him during his absence on the previous evening, opening the conversation with, "Kaisah hai paiyarah?—How art thou, beloved?"

Not far off there is a less picturesque but much more densely-crowded market called the "Chine Bazaar." It runs along the filthiest part of the city, and leads to a stone pier devoted to the native population and to the loading and unloading of native craft and vessels. The people who inhabit this part of the city are chiefly Lascars, or native sailors, and foreigners from different parts of the East. On any day and at any hour one may see what seems the entire produce of the East piled on this stone wharf; merchandise and mankind are in great masses here. Every inch of ground is thronged with moving forms, presenting a wild masquerade of extravagant dress and of the most perfect undress. Everywhere there is more filth and dirt than is possible to conceive at first sight; odors of ghee, or clarified butter, and fish in every stage of decomposition, assail you amid all manner of deafening sounds.

On one occasion, when visiting this part of Bombay, I saw the landing of some pilgrims from Mecca—a dirty, ill-looking set of men, but the moment they touched land the crowd was hushed; they walked in file counting their beads through the parted crowds, who almost to a man salâamed in abject reverence to the holy strangers.

I also saw some beautiful girls landed here, and that they were slaves, brought for private sale among the rich natives, I could not doubt. I afterward learned that women were brought here every year, and disposed of privately to fill the hareems of the rich Musulman merchants in spite of British laws. Riding through these bazaars, it has impressed me that whatever Great Britain might do for the improvement of the island of Bambâ Dèvi in the way of governing it, it would take very many centuries before she could destroy its purely Oriental character.

At one time a very curious organization existed in Bombay for upward of thirty years, consisting of a body of forty or more individuals who bound themselves into a sort of secret society, the sole object of which was systematic plunder. This society had in its employment about three hundred men as subordinates, instructed to receive goods stolen from the merchants' ships. The harbor was the chief scene of their secret operations. Here those of the members who were on duty were ordered to distribute themselves at the various wharves and piers, whence boats went off to ships either when loading or unloading. These employés of the secret society either detained the boats' crews in conversation, and thus purloined goods, or hired themselves for a very low sum of money to work with them for the night. In this way they managed to drop into the water or into another and confederate boat some of the goods surreptitiously obtained. The plunder was then conveyed openly to the shore, and sold by auction next morning, without any attempt at concealment, so far as the natives were concerned; and as few Europeans frequented this part of the native town, they had no fear of detection. It is said that the books of this robber society were scrupulously kept, the division of the profits made with strict honesty, and, what is more remarkable still, two shares of the profits were bestowed on charitable institutions among the various tribes and castes of Bombay. It was not until the year 1843 that this secret robber society was detected in some wholesale plunder; the chiefs concerned in it were brought to justice and the whole thing broken up.

The late East India Company, in order to protect the trade of the country against such societies, as well as against the hordes of pirates who have ever since the days of Alexander the Great infested the western coast of India, found it necessary to maintain an armed marine force.

Not far from the extreme point of the Oriental bazaars, so full of mystery, romance, and dirt, is a spot I have often visited, called Colabah—more properly Kaláaba, or Black Water—where the sea is of the deepest blue, and where an entirely different picture is presented to the eye. Bungalows, as the better class of Indian houses are called, with broad, open, and shady verandahs, each with its beautifully kept garden, stretch along this promontory, making a charming scene. These are the residences of some of the wealthiest inhabitants of the island. Bright, airy-looking dwellings, nestling amid the most graceful evergreen foliage, and standing as they do between two bays, they occupy the most beautiful spot in Bombay.

At the extreme end of this promontory are the European barracks, built with reference to the exigencies of the climate and replete with comfort for the British soldiers and their officers. It is really both pleasing and interesting to see that these are well cared for in this foreign land; but the curiosity and charm born in the native parts of the island, and especially in the bazaars, lessen by sure degrees as you see your countrymen quietly and comfortably established in a spot with which they seem so out of harmony in form and color. On the southern extremity of Colabah is the lighthouse, a graceful circular building standing on a desolate rock which stretches far into the sea and commands the entrance to the fort. It rises from the sea-level one hundred and fifty feet, flashing its light to the distance of twenty-one miles. I remember going to the top of it one moonlight night.

We remained there two or three hours, and saw the moon rise higher and higher, silently scattering the deep shadows one by one, revealing the half-hidden beauties of that strange shore; and at length, when she climbed over head and looked down in the full splendor of her light, the mountain-ridges, feathered with wavy palms, the glimmering peaks and spires of the land, were all magnificently pictured in richest and softest colors in the polished mirror of the sea.

The "Maidan," or Plain, is a fine esplanade in front of the fort. Here passing European officers, and those Europeans who are obliged by business or any other circumstance to live within the fort during the cool months, erect bungalows; some of these are remarkably elegant buildings, but wholly unfit to resist the violence of the monsoon. At the moment that the early showers of rain announce the wet season these temporary homes vanish and their place is very soon occupied by a vast sheet of water. The Esplanade serves to separate the European from the native part of the island, the latter being vulgarly called the "Black Town."

Toward the north of the island are scattered many picturesque and thriving villages amid native groves of mangoes, palms, and fine timber trees, cities of the dead, and some very interesting ruined portions once occupied by the Portuguese conquerors.

The village of Girgaum, to the south of the island, is, however, the most picturesque and most densely populated of all these native settlements. No other part of the island is so fascinating as night approaches. A blaze of light flashing on the surface of huge reservoirs of water, on citron- and orange-groves, flooding flagged courtyards surrounded with blooming tropical fruits and flowers, the brilliant colors and varieties of dress of the numerous attendants, male and female, together with the groups formed by different parties arriving or departing, with the sounds of all kinds of music and midnight revelry,—altogether formed a *coup d'œil* which I can never forget, and which can be only seen in a tropical climate. Parts of this village, I am told, are entirely given up to the dissipated and pleasure-seeking youths who may happen to be beguiled by these outward appearances. It presents a very different aspect in the morning light; the cottages amid its palm-groves look so quiet and secluded that it is still more attractive. In some parts there are vast plantations of cocoanut trees, with the neat little huts, here and there, of native planters stretching toward a portion of the island called the Back Bay.

Lying on the opposite side of the palm-groves of Mazagaum, a fishing village, about an hour's drive over a beautiful strand brings us to an interesting spot called Breach Candy. On our way, especially in the afternoon, we meet carriages full of handsome Parsee ladies, generally brilliantly attired in their peculiar costumes, surrounded by numbers of happy-looking children, taking their evening airing. Grand mohguls and nabobs, driving out in magnificent European equipages, drawn by two and not infrequently by four spirited Arabian horses, pass rapidly by. At length, leaving the grand and princely occupants of all these brilliant equipages, we arrive at a spot desolate and yet peaceful beyond description—the cemeteries of the dead of all peoples and all creeds. No sound is heard. One solitary Hindoo, robed in pure white, with his bare shaved head, is praying over a smouldering spot covered with hot ashes, which shows signs of a body having been recently burned there. These graves are separated, it is true, but hardly distinguishable from one another. Desolate homes of the dead, we cannot tell which are Christian and which pagan. All sleep quietly in the same dust. But kind nature has decked them in tender living green, with here and there a beautiful wild flower, while the ever-encroaching sea washes away every year, bit by bit, the tombs of Hindoo, Moslem, Jain, Buddhist, and Christian alike.

There is one place that one should not miss seeing in Bombay, and that is the Pinjrapoore, or the Jain hospital for animals. It is one of the most peculiarly Oriental institutions in the East, and the largest to be found in India—pagan in everything, even in that disposition which has become almost a natural instinct to the Hindoos, the Buddhists, and the Jains,* to feel respect not alone for what is stronger and more beautiful than themselves, but for what is weaker and more helpless, and even hideous. The Pinjrapoore is situated in one of the most densely-populated portions of the native town.

We were conducted by two very civil men, low-caste Jains, into what appeared a large courtyard. A number of low sheds and several other courts ran all round it. I must confess I was greatly disappointed in the appearance of the building itself; it was mean and wretchedly

* The Jains, a very curious sect found in India proper to-day, and known only to the learned in Europe as the sole representatives in Hindostan of the once-numerous adherents to the tenets of Buddhism in that region, hold an intermediate place between Buddhists and Brahmans, but approach more closely to the Buddhists. They hold that Mahavira the hero, their greatest teacher, and the last of a number of deified spiritual legislators called by them Tirthankaras, was the preceptor of the great Gautama, the Buddha, whose followers embrace nearly three-fourths of the human race even to-day. They have, like the Brahmans, castes, and abstain most rigorously from flesh of all kinds. But, on the other hand, like the Buddhists of Siam, Burmah, Japan, etc., they disavow the sacredness of the Vèdas and the Hindoo gods, but in their place worship twenty-four sanctified legislators or Tirthankaras.

dirty. But as for the aspect of the inmates, it was at once both ludicrous and pathetic. I felt inclined to laugh and cry by turns. Never was such a medley of sick and aged animals seen anywhere else. A number of sick oxen were undergoing treatment at the hands of several native physicians who live near the hospital, and whose sole care is to attend to its inmates. One poor old, lean cow was having her leg dressed, and she seemed to be pretty conscious of the physician's kind intentions, for she stood perfectly still and quiet during the operation, which must have lasted an hour at least. The other aged and sick cattle, some blind, others scarred, not a few with bandages over their eyes or with halting steps, presented a singularly pathetic sight. We passed into several small courtyards where cats and dogs and many aged greyhounds find a pleasant home. Some of these were old and infirm to such a degree that it was painful to look at them. One big dog was pointed out to me by one of the men as the "bura kahnah wallah," one who delighted in big dinners; they certainly did not aid in fattening him, for he was the leanest creature I have ever seen.

The monkey part of the hospital was the most entertaining. A big ape supported itself on crutches; another sick inmate was lying stretched full length on the floor, gazing most piteously into the keeper's face. It seemed to be an object of deep interest to all the other monkeys, who clustered around it. The native doctor shook his head solemnly, and if it had been a human being he could not have said more tenderly, "Bachara! bachara! whoo murta hai" ("Poor thing! poor thing! she is dying"). Almost all of the infirm inmates looked on their dying comrade with peculiar intelligence in their faces, as if they had a sort of vague idea of what was happening. As I looked on, I could not doubt but that each one had somehow divined the meaning of the doctor's foreboding shake of the head.

In these compartments were collected, as it almost seemed, every known quadruped and biped on the face of the globe. Old elephants, dilapidated buffaloes, deplumed ravens, vultures, and buzzards hobnobbed together with gray-bearded goats and most foolish-looking old rams; rats, mice, rabbits, hens, herons, lame ducks, forlorn old cocks, and sparrows, jackals, old owls, and geese, live here in harmony side by side. I have been shown through palaces which interested me less.

We waited to see this curious medley of inmates dine. When the food which suited each class was being conveyed by a band of attendant boys to their various pens, troughs, etc., the noise and confusion were deafening. The monkeys in particular, with the peacocks—birds the most sacred to the Hindoos and Jains—raised such a howl and were so importunate to be served first that we were glad to escape. Such is the extreme limit to which Oriental charity is carried. At first sight it seemed absurd beyond words.

Nevertheless, there is something very noble and touching about this "infirmary" for the brute creation. Every one who finds any animal wounded, sick, aged, or dying is authorized to bring it here, and here it is really well cared for until death comes to relieve it from all suffering. Who can estimate the power of an institution that is continually caring for the dumb mutes of the animal kingdom, who bear not only man's burdens, but his harshness and neglect, with the patience of almost sanctified beings?

In my first week in Bombay I received an invitation to a grand dinner-party to be given at the house of a rich East Indian lady, a Mrs. C——, the widow of what is called in British India an uncovenanted officer. So great is the prestige attached to the word "officer" in the East that every man is an officer of some sort or other, from the brigadier to the private soldier. A civilian, consequently, is an uncovenanted officer, and as for the merchants, they are Mohguls, nabobs, Badishas, or Kudawunds. Mrs. C——'s house was situated near Parel, formerly "Nonpareil," a most lovely part of the island. Our carriage drove through a long wide avenue of fine trees, and brought us before a large one-storied stone building, pillared and with a spacious flight of stone steps leading to it. On the steps were half a dozen handsomely-dressed servants in long flowing white robes called "angrakas," crimson-and-gold striped turbans, and bright blue-and-gold cumberbunds, or scarfs, folded round their waists; the effect was certainly striking. These salâamed to us, and with stately dignity advanced and helped us to alight. We were then shown by another band of ushers, magnificently dressed, into a sumptuously furnished apartment, where we laid aside our light wrappings. A fresh troop of dusky-hued, richly-draped, and turbaned individuals marshalled us into the grand drawing-room, where we found the rich widow seated on a yellow satin ottoman surrounded by a bevy of ladies and gentlemen. The ladies all wore low-necked dresses of the most exquisitely delicate Indian fabrics, Chinese crapes, gauzes, mulmuls, and silks; and some of them were young and beautiful.

At dinner numbers of dusky-hued attendants moved about us so softly that they did not seem to touch the floor with their feet; gliding noiselessly in and out, offering us costly viands and sparkling wines, laying down plates and removing them so dexterously as not to make the faintest sound, they seemed even to repress their breathing. Everything was done with magical effect. The punkahs overhead moved softly to and fro; the light fell from cocoanut-oil chandeliers in peculiarly softened splendor on the rare flowers, the glass, and the silver below. Everything went on with the ease and precision of clockwork, without the faintest echo of a click or sound. Even those domestics who did not wait at dinner-table stood with arms folded across their breasts under the shadows of doors or pillars, waiting their turn to serve, and so still and motionless were they that they might almost, save for the glitter in their eyes, have passed for bronze statues.

They impressed me very unpleasantly, and that in spite of all the laughter and merriment, the exaltation of British power and British supremacy in India. I had, somehow, a feeling of reserved force pervading those mute, motionless figures around us, and I involuntarily felt, for the first time, that it was a very solemn affair for the Briton to be in India luxuriating on her soil and on her spoils.

With those dark, restless eyes watching every turn, motion, and expression of our faces, in vain were the delicious coffee and the sumptuous dinner, the music of the fountains playing before each window. I was anxious to escape. If I laughed or talked or moved, those dark eyes seemed to observe me, even when they were seemingly fixed on vacancy. If I had dared, I believe I should have risen and gone away. But of course this would have been a shocking breach of etiquette, so I sat still, hushing secret perturbations and longing for dinner to end.

The conversation continued in a lively strain. I noticed that every one seemed to have a pet theory about home government and how it could best be administered; all of which I was then too young to comprehend, but I did comprehend, and that very painfully, that no one seemed to mind those dark, silent, stationary figures any more than if they had been hewn out of stone. On coming out of that house I drew a long deep sigh of relief and felt just as if I had escaped from some imminent danger.

There are no less than three government residences in the island of Bombay. One is within the walls of the fort, used for holding special meetings of the council durbars, or assemblies, and for various other public business. It has little or no architectural beauty, and looks more like a stadthouse in a German free city. The one at Malabar Point is a charming English cottage, situated on a rocky and well-wooded promontory, commanding a beautiful view of the sea, and is often washed by the sea-spray during stormy weather. The third is at Parel—a magnificent building, said to have been founded on the remains of an old Jesuit college which flourished here during the Portuguese supremacy in India. It was bought by a Parsee, from whom it was purchased by the East India government about a century ago and fitted up in its present style. A noble flight of stone steps leads to the entrance-hall, whence a fine staircase opens into two of the most spacious rooms I have ever seen in Bombay, about eighty feet long, one above the other, and each very handsomely furnished. It commands a fine view of the town and harbor.

There is a curious rock at the extreme point of Malabar Hill which is very difficult to approach at high tide. Here are the remains of an ancient Hindoo temple, and a hole famous as a place of resort for Hindoo devotees, who endure great hardships in order to get access to the hole and pass through it, believing that in doing so they are regenerated, born again, and purified from all their sins.

Among the places worth attention in the neighborhood of Bombay are Byculla and Mazagaum. The former has a fine English school-house for all classes of children. It

BANYAN TREE.

is placed under the supervision of a number of English ladies of high rank, who take turns in visiting it.

Mazagaum is a very old part of the island of Bombay, formerly a fishing village, which its name indicates, but now a densely-populated town, inhabited chiefly by the descendants of the early Portuguese settlers. The Roman Catholic church here is a most venerable and picturesque building, standing under the shadow of great forest trees. Their foliage is certainly magnificent beyond description. The mango, the tamarind, the graceful peepul, and the banyan attain great height and breadth, and are covered with marvellous specimens of huge parasitic creepers and plants forming miles of sheltered walks. The fruit-bearing trees come to great perfection here. But with all its beauty the spot is considered so unhealthy that it is often called the "white man's grave."

I have seldom seen a pleasanter sight than that which is presented at Mazagaum on every Sunday morning in the year, when the whole native Christian population turns out to church almost simultaneously. The streets are filled with handsome women and children. The women in their long flowing mantles and costumes, half Hindoo and half European, are very picturesque. But the men and boys present an appearance at once both grotesque and ludicrous. Most of them are dressed as Europeans, and not a few as English and Portuguese generals; gold lace, plumed hats, helmets, and striped pantaloons are the prevailing fashion. They seem to have no idea of the fitness of things. Their passion for European dress is carried to such an extreme that I have seen a native * Portuguese sailing down the lane without

* The descendants of the early Portuguese settlers who have intermarried with the Hindoos and other castes of India, and now form a very large portion of the population of Bombay and Goa.

any shoes on his feet, but sporting the military dress, with the cocked hat and feathers, of some English general. This love of dress is exceedingly queer, but it is quite as much a characteristic of the Portuguese men of education and culture in India as of the more ignorant and illiterate.

CHAPTER II.

Malabar Hill, and Domestic Life of the English in Bombay.

My first stay in Bombay was a comparatively short one, and was spent partly with friends at Colabah and partly in tents on the great green in front of Fort George.

My stepfather being connected with the engineer or public works department at the military station of Poonah, my life for a year or two was passed at that strange city. Upon the occasion of my marriage, however, I returned to Bombay for a settled residence, from which time I began my real experience of life in India.

We established ourselves at Malabar Hill, in a house completely isolated from the rest of the world, where my husband and I took up the study of the Sanskrit and Hindostanee languages. Malabar Hill is a rocky promontory on the south of the island of Bombay, and covered with beautiful houses, many of which are almost palaces. At its highest point, detached and alone, stands a lofty tower, the largest "dohkma," or "tower of silence," of the Parsees. Here the followers of Zoroaster deposit their dead. It is rendered not the less sombre by the birds of prey that hover around it in great numbers.

There are two other and smaller towers of silence on the island, all erected in the most isolated positions. No one is ever allowed to approach them save the Fire-priests and those who carry their dead. These strange towers or tombs are mysterious, grand, and barbaric in their very forms—at their base screened by huge branching trees from all human observation, open only to the blue sky, the free air, and the gloomy birds of prey hovering always near.

On the other side of this much-dreaded spot, and not far from a forest of palms which descends in graceful undulations to the very base of the hill, stood a solitary house, called by every one "Morgan's Folly." For full ten years it had found no occupant. Its owner and builder, having returned to England with broken fortunes and failing health, had entrusted the renting of it to a Parsee agent. By a happy accident this lonely house was discovered by my husband, who had it at once repaired, furnished, and fitted up for our use, and here we took up our abode after a few weeks' residence at Parel.

I wish I could do justice to this singular abode, on the portals of which the monosyllable "*Whim*" might fully be inscribed. It was the caprice of a rich English cotton-merchant, whose love for the feathered tribe amounted to an absorbing passion. The house was therefore designed and built at great cost to serve the double purpose of human and bird habitation. Foolish, capricious, extravagant, and incorrigible as he was called by every one, I for my part conceived an affection for this strange Englishman who built this fanciful place in which were passed the first few years of my married life.

Two fine roads led to the "Aviary," as we named the house, one of which was cut into the hillside and descended to the base of the hill, whence at low tide you might step from rock to rock away out into the bay. The other was connected with a beautiful road which winds along Malabar Hill, affording a favorite carriage-drive for the residents of the island.

As for the house, it was the most curious bit of architecture one had ever seen—so fanciful, it seemed more like something that belonged rather to the mysterious land we visit in our dreams than to an actual house made of solid stone and wood standing fast, bound to the hard, dull, practical earth.

The building consisted only of two stories, of great length, and a high chamber, called the "Teak Tower," which rose above the east corner of the house and commanded the most extensive and beautiful views to be found anywhere on the island. The upper story was the part designed for human habitation. The wood of which it was built was a fine-grained teak and very durable. The balcony, running all around the upper story, was elaborately carved. The lower part was chiefly of stone pillars, enclosing a spacious ground-floor united by screens of fine open wire wrought in Oriental patterns of the Persian rose and the Buddhistic lily. The pillars rested firmly on broad stone foundations, and the open wire walls let in all the wind, rain, and sunshine that the feathered inhabitants for whom the enclosure was intended could possibly desire.

But this was not all: on the ground-floor of the hall flourished some beautiful fruit-bearing trees. Right under our bedroom chamber stood that most exquisite of Indian trees, "the gold-mohur acacia," with its rich clusters of golden flowers; the slender, graceful pâpiya, with its heavy drooping leaves and round fruit of a rich yellow when ripe, so much sought after by birds. One gigantic baobâb, which had stood here, no doubt, for centuries, for whose growth and preservation the builder had made ample provision by leaving a well or circular opening through the lower and upper stories and in the roof, gave the house the singular appearance of growing around a great tree. Forcing themselves through this opening to the sky, the branches of the baobâb shot straight up on one side and overshadowed the tower chamber, covering it, after each rainy season, with masses of fragrant blossoms and fine fruit. It was very evident that in the course of time there would be, possibly, a prolonged but mighty struggle between the house and the tree, which should go first, and it was not hard to tell, for already the tree had found its way to the open sky, and its branches were seen pushing here and there and penetrating the woodwork of the chambers adjoining. There were one or two more trees that deserve mention. These were a beautiful Chinese pine and a heart-shaped peepul. The ground-floor of this hall was covered with weeds and a perfect jungle of brushwood. The gardener told me that it abounded in all kinds of reptiles, but I never saw any signs of them until some large snakes were called out one morning by a party of samp-wallahs, or snake-charmers. The fruit trees had long ceased to bear, and were gradually crowding out and killing each other.

All the more rare and beautiful birds with which Mr. Morgan had stocked this place had died or taken flight to homes less confined; only a few still remained. Among them were the sooruk, or scarlet breast, an exquisite singer; the mâina, the Java sparrow, the bulbul or Indian nightingale, and the zeenah, a little quarrelsome brown and red-spotted bird,—all hardy birds. They lingered here, partly from association and partly because of the grain still thrown in and around the "Aviary" morning and evening by the pious Hindoo employed by the Parsee agent to look after the garden.

The tower chamber was our favorite sitting-room because of its splendid views and being removed from the noise and vicinity of our servants. It was simply furnished—a table, a few chairs, mostly of cane, a couple of sofas and a Persian carpet, with gauze nettings to every door and window to keep out our worst foes, the gnats, flies, and mosquitoes. The rest of the house was furnished with the same severe simplicity; there were no curtains, no blinds, no carpets; the floors as well as the walls were painted in subdued half-tints, which gave them the air of being very handsomely fitted up.

In this place I began my first attempt at housekeeping in the East, and I can truly say, without the least exaggeration, that for months the house kept itself and my numerous servants kept me. To begin with, there were too many servants for so quiet and unpretending a household, but I soon found it would be still more difficult to do with fewer: "*dustoor*," custom, was flung into my face morning, noon, and night. I implored my husband to send half of them away, but if he sent one off, either the whole gang disappeared like a flash or else the work of the banished servant was scrupulously avoided by every one in the establishment. There was, in short, a servant for every distinct thing to be done in the house. There was a *khansamah*, or native butler, a high-caste Hindoo, who was supposed to keep all the servants in order, but who invariably incited a revolution in the camp if I wished anything to be done my way and not his. Then there was a cook, a *kling* (a name for a certain race natives of Madras), who got drunk whenever we happened to have friends to dinner; there was a cook's mate, who was inclined to be musical just as we were going to sleep; there was a *buttee-wallah*, or lamplighter, a stripling, some near relation of the butler's, whose friends and relatives were always dying, and who asked permission three times in the course of a few months to be allowed to go and bury his mother. When I very gently, because of his flowing tears and doleful expression of face, reminded him that he had already buried or burned her twice, he burst into a passionate sob and said, "Oh! that one was my aunt's mother, and the last one my father's mother, but this is my own, own mother." Of course I had to let him go off for two or three days, and the butler too, who was also a mourner. Then there were besides these an *ayah*, or lady's-maid; a *dhoby*, or washerman, who came to the house once a week for the clothes, and stayed away sometimes for three weeks, owing to that chronic epidemic, death, in the family; a *bheestie*, who filled the tubs in the bathroom with water, and did nothing else; a *jarroo-wallah*, who only came each morning and swept the house and grounds, and then disappeared till the next time; a coachman, a groom, a *pundit*, or professor of Oriental languages; and lastly, a tailor, whose name was Tom. He, Tom, was a Portuguese Christian, and attended to the mending of the household linen and the making of our clothes. He was the least manageable of the whole lot. He would not answer to the name "boy," a generic name for servants in India and a corruption of the Hindostanee word *bhai*, brother, but insisted on being called "Tom." This put me very often into an awkward position, as this was the familiar name by which I had learned to call my husband, not knowing that there was another "Tom" attached to him from his bachelor establishment. Once or twice, forgetting this fact, I happened to call "Tom! Tom!" after my husband, who was hurrying off to town, when who should pop into my chamber but the grinning tailor-boy, balancing a pair of huge scissors on his right ear and with a number of needles full of long threads stuck into his woolly head, which served him as a needle-case? There was nothing left me but to change my husband's name.

But this was by no means the beginning and end of my troubles of housekeeping in Bombay. I happened to awake very early one Sunday morning. It was a lovely sunrise: the first blush of dawn was mounting the horizon; the trees in the garden were unfolding their leaves; birds of all colors were perched upon their branches opening their "ruby eyes" on a newly-born day. But as I stood there, entranced with the beauty of a tropical sunrise, my eyes fell on the figure of Tom the tailor going off to early mass attired in my husband's best dress-coat and an embroidered vest which had been a chief object of my girlish admiration. In addition to these he sported pointed shoes, worked stockings—one of the finest pair in my possession—and a frill six inches deep projecting from his shirt-front, with a huge cocked hat, over which he held one of my smallest parasols to protect him from the mildest of morning suns, which had only just mounted the hillside. When I remonstrated with him on his return from chapel, he burst into a passion of tears and sobs and flooded me with such replies as these: "Your godship, you are my father and mother; an unkind, unjust word from your divine voice will break your poor slave's heart and consign him in the prime of his youth to a lonely and desolate grave," etc. I absolutely began to feel that he was the injured party, and that I was anything but a kind, generous mistress and a Christian. It ended in my presenting him with the clothes he had worn, but nevertheless he went about the house for days in a state of sorrowful dejection at my unkindness, which he persisted in saying had caused his heart to bleed to death.

Not long after this in a rash moment we resolved to give a dinner-party to some of our friends in Bombay, and to invite the rich East Indian widow, Mrs. C——, who had shown us many kindnesses. Never in my life did I pass through a more perplexing and fiery ordeal.

The viands were all ordered and sent from town, and

had arrived in good season. But no sooner had they been deposited in the kitchen than the butler reported, in his quiet and unconcerned manner, that the cook had gone off to town to get help, and would probably not return in time to prepare the dinner. The butler and the lamplighter were Hindoos, and could not touch beef or ham, or, in fact, any kind of flesh. The butler had no objection to putting these articles on the table when cooked, but as for cooking them, he would lose caste. There was nothing left to be done but for Tom the tailor-boy and I—who, being Christians, had no such scruples—to set about and cook the dinner.

About four o'clock everything was in a fair way toward being cooked, the capons, ham, soup, and vegetables were all in their places on the fire, when suddenly the cook returned, looking very strange; I thought he was only tired and sleepy. He insisted on taking possession of the kitchen, declaring that it almost broke his heart to see me spoiling my nice dress and ruining my complexion over the fire. "What am I good for," said he, striking an attitude and looking queerer than ever, "but to cook you a grand dinner and be your slave for ever?" Thus assured, I quitted the kitchen with all the dinner cooking away at great speed, and betook myself to making various other preparations. It was almost the dinner-hour before I was fairly through with the glasses and dessert and a thousand and one of the many requirements of a European dinner-party. No sooner had I put the last touches to my toilette than my husband returned with two unexpected guests, which called my attention at once, so that I had no opportunity to revisit the kitchen to see that all was as it should be.

The last of the guests had no sooner arrived than the butler threw open the dining-room door and announced in a solemn tone, "Kannah teyar hai Sahibloke" ("Dinner waits, ladies and gentlemen").

We marched gayly in, eager, happy, and very hungry. But, alas! no sooner was the soup-tureen uncovered than I divined from my husband's expression that something was wrong. The soup was sent away with some playful apology, but when dish after dish was set on the table, uncovered, and removed without my husband's even making a pretence of offering the guests anything to eat, it was too much for me.

At this juncture kind-hearted Mrs. C—— came to my rescue by saying, "Let us all go off to the kitchen and find out what is the matter with the cook," and coming to my side, gave me an opportunity to recover myself, which I did under her gentle smile and oft-repeated adage, "My dear, accidents will happen in the best regulated families."

The gentlemen returned from their survey of the kitchen and reported that the cook was "drunk and sound asleep in the middle of the floor," and that the remainder of the dinner was burnt to cinders, but still in the pots on the range. If it had not been for the kind-hearted Mrs. C——, I do not know what we should have done. She insisted on our all driving out to her house and taking tea with her.

I must not omit to mention another incident which is characteristic of life in India. My husband was in the commissariat department of the army, and had a great deal to do with native dealers. The Parsees, however, because of their honesty, had the monopoly of the contracts for supplying the British troops in Bombay. One morning a number of *Borahs** were ushered into the

* The Borahs are natives of Guzerat, converted to Islamism about five and a half centuries ago. They are remarkable for their extraordinary intelligence in trade. The name "Borah" signifies merchant

"Aviary," and laid before me on the table what seemed to be a tray filled with sugar candy, raisins, and almonds. Not understanding the meaning of this gift, and not having quite outgrown my love for sweets, I took up a handful of the good things, when, to my surprise, I found lying below the candy a number of gold coins called "mohurs." I hastened to inform my husband of the magnificent present waiting for him, but he no sooner heard of it then he turned the Borahs out, tray and all. It was simply an attempt to obtain contracts by bribery. The Borahs seemed in no way discomfited; they bowed most politely on my husband's prompt dismissal, and departed as if it were with them no unusual occurrence to be turned out of doors.

Such are some few of the most prominent features of housekeeping and life in India.

The native servants have some good points, however. They will rarely quit your service, even to better their fortunes, unless driven away. They contrive, too, to have their own way without ever being disrespectful to you. They bow or salââm at all times, move so softly about the house with bare feet that you hardly ever know that they are there, and, on the whole, they attend pretty well to their own peculiar province in the houschold; but as for helping in what is *not their province*, it is not to be expected.

They are never away a day except for sudden deaths,

in the Guzerati dialect. These Borahs are a distinct sect, followers of one Moolah Allih, who is buried in the old city of Cambay. They pay reverence to Mohammed Hussain, called in the records of the Crusaders "The Prince of the Assassins" and also "the Old Man of the Mountains." They transmit a fifth of their gains to the Saiyads of Medinah, and pay eleemosynary contributions to the chief of their learned men, who distribute alms among the poor. (See *Asiatic Researches*, paper by H. T. Colebrook.)

which take place in the various branches of their friends or relatives once a week, on an average. They are always clean, arrayed in their long flowing white robes and handsome turbans, and they never address you without some flattering or grandiloquent phrase, which helps not a little to smooth over your wounded pride.

Our pundit,* Govind, was not a servant, but a high-bred gentleman. He came to the "Aviary" morning and evening to give us lessons in Hindostanee and Sanskrit. He was a learned high-caste Brahman and a remarkably interesting specimen of a Hindoo gentleman.

Almost directly to the right of the "Aviary" was the government summer-house already mentioned; just opposite, situated on the summit of a steep acclivity overlooking the sea, was a grand stone house, the home of our Parsee friend and commissariat contractor. On the west, embowered in a thick grove of mango and tamarind trees, was the prettiest of little Hindoo villages, the village of Walkeshwar, sacred to the god of the strand or beach.

We spent a day here on a certain festal occasion accompanied by Govind, our pundit. We lunched under the porch of the Hindoo temple by permission obtained through our pundit. Perfectly nude dusky children were clambering about the stones watching us with eager curiosity. Our visit here was to witness the feast of Rama, the hero of one of the Hindoo epic poems, Ramayána, and his wife, Seeta, which did not begin until the afternoon. Hindoo women, black-eyed and singularly graceful in their movements, adorned with gayly-colored robes and most antique-looking bracelets and armlets, went to and from the pool, still called "Rama Talai," or Rama's Pool, bearing water in jars piled in tiers on their heads, others bathing and frolicking in the pool. There were at the

* A professor of Sanskrit or other branches of Indian literature.

same time some dozen Brahman priests at prayer, seemingly abstracted from the scenes around them, going through with all kinds of motions with their bodies while their lips moved incessantly, but inaudibly, in prayer and praise. Our pundit told us that this was the traditional spot where the hero Rama rested when on his way to Lanka (Ceylon) to recover from the tyrant Rawana his beautiful wife, Seeta.

The Rama Talai stands in a group of small temples—some of which are very pretty—surrounded by gardens. About two in the afternoon the officiating priests began to arrive, followed by thousands of Hindoos. The doors of the temple were thrown open to all comers. The priests placed themselves at the foot of the shrines, on each of which were several idols—Siva, the chief god, above, and Rama and Seeta below. The people poured forth their offerings to the priests. Those who could not get into the temples pressed around the sacred pool, throwing themselves into its holy waters and coming out free from all impurities. A great many young women with peculiarly interesting faces were kneeling outside of the temples and praying, with their eyes closed and their hands folded, for some especial blessing. It was an interesting sight, but for the fakeers and gossains, who make a disgusting spectacle of themselves, and, strange to say, are encouraged by the pure, mild, and modest Brahman priests to do so. As it was, we returned home shocked with the nudity and filth of these sacred beggars, but very much impressed with the perfectly pure and religious nature of the Hindoos, who have very beautiful forms and faces, and even those that are not absolutely beautiful have so much grace and gentleness about them that they attract the eye and remain impressed on the memory with something of the charm of a beautiful painting.

Bunder Boat.

CHAPTER III.

The Island of Shashtee, commonly called Salsette.—Gharipoore, "the Town of Purification," or the Island and Caves of Elephanta.

EARLY one morning, after almost a week's preparation for the trip, we found ourselves in a large roomy bunder-boat flying before the wind straight for the beautiful island of Salsette. which lies to the north and is united to the smaller island of Bombay by a causeway erected during the administration of Governor Duncan, chiefly to enable the natives of the larger islands to bring their produce to the Bombay markets.

Presently we entered upon a wonderful river, flowing through the land out of the sea and dividing this island from the continent, at the very mouth of which are the bleak, barren island and mountains of Trombay, the latter rising up nine hundred feet high. We passed along reefs of gold, now over wide swamps, our boat riding above and crushing down the tall waving grass, and anon we would suddenly shoot almost within touch of dark hollow caverns, and looking up see the high beetling cliffs piled one above the other, surmounted by the ruins of some of old Portuguese or Mahratta forts or castles, covered with wild flowers and huge creeping plants. The scenes along the banks of this river are wild and romantic enough to satisfy the most enthusiastic lover of nature. We cast anchor at length at Tannah, having reached "a land all sun and blossom, trees as high as heaven, amid every bird that sings."

Tannah, the chief town of the island of Salsette, was

taken by the troops of the East India Company in the year 1774, and by a treaty then entered into the Mahratta king, Raghu Nauth, ceded in perpetuity to the company Bassein with its dependencies, the island of Salsette, the entire districts of Jainbhosir and other valuable provinces adjoining it in Guzerat. It is chiefly inhabited by Roman Catholic Christians, the majority of whom are converts from Hindooism. The interior of the island is inhabited by a peculiar tribe of peasants who are to this day in a condition as wild as the Bheels and Konds of Guzerat and Central India. These peasants are burners of charcoal; they dwell together among the hills, but apart from all other tribes, and have neither intercourse nor any social bond with the Hindoos of the plain. At stated times they bring down their loads of charcoal in rude carts drawn by buffaloes to particular spots, whence it is carried away by the Hindoo or Portuguese buyer, who, according to a settled custom among them, deposits in its place rice, clothing, and iron tools. This excessive shyness is said to be owing to the contempt in which the natives, as outcasts, are held by their Hindoo neighbors.

We were met on our landing by a very polite and obliging native Portuguese, the elder brother of my husband's tailor Tom, in whose company we walked about the town and at whose house we stayed during our visit.

Tannah, the chief town of the island of Salsette, takes its name from the beautiful river which flows at its base, and which was anciently called *Tainnah-Dèo*, "the Limb of God." It runs deep and narrow in front of the town. It is a place of great antiquity, probably dating back to the days of Vicrâmaditya, of whose universal and beneficent rule, 57 B. C., tradition is yet eloquent throughout India. The ruins here are few and not very interesting. There are some massive walls of a great square building that was once a Mahratta citadel, and some ponderous old arches that have fallen and are now covered with beautiful wild creepers; also a Hindoo temple, a vast, shapeless mass of architecture, but almost animate with the innumerable gods and goddesses that grin and smirk at one from every cornice and entablature of the building. There is here a small but perfect little fortress, from which, during the last Mahratta war, the famous Trimbukjee escaped, occupied by a small European garrison. The government prison is also well worth visiting. We were surprised to see the manner in which the prisoners of all ranks, creeds, and nationalities worked together within these walls. Most of the prisoners, however, were of the Takhor race. They were busily employed in the manufacture of very valuable striped cotton stuffs much prized by the natives for scarfs, cumberbunds, and waist-cloths.

The cavern temples that are found in this island are the chief objects of interest.

On the morning following our arrival, furnished with two guides and accompanied by our pundit, we started off to visit some of these remarkable excavations in the mountains that stretch across the middle of this island. At first, the road, though very narrow and rugged, lies through a most beautiful valley formed by hills of moderate height, covered with forests to their summits, with here and there patches of bare rock, while the ravines and the valley itself were planted with groves of mangoes and several varieties of the palm. For some time we saw but few traces of inhabitants; we passed during a ride of more than eight miles but one small village, a collection of most miserable-looking huts, a few half-starved looking children, and a troop of pariah dogs, who rushed out to bark at us.

At another small village, named Viarè, we came upon

what seemed a jungle, open in some parts and in others densely thick, abounding in hyenas, tigers, panthers, and the wild-boar; passing through this with anything but pleasurable feelings, we reached Toolsey, named after a famous Hindoo goddess who, like the Greek Clytie, loved some Hindoo god, and was by him, out of pity for her unrequited passion, transformed into the beautiful toolsey-plant, whence her name. This is a lovely spot, encircled with hills, the highest of which is Khennari, its face perforated with no less than one hundred cavern temples. Under a fine banyan tree which stands in an open plain we passed the night. In northern latitudes one can form no idea of the peculiar beauty of the night with a bright moon shining overhead.

Almost at dawn next morning we set off for the temples. The ascent to the Khennari Hills is somewhat steep and difficult, but after a hard climb we gained a platform, and was confronted by a stone porch leading into an arched cavern temple of great majesty and beauty. These cavern temples are scattered over both sides of a high rocky hill at many different elevations, consisting of no less than six stories or tiers of caverns, of various sizes and forms, all excavated out of the rocky surface of the mountain and connected with each other by narrow stone steps cut in the rock. The façades and great court are most imposing.

Entering through a fine lofty portico, we saw a little to the left hand a curious octagonal pillar, detached from the rock and surmounted by three well-carved lions seated back to back. Passing this, we were suddenly introduced into an elaborately carved vestibule, at the end of which is a colossal statue of Buddha, with his hands raised in the attitude of benediction. The stone screen which here separates the vestibule from the body of the temple is

Cavern Temples at Khennari

covered with a row of male and female figures half nude; the expression of the faces of these figures is remarkably calm and thoughtful, and the whole is executed with considerable spirit. Above them the rocks are carved into a profusion of graceful sculptures.

The great temple or cave is divided into three aisles by regular colonnades of octagonal pillars; of these, the twelve on each side nearest the entrance are ornamented with exquisitely carved bases and capitals in the style usual in Indian temples. The arch of the vault is occupied by a dagoba or mausoleum, perhaps of some early disciple of Buddha. It is cylindrical in the shaft and surmounted by a cupola. On the right and left of the portico are two colossal figures of Buddha, perhaps twenty feet in height.* The ceiling of this cave is arched semicircularly and ornamented with slender ribs of fine teak-wood, disposed as if for the support of the ponderous dome overhead, but in reality for the floral decorations which on solemn occa-

* The following extract from Dr. Bird's *Caves of Western India* may prove interesting to the curious reader:

"The tope (a monument erected over a Buddhist relic, sometimes resembling a pagoda) at Khanari was opened by me in 1839. The largest, being selected for examination, was penetrated from above to the base, which was built of stone. In this tope the workmen found two small copper urns, in one of which were a ruby, a pearl, and a small piece of gold mixed with the ashes. In this urn there was also a small gold box containing a piece of cloth; and in the other ashes (probably of some cremated saint) and a silver box were also found. Outside, a circular stone was found, and to it were fixed two copper plates in the Salh or cave characters. The inscriptions read thus: 'Whatever meritorious acts proceed from cause of these the source Tathagata (Buddha) has declared; the opposing principle of these the great one of golden origin has also demonstrated;' or, in other words, Whatever merit may proceed from these acts, Buddha has explained its source to you, and also the opposite principle of these acts; he has also demonstrated to you the one of golden origin. This discovery establishes the fact that these caves are of Buddhist origin, and probably date from the beginning of the Christian era."

sions were hung from them. A flight of steps cut into the same mountain leads by various intricate paths to smaller caves or cells, consisting only of a portico and two small chambers, with everywhere seats for the disciples or the recluse cut into the rock. To each cave there is a cistern for the preservation of rain-water, some larger and more elegantly carved and finished than others. The whole appearance of this excavated hill of Khennari is that of a Buddhist monastic city, the cells and temples, the apartments and cisterns, hewn in the rocky sides of the mountain.

On Sunday we attended the Roman Catholic church, which is a stone's throw from the home of our Portuguese friends. Early on Sunday morning the streets were filled with men, women, and children, entirely of the Portuguese population. The men were, with a few exceptions, quietly dressed in the ordinary European attire, which the majority don only on stated occasions, with the black silk hat of modern fashion, carrying prayer-books, fans, and footstools of the ladies of their party. It was a pleasant sight. The Portuguese here are entirely independent of the Romish Church, and from simple contact have adopted the mode of life and a great many superstitions of the Hindoos. One finds everywhere in India not only Hindooized Mohammedans, but Hindooized Christians. Their priests are natives of the country, under the jurisdiction of the archbishop of Goa, who is a sort of Indian pope. Their worship is so much more pagan than Christian that when in a Roman Catholic church in any part of India one finds it difficult to believe that it is not the worship of Khrishna or Brahm.

The native Portuguese are darker than the darkest of the better class of Indians, showing a mixed and degenerate race.

I accompanied our host and his family to church. The children were charming with their little pink trowsers, lace over-slips, pink shoes, and were adorned with jewels; the only difference between the dresses of the little boy and the girls was that the boy sported a hat like that seen in the pictures of Bonaparte, which gave him a most whimsical air, and the little girls had white handkerchiefs tied neatly under their chins. I took little Marium's hand, and off we went; looking toward the deep flowing river, I saw a string of Brahman priests marching solemnly along the steep banks preparatory to beginning their morning services, for our Sabbath is also their day of sacrifice and prayer to Suriya, the sun-god. I was very much tempted to abandon my Christian friends and follow the Brahman priests, but I restrained myself, and was soon within the *temple* of Jesus Christ. I say designedly the *temple* of Jesus Christ. It was crowded with images—perhaps one ought to say idols—of God the Father, Christ the Son, the Virgin Mother, and the Holy Ghost, besides quantities of relics, sacred vessels, tapers, candles, incense-burners swinging from the roof, flowers both natural and artificial, and all kinds of beads and shells on the altar. High above the altar was a great porcelain figure of the Virgin jewelled and crowned as queen of heaven, with her arms stretched out in benediction.

We pressed in. The service had not begun. All the men, women, and children prostrated themselves—some at full length; others, being crowded for room, squatted down and touched the brick pavement with their outspread open palms and then their foreheads; after which the rich, among whom were classed my friends, took their seats, and the crowd remained kneeling on the bare floor. Presently the priests, of whom there were no less than a dozen, appeared, gaudily dressed in tinsel and lace, and took their places before the altar, keeping their heads covered. Now the service began, which consisted of some chants in a kind of Latin known only to the priests, and not fully understood even by them, with dressings and undressings, perpetual genuflexions, turning from the altar to the people, swinging of censers, marching and countermarching with the baby figure of Christ and a pretty wax doll which represented the mother; these the men, women, and children kissed with apparently genuine pleasure. This done, boys dressed as angels in long white robes and with wings attached to their shoulders, entered, each bearing a lighted candle and a lily, as do the Buddhists at prayer, chanting some beautiful hymn, of which no one understood a word, and even the music was wild and Oriental. Then finally came the ringing of multitudinous little bells (another Buddhist custom when about to exhibit a tooth or any other relic of Buddha), and up rose the Host, as large as an ordinary fan, composed of glutinous rice. In the centre was a white spot, and around it rays of gold proceeding outward. All fell upon their faces; little Marium and I alone were the lookers-on, but suddenly my gentle hostess gave her little daughter a vigorous push, which sent her head foremost to the floor, whispering, "The body of God!" I bowed my head out of respect for the poor human hearts that worshipped here, and not without a deep sense of humiliation at witnessing the complicated and ingenious ceremonies by which these ecclesiastics, an outgrowth of the Church of Rome, cultivate and foster the credulity and ignorance of the people, whom they teach to rely more on certain forms and the supernatural agencies of the Virgin and relics of deceased saints than upon religious and moral truths. After the "body of God" a bone of some martyred Indian saint who had been converted to Christianity was held up for adoration; again the people bowed down; and then came the end, the benediction, amid more ringing of bells and swinging of censers.

Who can witness these imbecilities and not hold the native Portuguese clergy accountable for withholding the true knowledge, the simple teachings of Jesus, the true Bread of life, and for substituting superstitions and pageantries not one whit superior to, but in some respects even more degrading than, the most debasing paganism which they have supplanted? Forms are the same, the names alone have been changed; otherwise, the Roman Catholicism I have everywhere witnessed in India is essentially the same as the lowest forms of paganism.

Before dawn next morning we took leave of our kind friends, and in our comfortable bunder-boat started for the island of Elephanta, or Gharipoore. After a couple of hours or more of pleasant sailing we reached the island. I found it larger and more beautiful than I had expected. A good part of it is under cultivation, especially all around a village of tolerable size, above which a couple of clearly-defined hills rise from the sea to a considerable height. The view as you ascend to the right is simply magnificent: the twin mountains seem to be knit together by a grand old forest, the one rising slightly higher than the other. The name "Elephanta" was given to it, some say, by the Greeks, others by the Portuguese conquerors; however that may be, the name of the caves was anciently "Gharipoore," or, "the Town of the Rock," or, according to some, "the Town of Purification."

We ascended a long flight of stone steps, in the wake of a party of fakeers, Hindoo priests, and half-nude men beating tomtoms, which at length brought us to a very handsome and spacious platform shaded with some fine old trees.

Here the party of Hindoo priests, drummers, and fakeers sat down to rest, while we went on a short distance and reached the entrance to the famous caves of Elephanta. The principal cave is of great extent, excavated out of the solid rock; the colossal columns of the portico seem to hold up the mountain above them. On either side of the entrance great creepers come down in heavy masses over the mountain. Rows and rows of columns handsomely ornamented appear within, growing beautifully less in the distance and vanishing amid gloomy shadows and a thousand fantastic shapes. The gateway or porch is still in excellent preservation; it leads directly through the heart of the mountain. The different shrines, which contain objects of Hindoo worship, are placed on each side. In the centre there is seen by the light of torches a majestic altar of stone, now in a state of decay, supporting a gigantic bust of three noble heads, two of which are in profile. The Hindoo Trinity, Maha Dèo, the Great God, commonly called Brahm, the Hindoo Creator, occupies the centre in full relief. The eyes are half closed, the expression serene and tranquil. It seems to be carved from a living model, and is a perfect Oriental ideal of masculine beauty, with the delicate and refined outline of the features and the deep contemplation expressed in those large downcast eyes. The forehead is crowned with a lofty diadem exquisitely carved, not unlike the mitres worn by the bishops of the Roman Church; the right arm, which is very much broken, once grasped the head of a cobra da capello, which, our pundit explained to us, here typifies in its sublimest sense the masculine or creative energy of the world.

Siva, to whom this cavern temple is said to be dedicated, and who is seen in another compartment with his consort Parvati, with a chaplet of skulls round his neck, eight-

Entrance to the Caves of Elephanta.

handed, and bearing the cobra, and whose name in Sanskrit signifies either happiness or pleasure, is seen in profile on the right. In a hand outstretched from the altar he also grasps a cobra, but with its hood extended wide. In his hand the character of the symbol is transformed with the god into that of the avenger or destroyer. The god's mouth is distorted with grimaces, and he puts out the tip of his tongue, by which, according to our pundit and guide, he mocks at the sensualist, and says as plainly as our Bible, "The wages of sin is death."

On the left side of Maha Dèo is Vishnu, in the grand character of preserver; the head is very noble and the face of no common beauty; it wears a tender and smiling expression. He no longer holds the symbol at once of masculine creative energy and of sensuality, but a peculiar oblong lotos-shaped cup or flower, the higher and purer symbol of maternity. Our pundit gave this wonderful bit of sculpture, which reaches from the low altar to the ceiling of the temple, the name of "Maha Trimourtri, the Great Three-in-One." By some it is called Bhava Natria, "Love threefold." Whatever else it may be called, it certainly makes a wonderful impression seen high above from the principal aisle, guarded on all sides by gigantic and well-proportioned caryatides. The shape of the largest cave is cruciform and resembles the plan of an ancient basilica.

The massiveness and strength of the pillars, which find their deep foundations in the earth below, supporting the elephant-shaped mountain above, is rendered more and more striking by the thousand and one scenes of Hindoo, and particularly Saivic,* mythology, in part solemn and

* The Saivi Hindoos are those who worship Siva or Shiva, one of the Brahman Trinity, as chief god; the lingam or phallus is sacred to him. Their chief act of worship is performed on the fourteenth night

majestic, and in part grotesque and absurd, that fill every part of the walls; gods and goddesses, heroes and .monsters, almost stand out of the rocks. Here are carved strong and clear the story of the babe Krishna and the slaughter of the infants by his uncle Cansa. Everywhere are curious and venerable specimens of sculpture, which, though shamefully mutilated in parts, still show so high an advance in art, and possess so indescribable an aspect of animated life, that one half expects the stone figures to move or to speak. A great number of the pillars have been undermined by the accumulation of water in the cavern temple; the capitals of some and parts of the shafts of others remain suspended from the ceiling like huge stalactites. Enormous creepers and trees have forced themselves through certain cracks and crevices in the mountain, and the whole scene is very wild and pagan; which enhances the beauty and mysterious appearance of the caves.

On going through a passage guarded by stone lions the pundit took a little tin box out of his pocket, opened it, and scattered some odoriferous snuff on the head of the lions, and then took a little pinch himself. His explanation was, that he had taken cold, and snuff was his remedy for it. "But," said I, "the stone lions haven't taken cold too?"—"Oh, that," said he, "was a propitiatory offering, lest I should sneeze in their sacred presence."

of the dark half of every moon. They fast during the day, and at night repair to their temples, repeat the names of their god—of which there are no less than one thousand, all expressive of certain spiritual and physical qualities, passions, acts, etc.—pour the leaves of the bheel tree, sacred to Shiva, because they are heart-shaped, over the lingam, then rub it with oil, and finally sprinkle it with consecrated water. At the Shivaratri, or the night of Shiva, which falls once a year on a dark night, a fair is held at the caves of Elephanta during the day, and a night-vigil from eight o'clock till five in the morning, accompanied with music, prayer, and other strange ceremonies.

As we went out of the great stone porch the declining sun sent a long line of light through the aisle, the wind blew softly, and the island stretched away green and beautiful, surrounded with the sea all a-glitter with the rosy hues of the setting sun. In many places we noticed traces of color, but everywhere are to be seen the ruthless mutilations this cave has suffered both from the conquering Mohammedan and Portuguese soldiers; most of the colossal statues are defaced and broken, the arms and limbs of innumerable figures are prostrate. Long lines of pictured story and inscriptions are effaced, but there are still standing rows and rows of gods and goddesses, their heads crowned with garlands. These figures, although much defaced, still show that the artist carved some of the female forms with only one breast, like the famed Amazons of Greek story. The temple or city of purification was desecrated centuries ago, and it is now deserted, save for an annual fair and occasional visits from Brahmans and fakeers; it can boast of none of the splendors of its palmy days.

About fifteen miles from "Gorabunder," on the mainland, lies Bassein—or, as it was anciently called, Vassai—once a proud city and the chief seat of the early Portuguese settlers in this part of India. But for nearly three-quarters of a century it has ceased to be inhabited. The city is of considerable size, and surrounded by a regular fortification of rampart and bastions. It is kept locked up under a small body of soldiers and an English conductor of ordnance.

By permission obtained from the authorities at Bombay we spent a very interesting day wandering over this deserted city, its ruined towers, cloisters, convents, monasteries, and churches, that once belonged to the Jesuits, which are here crumbling away unheard of and unnoticed.

The only building in good repair is a small pagoda raised over a Mahratta saint amid a display of the most melancholy of ruined houses, churches, and colleges. In the vast jungle-covered cemetery of the dead Portuguese are the tombs of the great Don Lorenço and the famous Albuquerque. In one of the largest of the churches there is a monument to a certain lady, Donna Maria de Souza, of the date of 1606.

Bassein was wrested from the Mahrattas by the Portuguese in 1532 A. D. But the Mahrattas laid siege to it again under the renowned Chinaje Apa, brother of the Peishwa Baji Rao, and after a desperate struggle the Portuguese were forced to capitulate. It is said that the English in Bombay might have saved them this defeat and humiliation, but from a feeling of jealousy of the power and influence of the Portuguese in India refused them all aid, except that of advancing fifteen hundred rupees, for which they took some very valuable church plate and some brass guns, which were actually removed from the defence of Bassein as security. They were finally induced, however, to make some amends for this barbarous treatment of fellow-Christians, and sent boats with a strong escort to convey the refugees to Bombay, whence they started for Goa, but were once more attacked and almost annihilated by the Mahrattas. In 1780 the English attacked, stormed, and captured the city of Bassein once more from the fierce Mahrattas, and have held it ever since, a melancholy monument of the departed greatness of the Portuguese conquerors. Such is the fate of conquering nations. It can hardly be doubted that if the English were now expelled from India the few relics left of their religion, their power, and their civil and military magnificence would be swept rapidly away, and would in the course of a century or two leave not a trace behind them.

CHAPTER IV.

Sampwallahs, or Serpent-Charmers.—Jâdoowallahs, or Miracle-performers.—Nuzer-bundyânâ, Mesmerizers.—Yogees, Spiritual Jugglers, and Naga-Poojmi, or Serpent-Worship, in India.

LIFE in the East is altogether so novel, so full of dramatic sights and sounds, that one's curiosity seems to grow with the abundant nourishment it finds everywhere. Now one sees a Mohammedan funeral, or the procession of gorgeous Taboots of Moslems, or gods of the Hindoos; anon the body of a Hindoo or a Parsee borne on an open bier by white-robed priests, the one to be burned, the other to be abandoned to birds of prey in their strange silent "towers of the dead." Sometimes a gay procession of dancing-girls, followed by troops of men and elephants richly caparisoned, waltzing all the way to the temple and keeping time to the pipes, cymbals, and the beating of most discordant drums; at others, a poor funeral of some low-caste person, quiet and unpretending—an open bier, on it perhaps an only child in its every-day soiled garments, followed by women wailing and beating their breasts and throwing dust on their heads. This wailing is inexpressibly mournful. One morning, as I sat at work in my room, there came floating upon the breeze toward the "Aviary" a sharp, penetrating, and very peculiar cry. While I listened there came another and another of these unearthly sounds; again they were repeated, and all at once there appeared in sight a band of half-naked men accompanied by two women and a perfectly nude little child—all so strange and weird-looking that I almost felt the victim of some illusion.

They were a band of sampwallahs, or serpent-charmers, and in rather a bewildered state of mind I watched the gang approach the front of the house and take their places around the doorsteps. Having deposited their bags and baskets, they proceeded to salââm before me. I could not summon resolution to send them away, as my curiosity was gradually getting better of my fears, nor could I bring myself to witness their performance in the absence of my husband. I therefore sent a message to the one who seemed the headman of the band by my "ayah," or maid, to inquire if they would not go away now and return in the afternoon about four o'clock. "Return? Why, what is to prevent us from remaining just where we are until the master comes home?" I could see no just reason save my own fears to have them lounging around my lonely house, and in spite of these concluded to let them stay.

Strange it was to see these, to me almost supernatural men and women, enjoying themselves as naturally and innocently for three or four full hours as did this company of wild serpent-charmers and jugglers. The two women of the party searched for the most delicate and polished pebbles to be found in the gravelled walks of the garden, and entertained themselves by digging holes in the sand and rolling their pebbles with great skill into these, hitting off one with another, and seeming to think it capital sport. Some of the men took some caiah, or cocoanut-fibre, out of their bags and proceeded to twist a rope out of it. Some lighted long pipes and began to smoke quietly, stroking down the cobra de capellos, who would poke their heads from under the baskets by their sides. The boy of the party had a bit of rag spread for

SERPENT CHARMER.

him under an adjoining tree, and here he stretched himself at full length to sleep, with a basket of snakes for his pillow. Every now and then the upper lid of this basket seemed to open and a snake would thrust out his head, as if to survey the sleeping boy, then as suddenly withdraw. All the while the beautiful sea gleamed and sparkled and dashed against the rocks in front of the "Aviary," and completed this strange picture.

A little after four o'clock my husband arrived, and, seated on the steps of the "Aviary," we witnessed some most astonishing performances. Before beginning his music, and while the women were girding themselves for action, the snake-charmer paid us some very startling and original compliments. All at once, seizing his bagpipe-like instrument and puffing out his polished black cheeks, he produced the same queer melody that I had first heard, with its endless reverberations, creating a strange effect upon one's nerves. The women kept time to these sounds by motions the most gently waving that one could conceive of. When the sounds were low and faint they waved their arms and bent downward in graceful undulating curves; then again, as the sounds began to be shrill and piercing, they raised their arms aloft, turned up their faces to the sky, and, poised on tiptoe, beat a rhythmic movement to the sound. The dance was in itself a wonder of grace and flexibility. But, strangest sight of all, the serpents were equally moved. In raising their heads they had thrown off the covers of the baskets, and presently every snake, large and small—and there were no less than six—had begun to take part in this dance, their eyes glistening, their forked tongues extended, their hoods spread to the utmost; they raised themselves on the abdomen and swayed their heads to and fro, following the movements of the charmers and seemingly ravished with the strange sounds. There was not a doubt in my mind, as I watched the serpents, that they distinguished the varieties of sound, for with every rise and fall of the music they kept time with their inflated hoods and slender forms.

Suddenly the serpent-charmer started to his feet and began a wild circular movement, accompanied with wilder and more energetic sounds, which were reverberated from every rock of the hill. After a few minutes he stood still, and, taking for a moment the instrument from his mouth, uttered a sudden "Ah!" short, sharp, and guttural, and all at once resumed his former movements both of sound and action. We involuntarily turned our eyes in the direction of those of the serpent-charmer, and noticed a slight movement in the grass and brushwood that covered the ground-floor of the "Aviary;" and as we looked the head and neck of a cobra de capello of large size rose above the grass. The strange reptile approached nearer and nearer. He passed with folded hood through the open wirework of the "Aviary." Out of it, he once more unfolded his hood, and, waving it to and fro, looked like one suddenly awakened to some subtle and purely spiritual influence; he leaped rather than crept toward the sound of the charmer; every curve, every change of motion, and every movement of the body betrayed an exquisite apprehension of the peculiar waves of the melody. The serpent, followed by another more slender in proportions, leaped almost into the arms of the charmer, and, swinging their bodies to and fro, both snakes seemed to give themselves up to the enchantment of sound. Very slowly but deliberately the serpent-charmer dropped one hand, and, stooping over the head of the largest serpent, playing all the while, grappled it just under the head by the thumb and forefinger and handed it to one of the men. This done, he proceeded to enchant and capture the smaller snake, which was accomplished in the same way. Then he dropped his instrument, took a curious flint knife out of his bag, and, pressing tightly the windpipe of each of the serpents in turn, cut out the bags containing the poisonous fluid and dropped the deadly reptiles, now rendered for ever harmless, into the bags. This was done in broad daylight, in the open air, where no deception could have been practised.

Some persons have suggested that these two snakes might have been brought by the band and let loose in the "Aviary." Even if this were so, it could not destroy the mystery of the influence which certain sounds evidently exercised over the serpents, who voluntarily returned to captivity even before the poison-bag had been cut out, the removal of which, according to all testimony, renders them harmless and agreeable pets. As far as my observation went, I am inclined to believe that these snakes were perfectly wild till caught by the serpent-charmer.

When I asked him by what power he compelled these snakes to abandon their holes and come out to hear his music, his reply was characteristic. "Asmani ka jore se, Maim Sahib," translated into English, would mean, "By the secret power of the heavenly motions."

The other tricks of the band were very wonderful, but not as absorbing as serpent-charming. They appeared to cause a seed to bud, grow, blossom, and bear fruit in the open air in a short space of time and with but few contrivances. They showed us a mango-seed, which they planted before our eyes in a pot of prepared soil brought with them; this they watered again and again with a peculiar liquid, also in their possession. Each time that there was a positive growth in the tree the round basket which covered it was removed, and our attention called to the fact that it was growing. When the tree had outgrown the basket a large cloth was thrown over it. Finally, it was presented to us full grown, and, though dwarfed in stature, with ripe mangoes hanging from its branches. They invited me to taste the fruit, which I did, and found it decidedly inferior in flavor to the most ordinary mango produced in the natural way. The curious part of this feat is this, that the tree itself, supposing they carried it about with them, had that fresh and vigorous look of active life and growth which it could not possibly retain out of the earth in a hot climate for any length of time without a very delicate and careful knowledge of how to preserve plant-life on the part of these apparently savage jugglers. I have also seen them produce flowers on plants in the same way.

A great many other feats and tricks were performed, such as throwing up a top, and not only catching it on the end of a slender stick, but balancing it on the point of the nose, and causing it, without any new impetus to stop or to go on spinning at the request of the spectator.

Some of the tricks are called *nuzzerbund*, "blindfolding" or mesmerizing the spectator. A ring is placed in your hand and you are requested to hold the hand tightly between your folded knees, and when you look again you find a little dust. One of these tricks, called *khano-nuzzerbund*, "ears and eyes bound," is that of a small boy being put into a basket and made to disappear and reappear. Our juggler produced a small basket and beckoned to the boy to get into it, which he did; two of the men then produced instruments that looked like flageolets and began to play, moving round the head of the child. This seemed to have a peculiar effect on the boy, who appeared like one in paroxysms of pain. It was very distressing to witness his convulsions, and even while we looked the child began to disappear in the basket. The moment he was out of sight the musicians seized long knives and fell upon the basket and pierced it with many thrusts, and it seemed certain that the child was not in it, nor could we see him anywhere. Presently they straightened out the basket and resumed their music, when, all at once, from afar the clear answering voice of the child was heard; nearer and nearer came the sound, until the basket swelled and distended, and, lo! there was the boy peering from under the lid serene and smiling.

These jugglers call themselves Jâdoo-wallahs, and are of the same tribe as the Yogees who follow the Mohammedan processions and cut themselves with knives and sharpened flints in order to extract money from the more tender-hearted of the crowds who always frequent such spectacles. The name of Jâdoo-wallah is a corruption of the words Yahdèo-Wallah, "filled with god-power." The common people believe that these powers are bestowed upon them by the gods, and thus do everything and anything in their power to propitiate the goodwill of the Jâdoo-wallahs. As acrobats they far surpass the Europeans. One of the men who performed for us received on his right shoulder, as lightly as if it had been a feather, a heavy weight which was dropped from an overhanging branch of a tree above.

It was dusk before the jugglers and serpent-charmers finished their astonishing feats and performances. We handed them five rupees, and they were delighted with this liberality, though I had feared they would not think it enough. They departed with the usual benediction, "Both burrus Jeho Sahib loke. Tumarra bucha kè bucha Ingrage kè guddee per bait jowoh" ("Long may you live, gentlefolk, and may your children's children seat themselves on the British throne").

Not long after we had an opportunity of witnessing the grand serpent-festival held in Bombay and other parts of Hindostan in the months of July and August. It is called "the naga-poojmi," literally, "serpent-worship." There are many tribes in India who have assumed the name of Nagas or Serpents from the earliest times. Diodorus supposes that the snake had been used as their crest or banner. There are three kinds of serpent-worship practised in India, and each is peculiar to a distinct class of people, although all the natives of India, except the Mohammedans, either from dread of the deadly serpent or from a feeling of veneration, join in the festival of the naga-poojmi.

The first of these is the worship paid to the serpent by the high-caste Brahmans, who adopted the early serpent-worship from the non-Aryan populations, placing the serpent, as a symbol of the masculine energy of the world, in the hand and sometimes around the head of Brahma, the chief god of their trinity; they adroitly represent that on the day sacred to the serpent, Krishna, their last incarnation, slew the great serpent Kali, who was just in the act of swallowing up the sun and moon. The second is the worship made to the serpent-gods carved in their temples by the non-Aryan and low-caste races of India, by whom the serpent is regarded in the light of a benefactor and friend, and to whom it was at one time customary to offer annually a human victim to propitiate its deadly sting. And, last of all, is the worship paid to it by the professional snake-charmer, to whom the art of taming the serpent has been transmitted from father to son, and in whose eyes the serpent is an oracle of wisdom, the harbinger of all good things, and last, but not least, a means of livelihood to the tribe.

On the last day of the waning moon at the end of July we rode out, accompanied by a party of friends, to the native part of the city, where we were told the chief of the serpent-worshippers were assembled. Here we found an immense throng of men and women gayly dressed, bands of handsome dancing-girls in flowing veils and glittering jewels, and rows of young maidens beautifully attired, with offerings of rice and milk, and some with fruit and flowers tastefully arranged in baskets which they carried on their heads; others with baskets filled with such flowers as serpents are reported to delight in—the champu, the marigold, the water-lily, the tuberose, and quantities of the snake-plant commonly called *sampkèmah*, "the mother of the serpent." We passed through the crowd and succeeded in reaching the centre of a great *maidan*, or open plain, where we stood.

Not far off clustered a vast number of serpents, with their charmers and worshippers. Immediately behind this curious assembly was a temple dedicated to the snake-god. From within these walls the lights, kept burning in great numbers, could be seen pale and ghastly amid the daylight, and the sounds of the tomtom and gongs beat in honor of the idol were heard; some noble old peepul trees surrounded the temple. Right in front of the temple were placed great basins containing milk and a preparation of rice and milk called *khir*, for the serpents. Those, however, that fed out of the basins were mostly all tame; they coiled in and out and round about the worshippers in a careless and easy manner. But farther on, beyond the stone basins and amid flowers and floods of sunshine, women dancing and men and boys singing, might be seen the deadly cobra de capellos now and then inflating their hoods and keeping time to the music.

The Brahman worship of the serpent is characteristic. Regarding the snake purely as a symbol, each priest prepares a clay figure of a cobra and winds it when in a plastic state round a tall pole, the upper part of which is ornamented with a ring, which in its turn typifies the feminine powers of nature.

On the day of the festival thousands of Brahmans, each with his pole thus ornamented, accompanied by musicians and dancing-girls, the former playing on their instruments and the latter keeping time to the music and performing a mystic circular dance, surrounded by half-naked fakeers and gossains, who keep shouting and leaping about, traverse the length and breadth of the native town till they reach their temples. Entering these, they plant their poles in front of the shrine of Siva, after which they make over the clay serpent a wave-offering of fire, pouring over it the oil pressed from the "telah," or sesamum-seed, sacred to the serpent, and repeat the prayer, "Life has sway over all in earth and heaven; protect us as a mother her children; grant us life, prosperity, wisdom," etc.

On this day every Hindoo and Brahman woman places seven wicks in a dish of silver or other metal, fills the dish with telah oil, and at nightfall waves it around the portals and windows of her house. When her husband returns he makes her a present, generally of a scarf, and she then performs a curious and very mysterious rite: placing her hands on her own hip-joints, and touching his with the tips of her fingers, she prostrates herself before him and implores for him, from the god of the day, renewed vigor, health, and strength.

The Nagas, or low-caste serpent-worshippers, assemble with the snake-charmers in open plains, where all the tame snakes in the country are brought together. After having fed these creatures, they offer up prayers, each to his own deity, but mostly to the god Siva, for long life and for protection from its deadly bite, making offerings of the snake-plant, and to the priests of little lamps lighted with one or two wicks for the altars.

The common people in the Hindoo villages also make clay images of the cobra and pray to them. Most of the abandoned characters turn out on the occasion of these festivals, and the night is spent in licentious merriment, music, and song, while the snake-charmers, jugglers, and Yogees obtain large sums of money and presents from the people, who regard them in the light of divine benefactors to their race.

To understand the worship paid to serpents we must remember that the earliest feeling which mankind had of a relation to invisible powers must have been a compound of dread and gratitude, and in the mingling of these emotions dread predominated. The dreaded serpent alone, says Fergusson,* without arms or wings or any of the usual appliances of locomotion, still moves with singular celerity and grace; its form is full of elegance, its colors are often very beautiful, its eyes are bright and piercing. A serpent can creep, spring, climb, swim, expand, constrict, suspend itself by the tail, burrow in the ground, and even raise its body almost erect. Its muscular irritability is remarkably great and persistent, depending on its nervous energy. The heart palpitates long after death; the jaws open and shut even when the head is severed from the body; the outer skin is shed more than once, and the ancients believed that by this means the snake renewed its youth. It does not need food for long periods when casting its skin. It often changes color at will, and, above all, its longevity is so great as still to make the superstitious ascribe to it immortality. It makes no nest (except in the case of the python, who hatches her eggs by the heat of her own body); no food is stored for the

* See Fergusson's *Tree- and Serpent-Worship.*

young, who are born with all powers in full perfection. Then the poison of a serpent is so deadly and subtile that it excites in the heart of the savage the greatest dread and mystery, and even more startling and terrible than the poison of the cobra is the flash-like spring and fascination of the boa constrictor, the instantaneous embrace, the crushed-out life,—all accomplished faster than the human eye can follow. These are the powers that must have impressed the primitive races of the East with dread and terror, and wherever the serpent was found, there he seems to have been propitiated by man with prayers, supplications, and all forms of worship. It is perhaps strange that the serpent in the early period of the worship was not so much dreaded as loved—whether from a feeling that it was not as deadly as it has in its power to be, or for some other reason, it is now impossible to determine. However, in the history of this peculiar religion it is found that in course of time the serpent began to be regarded as the harbinger of good gifts, the teacher of wisdom, the symbol of subtlety, the oracle of the future, and even the healer of all diseases.

All the gods, and even the kings and queens, of the old world are usually represented with serpents coiling about their heads or arms. The Hindoos most probably adopted this symbol of the serpent from the aboriginal populations among whom they settled. "Sance," the oldest rock-sculpture of the Hindoo "Saturn," the presiding deity of the seventh day of the week, has serpents for her belts or rings. She rides on a raven, a bird of ill omen sacred to her, and no Hindoo will undertake any new enterprise on the day over which she presides. As one wanders through the forests of India one finds that many of the finest trees served as altars to a generation long gone by. Their huge old trunks have been hollowed out and carved in the form of oriel chapels or windows, in the inmost recesses of which may be still traced the faint remains of what was intended to represent the cobra de capello or hooded serpent of India.

Sacred trees have from very early times shared a portion of the homage paid to serpents. It would appear that while the serpent was made to symbolize both the beneficent and dreaded powers of nature, the tree represented man. The wondrous spectacle of a new creation every year, the forest trees gathering their fresh leaves every spring, became to the primitive man a steadfast promise of a similar resurrection, and perhaps caused him to associate the tree with the serpent because of the analogies that exist between them. The one shedding its leaves, the other its skin, their mutual inactivity in winter, their awakening to life in the spring, their longevity, the twig-like form of the serpent, and a last, but not least, important fact is this, that wherever, in India, the deadly serpent is found, there also abounds the mungoose,* or snake-plant, with convex flower-clusters and long serpentine roots, possessing the mysterious power to cure the deadly bite of a snake.

Thus, in the course of time, the serpent became an endless writing on the wall, so full was it of mysterious significance and dread to the ancient races of the world. In fact, serpents play an important part in the mythology of every nation of the earth. Even to-day the snake-charmers will tell you that the circles on the head of the cobra de capello are spiritual eyes which enable it to distinguish

* This plant is named after a large rat common in India and called mungoose by the natives. It is said to have a deadly antipathy to snakes of all kinds. It will hunt and destroy them wherever they are found. If, however, the mungoose happens to be bitten by a snake, it is said that it instinctively runs to this plant, gnaws at its roots, and thus cures itself of the poison.

between good and bad men. If a good man is bitten to death, they account for it by declaring that he must have committed some deadly sin in a former state of existence, hence his punishment in this.

It will not be amiss to conclude this chapter with a mention of some of the symbols for which the serpent stood in ancient times. It stands for the higher and lower forms of the creative energy of nature; for the emblem of evil; for wisdom and subtlety, as we all know, being self-supporting from the moment of birth; for immortality, because of its fabled longevity; for death, for new birth, and resurrection, from its casting its skin and from its awakening in spring from the torpor of winter. In the oldest hieroglyphics the serpent with its tail in its mouth stood for cycles of time, for the horizon, for eternity, and for life to come. Twined around the crown of ancient Oriental kings and queens, it symbolized the fatal sting lurking beneath the power entrusted to them; and bound round the royal sceptre, it typified national life, vigor, and strength.

CHAPTER V.

The Parsees, or Fire-Worshippers, of Bombay.—A Visit to a Fire-priest and Astrologer.—His Astral Predictions.—The Gâthas.—Zoroaster.—His Life and Religion.—History of the Settlement of the Parsees in India.

THE race which more than others attracted my attention in India was the Parsees in Bombay. As we drove almost daily to or from the fort to Malabar Point, we passed a Fire-temple, and there are also two others in the old fort. These are held very sacred, and none but Parsees are allowed to enter them. The one, however, which stood between the fort and our house was less guarded, by which means it was more accessible to strangers and visitors.

At my earnest request, I was invited by the wife of our Parsee neighbor to witness the worship of this interesting people. It was on the occasion of the "Khurdad-Sal," the anniversary of the birthday of Zoroaster, that I repaired to the above-mentioned Fire-temple. Seeing a large crowd centred about the building, I ventured to peep in, in the hope of seeing my friend. No one paid the slightest attention to me; presently a young Parsee lad came forward and conducted me to a quiet corner, and I found myself the sole spectator of a very curious and interesting worship performed by the Fire-priests alone, with a crowd of Parsee women and children, and some very aged Parsee men scattered here and there among them.

The building was quite small, circular in shape, with a

sort of pent roof, small iron-grated windows, and an iron-bound door, which was padlocked the moment the service was over. Under the central arch of the temple was a low altar on which burned a clear bright fire; the smoke had no means of escaping but through the windows, which made the place rather unpleasant to stay in for any length of time. A number of priests clad in simple white robes and quite unadorned fed the sacred fire * with the dif-

* Minute instructions for the preparation of this sacred fire in case of its accidental extinction or in the first building of a temple are given in the "Fargard," one of the books of the Zend-Avesta. Fires from sixteen different places are necessary. One of the most indispensable ingredients in the building of the Fire is the flame by which a *dead body is burned,* though the body itself is held as the most impure of all things. Still, the fire which has consumed it is essential, as containing the most mysterious of all created substances, "electricity," which is thought to be more abundant in the human body than elsewhere in nature; it is called "naçupâka." This fire is purified by a very extraordinary process. A certain number of holes are prepared in the ground called "handarèza," or, in modern Parsee, "andaza," a measure. The fire is then placed in each of these holes in turn, prayed over by the chief priest with closed eyes, and blown over with the breath, already purified by the prayers just uttered.

The dyer's fire, the potter's, the glass-blower's, blacksmith's, bricklayer's, gold- and silversmith's, with phosphorus, beeswax, odoriferous gums, many different kinds of wood, the ashes of the rose and jessamine-flower, salt of various kinds, etc.,—all these fires and substances must be brought, after having been purified by the prayers said over them, to one and the same hearth or altar, called in the ancient Pehlevi Dâityo-gatus, now corrupted into "Dâdhgah." The collective fire, combined into one and thus obtained, represents the essence of nature, the mystic wine of the poets, pervading the whole universe, even to the most distant stars. This "mystic wine" or "life-water" is held to be the cause of all the growth, vigor, and splendor of the physical and mental qualities of animals, men, birds, beasts, and plants. It is therefore regarded with the deepest reverence. Before the collection and preparation of this fire the priests who are to take part in the ceremony must undergo great purification for nine nights, nine being the most sacred number, as it is the period in which the human offspring is perfected. The priest must drink the urine of a cow, sit on stones

ferent kinds of precious woods, and while some chanted, passing each his sacred thread through the fingers of his hands, others dropped perfumes and consecrated oil into the Fire.

The Parsee women and children sat or stood around this central fire, most of them beautifully dressed. I was struck with the beauty and nobility of their faces as they worshipped here with their hands folded, their eyes closed, listening reverently to the chants or praying silently to themselves.

A great many silver trays full of fruit, sweetmeats, and white robes were placed on one side, offerings from the women to the Fire-priests.

At the close of the service the entire congregation folded their hands across their breasts, and, having bowed their heads, retired, leaving the priests to heap precious fuel on the sacred fire, so as to preserve it from going out, for which purpose the temple is regularly visited during each day, and the fire is carefully preserved from year to year by certain priests who take turns to perform this most religious duty.

One evening we went to visit, by appointment, one of the oldest Fire-priests in Bombay, who was also a famous astrologer. The appointment was made by our nearest European neighbor on Malabar Hill, a Mr. S——, an Englishman who had lived a long time in India, and one of our intimate friends. Although Mr. S—— was personally acquainted with him, the old priest had declined to receive strangers until prevailed upon to do so by Mr. S——'s Parsee friend and partner in business.

within the enclosures of certain magic circles; while moving from one circle to another he must rub his body with cow-urine, and then with sand, and lastly wash himself from head to foot nine times in pure cold water.

We started about six o'clock in the evening, and after a long drive through the Parsee settlement of the native town and through a crowded and noisy bazaar, our carriage drew up before a high, dilapidated wooden building. The balcony projected into the street, supported by rickety wooden pillars, under which there was a small garden filled chiefly with herbs and plants. Mr. S——, who had often visited the house and was familiar with its ways, led us through the little garden and up a great flight of wooden steps into a corridor or hall, crossing which we at length stood before a very old door which was slightly ajar, through the opening of which a light streamed upon us in the dark passage. Mr. S—— tapped, and a voice feeble and tremulous bade us enter. We did so, and in another moment we were standing side by side with an old Fire-priest, perhaps the oldest in the world. He did not move or speak, or even turn his eyes upon us.

An old Ethiopian servant present pointed to us to be seated on some cushions near by until his master had finished his evening prayer. We silently took our places on the seats and looked on. In the centre of the room, which was woefully shabby and coarsely built, stood a three-legged stand, and on it was a round earthen lamp filled with cocoanut oil and containing depressions at the sides for wicks, of which there were just seven burning. Before it stood the Fire-priest, his dress, a long dingy-looking robe which might once have been white, flowing down to his emaciated feet, which were bare. But as his lips moved in prayer, and his thin dark fingers passed over and over his sacred thread or girdle, that mystic emblem of his faith, there was an indescribable reflection of some unseen interior light on his wan and pallid features; he hardly looked old, so wonderfully was his countenance lit up with a serene and beautiful expression of peace and happiness.

The floor of the room was made of planks roughly hewn and rudely put together. A number of curious old parchments were piled up on one side; pots, earthen lamps, vases, flowers, shawls, carpets, bedding, and a number of embroidered silk cushions lay in seeming confusion about the floor. The Ethiopian attendant, who looked almost as old as his master, grinned at us from his corner, showing plainly that he had lost nearly all his teeth; but no word was spoken.

His prayers over, the aged Fire-priest put off his long robe and dark conical cap, which were replaced by a short gray angraka, or coat, and close-fitting skull-cap, revealing a few locks of long scanty gray hair. He then turned to Mr. S——, took both his hands kindly in his own, and saluted him by raising them to his forehead three times, and then he did the same to us.

After an interval of about an hour or so spent in pleasant conversation, during which we learned that the Dustoor or Fire-priest Bhèjah was a native of Surat, and had come to the island of Bombay about forty years before with his family, every member of whom he had survived save some distant connections still living in Surat, we begged him to read our horoscopes for us.

The old Dustoor rose at once, as if pleased at our request, and with great alacrity led the way through a long narrow passage and up another old wooden staircase into a small chamber open to the sky by a curious contrivance, a sort of trapdoor, which was let down in rainy weather. There was a bench in one corner of this room; in the middle a circular table which revolved on a pivot, painted with curious hieroglyphics, and beside it a three-legged stool. As soon as we had taken our seats on the bench, the Dustoor drew out from under the table a board chequered black and red and a piece of chalk, and, taking the dim horn lantern that stood in a niche in the wall, set it on the table. This done, he turned to me and questioned me very closely in Hindostanee about the day, year, hour, and almost moment, of my birth. All such questions as I had it in my power to reply to he put down in what seemed to me signs and figures in one of the squares on his peculiar black and red board.

This was a work of some time, for every now and then he seemed doubtful of his operations, rubbing out and replacing the signs and figures in new squares. When he had scrawled on the board to his satisfaction he began to compare it with the hieroglyphics on his revolving table, deciphering and studying the stars on each of his tablets with the utmost care. He then turned up his wan face and began to gaze alternately at the bit of sky seen through the open trapdoor and to examine the strange hieroglyphics on the table. The stars presiding at my birth were evidently unpropitious. He foretold for me many deaths among relations and friends, long and cruel separations by strange seas and oceans being placed between my friends and me; softening it off, however, by predicting a long life, a happy old age, and a numerous progeny of grand- and great-grandchildren; which, indeed, are the chief sources of happiness in the Parsee household.

He then foretold my husband's future, which was even less auspicious, saying that a great shadow of one of the planets would cross his path in middle life, which if he survived he would live to a good old age, etc., etc.

It was not what the old astrologer and Fire-priest said so much as his perfect faith in his own rendering of the position of the stars that most impressed me. The floating locks of gray hair, the serious brow, the deep, thoughtful, contemplative look on that face, were all very striking: his head full of the mystery of the stars and his heart ever revolving the secret destiny of human life were as strange and marked as any of the many lives whose future he believed he could so easily decipher.

In the Zend-Avesta—or, more properly, the Avesta-Zand—the religious books of the Parsees, we find the Gâthas, or sacred hymns, of the ancient Fire-priests, and these in their turn may be traced directly to the Rig Vèdas, the oldest of the Aryan Scriptures, a collection of a thousand hymns, more or less, called "Mantras," or Mind-born songs, composed and recited by various priests and poets, the earliest of whom lived about three thousand, and the latest not far from twenty-six hundred, years ago. These hymns, some of which are very beautiful, composed and sung long before the Aryans left their home in the Hindoo Kush * Mountains, were inspired by its soaring mountains—"roofs of the world," as they called them—capped with snow, clear blue skies, and by the rushing waters leaping in gladness out of the heart of the hills.

"They found the mountains ever near mighty to defend them, the lakes and rivers eager to serve them." † "Sparkling bright with mighty splendor, she carries the clouds across the plains; the unconquered Sindhui, Indus, the quickest of the quick, like a beautiful mare, a sight to see; by their swiftness, depth, as well as by the sweetness of their waters; the birds by their delicious warbling; the winds by the fragrant dust of flowers which they

* The "Hindoo Kush," name for the Caucasian Mountains.

† See Max Müller's *The Origin and Growth of Religion*, p. 195, "The Gâthas, or Sacred Songs of the Parsees." See Haug's essays on "the Zend-Avesta."

bore along on their invisible wings, the clouds by their refreshing shadows."

Light, as seen in the sun, moon, and stars, dawn and sunrise, fire in all its mysterious forms—the spark struck from the flint, the fire that burned their oblations, the holy flames that were lighted on the domestic hearth—became their earliest objects of worship. These they celebrate in the Rig Vèda, and in these they saw, with their deep intuitive insight, thousands of years ago, an "all-productive cosmic energy."

Thus, the simple act of rubbing two dried pieces of wood together in order to obtain fire became a religious ceremony, and the tiny flint which served to kindle fire became their first idol, and gave those ancient Aryans the first hint of the wonderous power of heat, at once their god, the ministering angel of their lives, and their first step toward civilization.

This vital fire of the universe, with every upward dart of flame issuing out of the cold, hard rock, starting out of dried wood, streaming in jets spontaneously out of the heart of the earth itself, and flaming luridly from mountain-tops, was an object so full of mystery, so potent, ever present, even when invisible, ever within call, lurking in the rock and air, water and tree, waiting to be called into life, vanishing at a breath, naturally became the highest symbol of the unseen to those primitive worshippers of nature.

The early Aryan priest, who was to his race what our poets and thinkers are to us to-day, on awakening at dawn turned his face to the east, and, waiting for the light, cried, "Arise! arise! the breath of our life has come, the darkness has fled." The fire had to be kindled by men. "She, the Dawn, brought us light by striking down darkness.—Shine for us with thy best rays, O thou bright

Dawn! thou who lengthenest our lives, thou beloved of all, thou mother of the morning clouds, leader of the days, gold-colored and lovely to behold!" When the sun at last climbed the mountain-tops and shone upon his worshipper, he sang a deeper hymn of joy to the Creator: "In the beginning there arose the source of golden light. He was the first-born lord of all that is. He established the earth and the sky. He gives us life, he gives us strength—whose shadow is immortality, whose absence is death—he who through his power is the only king of this breathing and awakening world."*

These songs were not only sung, but transmitted from father to son, long before the age of a written alphabet, as a sacred, inviolable inheritance, preserved from century to century in the religious memory of the Aryan priest, even as they were recited to us evening after evening at the "Aviary" by our modern pundit without book or notes or text.

The pictures these songs present of the deep religious and poetic fervor of the early Aryans, both before and after their descent into the plains of India, of their pastoral and agricultural life, divided into separate and distinct classes, as priest, king, shepherd, warrior, and tiller of the soil, are in themselves the most comprehensive and valuable of historical records.

The first and most important fact to be found in the study of these hymns is that every home, every dwelling, has its own altar, which is the family hearth, called the "dâdgâh" by the Fire-worshippers—that "holy of holies" of which father and mother were priest and priestess. This fire is the ancient "avesta," to which were attached three mystical interpretations—first, "womanly purity;" second, the "inviolability of the family;" and third, "the sacred-

* See Max Müller's *Chips from a German Workshop.*

ness attached to the mother as the transmitter of human life."

There is no doubt that from the Assyrians, Chaldeans, and the early Iranians, who were then one with the purer Hindoos of to-day, this worship of nature, and especially of fire in its triple significance, was propagated southward among the Egyptians, westward among the Greeks, and by them introduced into Italy.

The Greeks met together to worship in their Prytaneia. Here they consulted together for the public good, and there was a constant fire burning on the altar, which was called "vesta." The Vestal Virgins of the Romans had their origin in the same idea. Many of the oldest and some of the most modern usages still to be found among the Parsees, Hindoos, Jews, Greeks, Mohammedans, and Roman Catholics bear reference to this early worship of the "household fire," and many of the problems, puzzles, and contradictions that are found in the religious symbols of the world stand clear and evident when submitted to this light.

The word "Light" is used in the New Testament as the highest symbol of Christ—"the Light of the world," "the Light that lighteth every man who cometh into the world." Every instance also of God's acceptance of sacrifice and prayer in the Old Testament is made evident to the people through the medium of fire, as seen in the case of David, in the dedication of Solomon's temple, and when Elijah demanded that extraordinary proof from Jehovah that Baal was not God. From Genesis to the Revelation, from the first offerings of Cain and Abel to "the city that had no need of a sun, neither of the moon, to shine in it, for the glory of the Lord did lighten it and the Lamb is the light thereof," this symbol of light is the dearest to the human heart, and ever recurring and conspicuous as the fittest and purest to be applied to the Deity.

It is as a symbol, not as a material element, that the worshippers of fire have clung to it through all times; and their adherence and tenacity are all the more remarkable when we consider the changes that have passed over all primitive institutions. We ourselves have had a succession of different religions and gods—the divinities of the Phœnicians, then those of the Greeks and Romans, which superseded the terrible gods of the Norsemen and the aboriginal deities of the Druids, our ancestors. All these in time have given place to the sublime teachings of Christ. Our religious forms are changing even to-day as religious convictions become wider, deeper, and more comprehensive than ever.

But the Parsees, those ancient Sun- and Fire-worshippers, still offer up their prayers in the old Pehlevi—a language which is the elder sister of the ancient Sanskrit—in which the Zend-Avesta, the sacred books of the Zoroastrians, are written, and older by far than the cuneiform inscriptions of Cyrus, Darius, and Xerxes;* still wear the same old conical cap in the form of ascending flame, preserved in the shape of the bishop's mitre in the Christian symbolic dress; still adhere to the rites, ceremonies, manners, and customs peculiar to their earliest fathers, invoking the invisible fire upon which they called centuries before the building of the temple of Solomon.

The race has survived the destruction of Babylon and Assyria—outlived the beautiful gods of the Greeks, who beat them down by land and sea. It has persistently overcome the hatred and persecution of the Scythian and Tartar hordes, the rage and fury of the Moslems, the

* See Max Müller's *Science of Religion*, Lecture IV., page iii.

intolerance and prejudice of all sects and nations, and, strange to say, even when placed between the currents of new ideas, which ceaselessly move and transform those around them, the Fire-worshipper, like the Jew, stands alone, as if he were beyond time and above change.

From the time of Xerxes, four hundred and eighty-six years B. C., we have to date the decline of the Persian empire. Even the old heroic name of Iran—Ayiran, from the Sanskrit Ariya, "the noble"—has passed away for the word Persia, which, whether we apply it to the country, to the people, or to the language, is a misnomer. Pars, or Fars, is only a province of the great empire of "Iran." It was owing to the fact that the language of its chief city, Shiraz, was considered the most elegant and fashionable speech of the Iranians that the name of the province Pars was gradually used to distinguish the people, the entire country, and the language.

To the ancient world Zoroastrianism was known by the name of "Mazdasnah" or "Mazdayasnah," the doctrine of "universal knowledge." It was revealed by the "Pure Spirit," called also the "Excellent Word," pure, efficacious —"the word that Zoroaster has conveyed to men," which is the "Good Law." The priests were called Madhi, or middlemen, go-betweens, corrupted into Magi, which name is very commonly applied to the priests of the Zoroastrian religion by the Greek authors, beginning with Herodotus, who had travelled in Media and confounded the name of the priests of Magism and the Median religion with that of Zoroastrianism.

It is impossible to fix exactly the era when the great reformer Zarathustra—"splendor of gold"—lived. The Greek and Roman historians make him very ancient. Xanthos of Lydia, 470 B. C., the first Greek writer who mentions Zoroaster, is convinced that he must have flourished about six hundred years before the Trojan war. Aristotle and Eudoxus place his era even earlier. Berosus, the Chaldean priest and historian, who translated the history of his native country, Babylonia, into the Greek language, and dedicated the work to Antiochus, one of the Greek kings of Syria, makes him a king, or rather founder of a dynasty which reigned over Babylon between 2200 and 2000 B. C.* The Fire-worshippers hold that their great priest and reformer lived about five hundred and fifty years B. C. They identify him with the great Kavan-Vistaspa of the Zend-Avesta, called Khai Gustasp in the *Shahnamah*.† But it is very evident that even the ancient Persians themselves were very uncertain as to who this Kavan Vistaspa was. It is clear, however, that Darius's father, who was also named Vis-

* See Rawlinson's *Ancient Monarchies*, where he identifies Zoroaster with the celebrated Median king Kudur-Nakhunta, and says: "A king of Elam, whose court was held at Susa, led in the year B. C. 2286 (or a little earlier) an expedition against the cities of Chaldæa, succeeded in carrying all before him, ravaged the country, took the towns, plundered the temples, and bore off the images of the deities which the Babylonians especially reverenced. This king's name, which was Kudur-Nakhunta, is thought to be the exact equivalent of one which has a world-wide celebrity—to wit, Zoroaster. Now, according to Polyhistor, who certainly repeats Berosus, Zoroaster was the first of those eight Median kings who composed the second dynasty in Chaldæa and occupied the throne from about B. C. 2286 to 2052. The Medes are represented by him as capturing Babylon at this time, and imposing themselves as rulers upon the country. Eight kings reign in the space of 234 or 224 years, after which we hear no more of Medes, the sovereignty being (as it would seem) recovered by the natives. The coincidences of the conquest, the date, the foreign sovereignty, and the name Zoroaster, tend to identify the Median dynasty of Berosus with a period of Susanian supremacy which the monuments show to have been established in Chaldæa at a date not long subsequent to the reigns of Urukh and Ilgi, and to have lasted for a considerable period."

† A collection of heroic poems on the ancient histories of Persia and her kings, by Firdoosi.

taspa, and the Kavan-Vistaspa of the Zend-Avesta and the *Shahnamah*, were entirely distinct persons.

There is very little doubt that this confusion of opinions is owing to the similarity of names. A very common habit even in India to-day is to name persons after heroic kings, great priests, or even after the gods, without any mark being added to distinguish them in after years; and when any period of time has elapsed it is almost impossible to separate the personality of the father from the son, or the disciple from the teacher, or the priest from the god. Zoroaster, or rather "Zara Thustra," means illustrious like gold, or, in another sense, simply high priest; and this being taken afterward as the proper name of the celebrated priest and reformer of ancient Iran, gavé rise to the endless confusion of dates and opinions which has always prevailed with regard to the age in which he lived.

There is, however, internal evidence in the language and religion which he reformed that he lived at a very early age, and there are many traces of his great antiquity in the Zend-Avesta itself. First, that he stands at the head of the extensive Zend literature,* which must have required centuries for its growth, and which was already in a state of perfection when Buddha, the founder of Buddhism, was born, from four to five hundred years before Christ; and secondly, that he is expressly called Aryana Veèdgo, "the celebrated one," in the Aryan home whence the Aryans, now called Hindoos, emigrated in times immemorial. This title, Martin Haug justly observes, would not have been given him had his followers not believed him living at that early time. Under no circumstance can we assign to him a later date than the year 1000 B. C.

* See Martin Haug's *Essays on the Sacred Language, Writings, and Religion of the Parsees.*

The causes which led to the schism between the early Fire-worshippers may be readily learned from the Zend-Avesta, where the gods of the dissenters are called "dèvas" (to whence our word devil) by the orthodox "Soshyantos," or Fire-priests. It was a vital and successful struggle against that form of the early religion which inclined to Brahmanism, and later to open idolatry. Thus, for instance, the Vèdic gods Aditya, Mitra, Varuna, and Indra became the devils of the Zoroastrian religion; and this struggle must have taken place when Indra was declared the chief of the gods by a large portion of the Aryans, before they had immigrated into Hindostan proper. In the later period of Vèdic literature we find Indra at the head of the gods; then in the great epics, the Mahâbhárata and Râmayâna, he gives place to the Trimourtri, Brahma, Vishnu, and Siva. A compromise was thus effected between the esoteric doctrine of the metaphysicians and the common forms of worship, giving rise to what was henceforth to constitute the orthodox system of belief of the Brahmanic caste. The Vèdic pantheon, however, is not altogether discarded in the Zend-Avesta; the existence of the old gods is recognized, but in a very different way from that of the mysterious triple divinity which represents not only the eternal, infinite soul, but Brahma himself in his active relation to mundane occurrences; and moreover, as the Trimourtri is never alluded to in the Zend-Avesta, where most of the other Vèdic gods are named, we are obliged to fix the religious struggle at a much earlier date than that assigned to the Indian poems.

The only source whence we derive anything like reliable historical facts, and those of the most meagre kind, respecting this great reformer Zoroaster, is in the Yasnahs, where he is distinguished by his family name S'pitama. His father's name was Pooroosliaspa. Of his children, only his son S'pitama and his daughter Poroochista are mentioned. In these fragments, rather than books, he appears to us as a real man, earnest, strong, and true, just and generous in every act of his life, taking a prominent part in the history of his country and the welfare of his fellow-creatures. It was he who struck a deathblow to the idolatrous practices that had crept in among the Fire-priests—who established in his own country a new community, governed by new laws; he called upon every man to take his part in the battle between good and evil, adding the firm assurance that good will always prevail. In his own works he calls himself a "Dutah"—*i. e.* "a messenger"—sent by the great Ahura-Mazda. His ideal of home, of father and mother living together under one roof in freedom and love and unity, cemented by a supreme and unalterable bond of love and friendship, has never yet been equalled save by Christianity.

This remarkable reformer, according to the Yasnahs, was born in the sacerdotal city of Ragha, near Teheran, the capital of Persia. His father was an aged priest named Poorooshaspa, a man noted for his purity of life. Like all such histories, his birth was miraculously ordained.* One evening as Poorooshaspa and Dhogdha his wife, a childless old couple, were praying in a lonely place, the atmosphere around them became suddenly luminous. They looked up, and saw a form of exquisite beauty standing in the midst of a bright cloud, and as they gazed upon this beautiful vision there was handed to them a cup fashioned out of an amethyst filled with the wine of heaven. "Drink this," said the angel, "and renew your youth, for

* The Persian writers of the Middle Ages ascribed to Zoroaster a long series of prodigies and miracles without end; to which both Pliny and Eubulus, giving the last echoes of popular traditions, allude.

Ahura-Mazda has chosen you to bring a savior into the world." Having drank the wine, they became the parents of one son, S'pitama.

It is related that the ruler of the city of Ragha sought to destroy the child; at his command he was snatched from his mother's arms and thrown into a narrow lane where cattle passed, in the hope that they might tread him to death; but, lo! in the evening a sensible and motherly cow brought him on her horns to his weeping, disconsolate mother. Then again, by the order of the same cruel governor, he was cast into a blazing fire; but he lay there unscathed, smiling so serenely upon his persecutors that they were at once converted into friends. In fact, every attempt made by enemies to destroy the infant is said to have been arrested by divine agency. At last the child was permitted to grow up unmolested with his friends and relatives, who were among his earliest followers.

Zoroaster did not so much reveal a new religion as reform the old Fire-worship of his country. He abolished stone images, necromancy, magic, witchcraft, all of which were identified with the worship of fire. He investigated astrology, and confirmed its practices as true and elevating. He inspired the old materialistic teaching of the Fire-priests with a new and more spiritual meaning. He made war on the idolatrous practices of his fellow-men, and banished from Iran all who still bowed down before wood and stone. At the age of thirty he completed a new code of laws, and also the Zend-Avesta, with the Izeshnee, a still more sacred book. He distinctly recognized, above and beyond all manifestions of sun, light, or fire, a purer, higher, unconditioned Being.* When moved by deepest awe he bowed his head and reverently called this Being

* The Uncreated, the Eternal. He has had no beginning, and will have no end.—*The Yasnahs.*

"the Truth of the Truth, the Wisdom of the Wise, the Purity of the Pure." So also in his famous prayer of one-and-twenty words, "The world is produced, and all that is good in thought, word, and deed, because of the Truth."

The problem of the origin of evil, the most difficult to be solved, seems to have been constantly before his mind. It seemed to him impossible that the Truth, whom he conceived to be eternally pure, good, just, and perfect, had created evil. The ancient Aryans attributed the struggles in the physical world around them to the strife between good and evil; Zoroaster seized this idea, applied it with the deepest emphasis to the moral and spiritual world, and it became the basis of his system of dualism. Together with Ahura-Mazda, the good principle, he admitted the existence of an evil principle or spirit equal in power and of a similar nature*—Angra Mainyus; in Persian Ahriman. This spirit is the author of all moral and physical evil, sin, disease, suffering, and death.

All things, created by Ahura-Mazda pronouncing the creating, pre-existing word "Honover," were pure, perfect, and beautiful as himself until spoiled by the evil influence of Ahriman. And though Ahriman, like Ahura-Mazda, has been eternal and self-existing in the past, Zoroaster declares that a day will come when three great prophets will arise, Ukhsyad-eremah, "the increasing Light," Ukhsyad-eretah, "the increasing Truth," Açtvad-ereta, "self-existent Truth," who will convert all mankind; everything created will become as pure as on the

* To reconcile the existence of these two absolute Beings, coequal and coeternal, the doctrine of the Zarvanians was conceived in later times. This sect, which flourished about the time of Alexander the Great, supposed an unconditioned existence prior and superior to Ahura-Mazda, Ormuzd, and Ahriman, called "time without limit," Zaravan-Akarana, from whom emanated the two spirits or principles of good and evil.

first day when it issued from the breath of the "Wisest of all Intelligence," and Ahriman will be destroyed and disappear for ever.

Such is the real doctrine of Zoroaster, while the hymns of the Zend-Avesta glow and burn with the assurance of the mystic and essential life of the soul with the spiritual essence of all pure thought. The pure heavens are like light; thought is likened to a drop of pure light, and the departing spirit has a sunbeam for its guide to conduct it to immortal light.

In the Gâthas, or Songs, he says: "God appears in the best thought, the truest speech, and the sincerest action. He gives through his pure spirit health, prosperity, devotion" (which, more properly translated, ought to be "love"), "and eternity to this universe. He is the Father of all truth and the Mother of all tenderness."

It is very remarkable that the early Aryans looked upon disease, deformity, and weakness in the same light that we are apt to regard the depraved and vicious. Health was the first and greatest boon, the gift they supplicated most earnestly from heaven. Health first, then immortality. They seemed to loathe consumption and scrofula, and many of their most energetic prayers are supplications to the Deity to be preserved "from this hateful indwelling sin," as they termed it. Their laws for the happy treatment of women, especially in certain conditions of health, of which I shall treat in the chapter on their domestic life, is full of that reverence for her health and happiness, as well as those of her offspring, which is seen to penetrate the whole life of the Fire-worshipper, passing as it did in the course of time into a rigid etiquette. Stern as it is, it is infinitely better than the careless indifference with which the mother, "the transmitter of human life," is so often regarded among us.

In the Zend-Avesta we find a moral code almost as perfect as our own, with rather a singular account of the creation. In one of the books, called "Desater," it would seem all animals being created except man, the dog was dreadfully lonely, and that man was created only out of compassion for him; and no sooner was man formed than all the animals, save the dog, broke out into open rebellion against the Great Spirit for having favored man with speech, reason, and immortality.

As in Genesis, so in the Desater, the Great Spirit brought the animals to Gelshadèng and made them subject to him, and he it was who divided them into seven classes. There is a curious dialogue that passed between the seven great sages of Persia and the seven different animals, and the reasons given why some are made fierce, others harmless, and yet others beneficent. In some passages great veneration is expressed for the cow, and great aversion to some animals, and to the human corpse; this is not permitted either to find a resting-place in the earth or in the fire, because of the sacredness of both these elements; and it is commanded that it be abandoned to birds of prey or to absorption by the air in enclosures set apart for the purpose.

However, in spite of many things that seem childish and absurd in their books (the unprejudiced student is not always certain that the right meaning of the text has been rendered, for the language is full of difficulties), yet so much is clear: that the "Gâthas" are very beautiful hymns and full of true religious feeling. They are addressed to the household fire, to the sun, moon, and stars, to the spirit of the hills, mountains, trees, birds, and flowers, to the earth, air, and sea. The earth is often called the "infinite, the all-nourishing cow," and the sun is consequently, by the same figure, designated "the fiery-winged one, the immortal bull."

Then there are prayers and songs to the spirits of the righteous dead, to the seven high angels around the throne, the planets then known. The most spiritual are those addressed to Ahura-Mazda, "the Everlasting Light," who is described as an ineffable Being, full of brightness and glory. Zoroaster discovers God in the eternal invisible Fire. His wonder and joy over the first kindling of the flame arose from the spiritual symbolism that interpreted all nature to him. In it he recognizes the type of the immortal Light and the spiritual resurrection of the soul. Thrilling with religious fervor, he bows before the radiant light as the most subtle and all-dissolving element, and in feeling its mystery acknowledges the mystery of God, its Supreme Creator.

Thus, all the rites and ceremonies of the ancient Fire-worshippers abound in symbols which typify the operations of nature, not only in the heavens, but also in the hidden recesses of the earth. They attribute the maturing of precious gems and metals to the peculiar influence of the sun, moon, and stars; and it is a curious fact that they called the seven metals by the very same names by which they denominated the seven planets, and the same peculiar hieroglyphic characters are used to this day to distinguish both. Among them certain stones represented certain virtues, and not a few were famed for their magical properties. The months of the year were spirits who exerted their influence over certain precious stones, which in their turn had power over the destiny of any person born during the period of their sway. Thus each month has its own presiding genius in the heavens and its appropriate symbol in the heart of the earth, bound up with the life and character of the individual born under their combined influence. The garnet, symbol of the presiding spirit of January, means constancy; the amethyst, of February, sincerity;

the bloodstone, of March, courage and presence of mind; the diamond, of April, innocence; the emerald, of May, love; the agate, of June, health and long life; the carnelian, of July, contentment; sardonyx, of August, happiness; chrysolite, of September, antidote against madness, sane mind; opal, of October, hope; topaz, of November, fidelity; turquoise, of December, prosperity.

Rings are still used among the more superstitious of the Parsees as charms and talismans against the evil eye, demons, and most of the ills inherent to the human flesh. Sometimes the virtue exists in the stone, sometimes in the magical letters engraved upon it, which are thought to have the power to preserve the owner from thunder, lightning, witchcraft, the evil eye, from sin, and from taking cold even when exposed to biting frosts and storms.

The ancient history of the Fire-worshippers presents no nobler picture than that of Zoroaster traversing the wilds of Persia to preach a purer doctrine to his fellow-men. Before his death he is said to have reduced the twenty-one books he had written to three immortal maxims: Pure thoughts, Pure words, Pure deeds. "All pure thought is spirit-worship, or religion," said he, going at once to the root of the matter, "and all pure actions are fed by the immortal dew of heaven;" this dew is *virtue*, and he calls it the vapor which the pure-hearted inhale from the heart of the eternal Sun.

What a nation does thoroughly, she does for all time. So it was with the ancient Persians: centuries after the death of their great teacher they kept their faith in one God firm and inviolate amid the most crushing persecution. On the final conquest of Persia the unrelenting soldiers of the Caliphat forced at the point of the sword one hundred thousand persons daily to abjure their faith. Thousands upon thousands were slaughtered daily; only a few escaped and fled to the mountains of Khorasan, taking with them a lamp lighted from the sacred Fire. From these mountains they were again driven forth by the Mohammedans four hundred years after, and the little band of Zoroastrians fled once more, to the beautiful island of Ormuzd, at the mouth of the Persian Gulf. Here persecution still followed them, and, driven out again, the little colony put to sea, still taking with them their sacred lamp, which had been preserved from extinction through all those troublous years.

They had hardly lost sight of land when a terrific storm overtook them, and their little fleet was soon deprived of all hope of escape. Voluntarily exiled from their native land, they had fled from place to place for protection; the mountains refused to hide them, the earth to shelter them, and now even the sea and all the elements rose up against them—all but their little feeble lamp, which, according to their historians, continued to burn brightly in spite of the dreadful storm. At length the high priest of Zoroaster resolved to hoist their sacred lamp as a signal to the tempest-driven little fleet to join in prayer. Up rose the horn lantern containing the sacred light to the masthead of the dahstur's (or high priest's) vessel. The little fleet of boats and ships tried to draw near to the precious beacon, but the winds blew and the tempest beat upon their vessels. All undismayed, straining their utmost and peering through the gloom, they turned them in the direction of the sacred light. Then up above the din and roar of that angry surging sea the prayer of that faithful little company ascended to the Invisible, the shining Ahura-Mazda, for help in their sore distress.

Next morning the storm had abated, and they landed at Diva, on the coast of Western Hindostan, where they disembarked, and remained nineteen years, whence they migrated in a body to Sajan, twenty-four miles south of Damaun. The Hindoo king, Ranah Jayadeva, granted an asylum to the fugitives.

After centuries of cruel persecution the exiles at length found refuge from the enemies of their faith among the Hindoos, who had separated from them in the dim dawn of history because of a religious feud, but whose antagonism touched only names and other non-essential rites, the worship of light as the Creator's highest symbol remaining unchanged for both. Though they had drifted farther and farther apart, the latter in the multiplying of symbols, while the former gradually dispensed with even those they once regarded as a part of their worship, they still remained united in their worship of fire.

In 721 A. D. they erected their first Fire-temple on Indian soil at Sajan, and the sacred fire was once more kindled on its altars by means of their little lamp, the flame of which they had so religiously preserved. To the Fire-worshipper this first temple on Indian soil seemed a resurrection of hope, of reality, striking deep into their fervent hearts and binding them to one another by a subtler and diviner fire. From this time the Parsees rose to importance in India. They greatly aided the Portuguese and Dutch settlers in the establishment of mills and factories all along the coast of Guzerat. Owing to their enterprising spirit, Surat, Cambay, and Baroda grew into large and influential cities and attracted all the extensive commerce of the East. When the island of Bombay was ceded to the British a colony of Parsees emigrated thither, and, having purchased a part of Malabar Hill from the British, built there a Fire-temple and a tower of silence, or tomb for the reception of their dead, and here was brought the same sacred fire and rekindled once more on the altar of their first temple in Bombay.

No country in the world has witnessed so many revolutions as Persia. Nevertheless, the moral and physical condition of the Fire-worshippers, who are still found centring about Yezd and Ispahan, has remained much the same as when they called the country their own. They certainly are superior in moral character to the Mohammedans of Persia to-day. In the garden adjoining the harem of the present shah none are employed save Zoroastrians, and this is because of their national character for purity. As for the Parsee women, they are remarkable for their chastity, an unchaste woman being unkown among them.

In Persia, however, the Parsees are subject to heavy taxation, from which the Moslem population is entirely free, and the distress to which the poorer Parsees are reduced in order to pay this tax is deplorable. Unheard-of cruelties are practised, and many as a last resource abandon their homes to escape the extortions of the annual tax-gatherer. All means of instruction are also closed to the children of the Fire-worshippers in Persia. "The Parsees of Bombay, hearing of the distress of their co-religionists, have recently caused schools to be established in various parts of Persia, where instruction is imparted gratuitously to the children of the Zoroastrians."

When we remember that the Parsees of Bombay are the descendants of a small colony of ancient Fire-worshippers who emigrated from Persia more than a thousand years ago under circumstances the most overwhelming, it is a matter of wonder that this people should have risen with the progress of British power in India to wealth, honor, and dignity in every condition of life. More than once, even after they had established themselves in Guzerat, they were all but decimated by the sword of the conquering Moslem. But up again they rose each time, creating anew the old life, starting afresh on the same old basis, nothing discouraged, remembering with deeper appreciation the old promise of their earliest priest and founder, "that to persevering mortals the blessed immortals are swift."

It is impossible not to be struck with the life and history of this people—a history of endless defeat and persecution, a life of the closest unity and steadfastness. And this oneness of purpose, by which they have distinguished themselves for so many centuries, has a still closer relation to their moral and religious character. Whatever may be the errors and defects of the religion of the Fire-worshipper, the comprehensiveness and unity of his national character demand our respect and admiration.

CHAPTER VI.

Domestic Life of the Fire-worshippers.—The Zend-Avesta.—Parsee Rites and Ceremonies at Birth, Marriage, Death, and Final Consignment to the Tower of Silence.

BEFORE we cross the private threshold with a view to take a peep at the domestic life of the Parsees it may be well to state that "Avesta," in one of its deepest significations, is said to be the symbol of womanly fervor and purity. Among the early Zoroastrians it was consecrated in the *fire* that burned on the hearth, which typified the inviolability of the family, through which the sacredness attached to Asha* as the centre and preserver of the order

* "It cannot be denied," says Max Müller in his *Origin and Growth of Religion*, "that in the Avesta, as in the Vèda, *Asha* may often be translated by purity, and that it is most frequently used in reference to the proper performance of the sacrifices. Here the Asha consists in what is called 'good thoughts, good words, good deeds—good meaning ceremonially good or correct, without a false pronunciation, without a mistake in the sacrifice. But there are passages which show that Zoroaster also recognized the existence of a kosmos or *rita*. He also tells how the mornings go, and the noons, and the nights, and how they follow that which has been traced for them; he too admires the perfect friendship between the sun and the moon and the harmonies of living nature, the miracles of every birth, and how at the right time there is food for the mother to give her child.

"As in the Vèda, so in the Avesta, the universe follows the Asha, the worlds are the creation of Asha. The faithful while on earth pray for the maintenance of Asha, while after death they will join Ormuzd in the highest heaven, the abode of Asha. The pious worshipper protects the Asha; the world grows and prospers by Asha. The highest law of the world is Asha, and the highest ideal of the believer is to become Ashavan, possessed of Asha—*i. e.* righteousness."

of the universe is reflected upon and consecrated in the mother as the immediate centre of the home, "the transmitter of human life," and the preserver of family bonds.

The ancient Fire-worshippers are commanded in their religious books to watch over the woman in the home. It is a religious obligation. In the first male child centre the past, present, and future glory of the father. Children have always been the desire, "the crown of glory," to an Oriental. Thus the mother became in the Zend-Avesta the "holy mystic one," through whom man himself was born again as a son. She was the goddess of abundance, the irradiator of his hearth and home.

While the procreative and nutritive offices of woman called forth deep religious enthusiasm and veneration, the peculiar physical difference which these entailed on her appealed to a dawning sense of chivalric generosity; and it was a tender regard for her physical liabilities that first led to the institution of distinct rules for her life at times and seasons when she was most likely to be overworked, oppressed, or unduly taxed; and these rules time has rendered fixed and absolute as the Medo-Persic laws. But all through this rigidness of custom are seen not only a tenderness for the weakness of woman, but a high appreciation of her ideality and beauty.

"A wife cannot be set aside, save for the crime of adultery alone. She may be superseded because of barrenness, but not a beloved and virtuous wife. It is better to be childless here and hereafter than to wound or grieve her for a moment. And in any case let her not be set aside but by her own consent and free will." In all such cases she must be supported and cared for tenderly until death. It was an unpardonable offence against *God* to leave a wife destitute and without support. Unmarried daughters—a very rare occurrence among the Parsees—are entitled to an equal share of the mother's estate. A wife is not responsible for the debts of husband or son, whereas they are held strictly responsible for hers, and the son is enjoined, as the highest duty to the gods, to support his mother after the death of her husband. In a husband habitual vices—such as profligacy, intemperance, cruelty—insanity, and impotence, were held sufficient excuse for aversion. She was neither to be punished nor deprived of her property in any such case.

A father is strictly forbidden to sell his daughter—*i. e.* to take money in any shape whatever when giving her in marriage, but is enjoined, on the contrary, to furnish her with a handsome dowry.

The Parsee woman is as independent in her home and marriage relations as the European, although the universal seclusion of high-born Hindoo and Mohammedan women has not been without its influence on her domestic life. The first use of the veil among the Persian women was as a symbol of dignity and honor rather than of concealment from motives of modesty. In the early days of the Zoroastrians woman was held not so much as an equal, but as something superior in the home. In social rights and home-duties the husband and wife shared alike, and side by side they ministered to the holy fires on their household hearths. In the "Prajapatya" form, which, though *Vêdic*, is equally binding on the Fire-worshipper, the bride and bridegroom are distinctly enjoined to perform together their civil and religious duties. But the poetic love and reverence which surrounded woman in the early days of the Aryans, and which is still unsurpassed in all their literature, struck deeper than laws or rules, and in a burst of generous and spiritual enthusiasm "all men were commanded to bow the knee in filial reverence before the mother of a family, declaring a mother to be greater, more blessed, than a thousand fathers." Thus we see how much the simple fact of maternity tended to elevate woman in the home. And the desire to foster and protect her led these early worshippers to typify womanly purity as ever sacred, and as ever ready to comfort and cheer the heart of man as is the carefully-watched fire that burned on their altars.

But, alas! the rules and obligations which were originally intended for her safety and happiness are now forged into iron fetters to bind her, too often a willing slave, to the caprice of man, and have been used, and still are urged, against her higher advancement to the privileges of a liberal education.

Nevertheless, there are among the Parsees even to-day a few old-fashioned observances which might be introduced with great advantage to the wife and mother among the laboring and even richer classes of European nations. For instance, even in the poorest families there are certain days when the woman is considered unfit to cook, wash, bake, sweep the floor, or light the house-lamp. So strenuous are the laws against her working at these times that among certain persons her touch is held to pollute the thing or person that comes into close contact with her. She is forbidden to perform even the lighter offices which may fall to her share in the house. She separates herself from the family on such occasions. If she is too poor to keep a servant, her husband is enjoined to do her part of the housework in addition to his own outdoor labor, whatever that may be. The same rules apply to all female servants.

During pregnancy woman is held sacred among both Persians and Hindoos. Their laws are fixed and absolute on all points relating to maternity, whereas in European countries women are often treated with less kindness and consideration than the household and domestic animals. Disregarded by man, she is too apt to neglect and overwork herself at such times. But in the Parsee code of laws maternity and childbirth are protected by deep religious obligations. "All harsh words, anger, sorrow, anything that will occasion pain of mind and body, are to be kept away from the woman with child." "She is forbidden all strong drink, all unhealthy intercourse with neighbors and friends; she cannot travel from home or from place to place, or look upon unsightly objects, or listen to any but pleasant and familiar sounds." In fact, woman at such times is to be guarded with an especial religious care, "as the household priestess or divinity, who is on the eve of unveiling the future greatness and glory of the family by the gift of a male child."

Another and a very old superstition among the early Aryans and Parsees, if we may call these tender observances by such a name, is that the living, thinking, intelligent soul (which is held to be distinct from the life) of the child takes up its habitation in the heart and pulse of the unborn babe forty-nine days, or seven times seven sunrises and sunsets, before its advent into the world. This curious belief makes them regard the mother at such times as overshadowed by the presence of a divine being. Hence, before the "holy breath" has animated the unborn babe the mother is conveyed with religious care to the ground-floor of the house. There are both spiritual and physical reasons for this step: that she may not be disturbed by the ordinary household cares and jars; that the child should enter into the world on the solid breast of the great mother of all, the earth; and that she may not undergo the fatigue of climbing stairs, which Oriental women very much dislike. Here she remains fifty days, and sometimes even more, before, and forty days after, the birth of her child, tenderly cared for by every member of the family, for to neglect her at such a time is to forfeit the blessings of the seven high angels who are about the throne of Ahura-Mazda.

In the centre of her chamber there is an enclosed spot, sometimes provided with a cot, and all around it is a low wall or a light fence to guard off all irreverent approach. At the time of delivery her women place her in this sacred spot, and here, in the heart and centre of the Fire-worshipper's *home*, the newborn child is ushered into the world.

Among the Hindoos, and even among the more uneducated of the Parsees, these observances have lost their original signification, and have dwindled down not only to a mere ritual ceremony, but are corrupted into a gross superstition. The poor mother is now looked upon as being impure,* and her seclusion from the rest of the family necessary to preserve the entire household from the much-dreaded pollution of childbirth; therefore none of the members of the household will approach or touch the mother—not from a fear of harming her, but rather of pollution to themselves—until forty days after her confinement and after she has undergone a series of purifications and performed a great many sacramental rites.

The whole course of the future life is carefully traced out for every child that is born unto the world. First of

* It is now very difficult to ascertain at what period the "dual principle" of good and evil formulated by Zoroaster was first applied to the sexes. It is clear, however, that in course of time the masculine energy came to be regarded as good and holy, and the feminine as evil and unholy; and there is no doubt that from that time the original idea of the mother as the household priestess or divinity underwent a slow but radical change; and at length the fall of woman from the lofty place assigned to her in the early Vèdic and Zoroastrian religions became an accomplished fact.

all, at the moment of birth it is the duty of the nurse and midwife to carefully observe the time, the hour, the signs, and marks, and any and every unusual occurrence which may happen at the moment of delivery, particularly the aspect of the heavens at the time of day; if at night, the appearance of the moon and stars, and all such phenomena. All these and the exact moment of the infant's birth are noted down. The newborn child is also carefully examined as to its physical conditions, and these also are commented upon and set down for the use of the astrologer. The mother too has especial attention bestowed upon her; incense is kept burning at her bedside; she is fumigated twice a day by means of a censer in which odoriferous gums are burnt; tapers are lit and sent as offerings to the Fire-temples, with wine, fruit, flowers, sweet oils, and frankincense and myrrh.

On the seventh day after the birth of the child an astrologer and priest are invited to determine the horoscope of the newborn infant. The former, having ascertained the moment of birth and all other notable things with regard to mother and child, begins by drawing on a wooden board a set of hieroglyphics in chalk as curious as they are complicated, and his dexterity in counting and recounting the stars under whose influence the child is supposed to be born is marvellous; after which all the assembled relatives press forward, especially the father, eager and trembling to hear the astrologer predict in a solemn voice the future life and prospects of the newborn babe.

According to these curious speculations, if the child is born at the point of Cancer he will be a great man; if at the point of Capricorn, he will be a great priest and reformer. Under the influence of the planet Saturn he will be distinguished for intelligence (though some priests hold the influence of Saturn to be dark and sinister over human life); if under Jupiter, for power and physical strength. If he happens to be born at the moment of the arrival of the sun at the summer solstice, the child is looked upon as the favorite of Heaven, and every good fortune is predicted as the result. Should the planet Mars preside at the time of birth, they foretell great trouble and sorrow; if Mercury, poverty and early death; under Venus, contentment and peace; and under the moon, a numerous progeny. The astrologer then enumerates the names which are the most appropriate for the child to bear, so as to mark his or her astral relations; the parents make a choice of one of them. The Fire-priest then takes the babe and places it on his knees, waves a lamp lighted from the sacred fire over it, calls aloud its name, and implores Ahura-Mazda to fulfil all the good and avert all the evil predicted by the stars of heaven at the hour of its birth.

After the expiration of the forty days, and having undergone seven purifications by fire and smoke and various incense fumigations, the mother returns to the family circle as before, but is exempted from much arduous work while nursing her infant.

I was fortunate enough to be present one evening at the house of Shet Dorabjee, a Parsee merchant of Bombay, when one of their most beautiful services was held. It was the simple act of lighting their evening lamp, which in every Parsee household is one of the most sacred duties. This lamp is poetically called "the dispeller of darkness." It is always lighted in the evening, but goes out at dawn. Besides this, an earthen and ever-burning lamp is preserved in almost all Parsee homes.

On the occasion when I happened to be present at the house of Shet Dorabjee the front door was gently closed at twilight. The family, of whom there were no less than forty-five persons, assembled around this "hearth-lamp." My charming hostess and friend, the lady Shet Dorabjee, repaired to the secret chamber, kindled her torch at the perpetual fire, mingled its flame with her breath by lightly blowing on it, returned, and lighted the hearth-lamp. Then the family all stood up—father, mother, sisters, brothers, children, and grandchildren—no stranger being allowed to join the circle. I stood aside and quietly watched the scene. With their arms crossed upon their breasts while the mother was lighting the evening lamp, they repeated this prayer (of which I obtained the translation): "O Ahura-Mazda, thou who dwellest where the sun never shines, where the lightnings flash not, from that world, thy secret hiding-place, kindle our hearts to worship the pure Lord of Purity;" to which the whole family responded, "So be it, O Divine Illuminator."

Consecration into the Zoroastrian religion takes place in the seventh year of a child's life. First comes the strange purification by washing the child's body and face with the urine of the cow. This curious and disgusting custom is said to be handed down from the most ancient times, when this liquid was regarded as a very effective remedy against any disorder of the bodily organs. This done, a prayer is repeated, and the body is bathed again in pure water. There is a second and a third process, each called purification; the second consists of standing face to face with the fire, and praying to the Light without beginning or end; the third in repeating, with arms crossed, the Zoroastrian creed and acknowledging the truth of the Zoroastrian religion.

The child is then seated before the high priest, who puts on him a linen garment of nine seams and a woollen girdle of seventy-two threads. These are the exact number of the sacred books of the Fire-worshippers. These two are called the "garments of the pure and faithful," and the whole ceremony is concluded with a benediction of fire and prayer, the former being waved round and round over the child, and the latter being chanted.

The last and peculiar initiation takes place when the youth has attained his fourteenth year. He stands clad in pure white among the priests and his assembled relatives and friends in the Fire-temple. Here he repeats his vows; the priests warn him of certain temptations that will beset his youth and manhood, and the shame and suffering that will follow him through life if he should prove unfaithful to the higher instincts of his nature. They then invite him to drink the "homa" or "soma" juice, and to join them in practising purity in thought, word, and deed.

The "soma," or moon-plant, is a round smooth twining plant peculiar to the Aravalli Hills; it is also found in the deserts north of Delhi and in the mountain-passes of the Bolan, and it is imported into Bombay. It possesses not only medicinal, but, when allowed to ferment, slightly intoxicating, properties. It is the privilege of the Fire-priests and the most devout of the congregation to partake once a month, at the time of the new moon, of this intoxicating juice. Those who are about to partake of it generally abstain from food from sunrise till noon, which is the hour for celebrating this ceremony.

A day or two before the appearance of the new moon the stalks of this plant are bruised with the tender shoots of the acacia and with pomegranates, extracting thereby an acrid greenish juice. This is put in a strainer of goat's hair, after which it must be pressed through by the priest's fingers; this juice, mixed with barley and clarified butter, is allowed to ferment, when it forms the "soma wine." On the first morning after the new moon is seen in the heavens the Fire-priests repair to their temple, where, after certain prayers and chants, the soma-juice is drawn off in a vessel; a portion is thrown into a sacred well as a libation to the earth, a ladleful is drank by the priests, and the residue is handed round to the people who are present. The priests then join hands and wait for the stimulating properties to reach the brain, whereupon they wheel round chanting a hymn full of mystical meaning.

Strange as it may seem to us, the exhilarating property of this drink is supposed to shadow forth the presence of divine life in the soul, and this life of thought and emotion is often poetically called "wine"—"the wine that fills creation's cup." *

The Parsees in worshipping the sun turn their faces to the rising luminary, and, holding before them branches of certain trees, chant aloud. In our early-morning rides on Malabar Hill, as the sun made his first appearance above the horizon, the white-robed priests of Iran were always before us, crowding the summit of the hill; they could be seen with their faces turned eastward, with branches of acacia raised aloft in their hands, singing their morning hymn to the god of day.†

We knew personally several of the Fire-priests of Bombay. They seemed less intelligent than the ordinary Parsees, and some of them went through their religious duties mechanically and without any of that religious fervor that I had noticed in the Brahmans; but I have seen others who were both intelligent and extremely devout.

* Omar Khyâm, astronomer-poet of Persia.

† The earliest mention of this practice is found in the eighth chapter and sixteenth verse of Ezekiel, where that prophet complains that the Jews turn their backs upon the temple to worship the sun.

Among the Fire-worshippers the marriage of one's children is the first and earliest consideration. Marriage is held a high sacred and religious obligation, and mothers often pledge their children in marriage before they are born, and if their children prove of the right sex their pledge is held sacred. In most cases, however, the priests are the go-betweens or the matchmakers. This is held as one of the most important of the ministerial duties that fall to the care of a Fire-priest. As soon as a Parsee sees what he and his wife consider an eligible mate for his son or daughter, direct negotiations are opened with the parents by means of the Fire-priest, who calls on the parties, and after some few preliminary questions with regard to the temper and disposition of the proposed mother-in-law on the part of the relatives of the young maiden, the Fire-priest (who cannot proceed until he has examined the respective horoscopes) demands the birth-paper of the little maiden in question, who, perhaps all unconscious of what is going on, may be frequently seen hiding behind her mother and peering timidly at the white-robed Fire-priest who is about to decide one of the most important events of her future life.

Everything depends on the positions of their respective stars. The stars once declared favorable, however, matters proceed rapidly and the betrothal takes place. This consists of an exchange of dresses from the parents of the young couple; but so rigid are their rules that the acceptance of this simple gift is held by each of the parents as the sign of an indissoluble bond between the children.

Even the day for the celebration of the marriage (after the children have arrived at the respective ages of eighteen for the boy and fifteen to sixteen for the maiden) is selected by the Fire-priests. Indeed, there are only a few days in the year held propitious for marriage by both the Hindoo and Parsee. So many marriages take place on these favored days that to a stranger it would appear as if the entire native population was being married off.

We were invited to the celebration of the marriage of Munchejee Sorabjee's daughter, a very beautiful girl and a great heiress in her own right, her late uncle having left her a very large fortune. We arrived early, so as to witness the whole ceremony from beginning to end.

It was a lovely place near Mazagaum. The house was approached through grand old groves; there were rustic seats here and there, and inviting grassy slopes whence one could catch glimpses of the distant sea. We were shown into a spacious hall, where we took our places, with several other European guests, on divans arranged along the walls.

Just before sunset the bridegroom's party arrived in full dress of pure white, all save the turban, which was of a dark chocolate color, ornamented with precious stones. Each of the gentlemen attached to the bridegroom's party had garlands of white flowers around his neck. Behind these came a long row of Fire-priests in flowing white linen robes, white turbans, and long white silk scarfs.

The nuptial ceremony must always be held on the ground-floor, and after all the guests, some three or four hundred Parsees, had taken their places round the hall, there was heard a gentle buzz of expectation. All eyes turned involuntarily to the great lofty door at the western extremity of the room. It opened, and for a moment the young bride stood still, hesitating at the threshold of the unknown future before her. Presently both bride and bridegroom entered. I never saw a more graceful or more beautiful creature than this young Parsee bride. Her dress was exquisitely simple—white satin trousers fastened at the ankle, above a pale blue silk bodice covered with some sort of rich white embroidery, and over it all, wound round her whole person, half veiling her face, was a semi-transparent flowing scarf, every curve and twist of which was arranged with the most artistic effect. They walked in side by side. A murmur of delight ran through the audience at the delicate downcast face, the grace, and the beauty of the half-veiled maiden figure before us. When the couple reached the centre of the hall they bowed down and performed a sort of mystic prostration to Mother Earth in the presence of the Fire-priests. They then stood up, joined hands, and waited for the auspicious moment. All eyes were turned upon the youthful pair; every one was almost breathless with tender expectation, save the Fire-priests, who watched the sunlight fading out of the sky. With the vanishing of the last shimmering gleam of light the ceremony began. Torches and lamps were kindled with fire from their temple by the Fire-priests, who approached the young couple, and, waving round them the sacred light, sprinkled them with consecrated water; then taking an immense "purda," or veil, placed it over one of their number and over the bride and groom, who were shrouded beneath its folds for some minutes; meanwhile other priests chanted the following hymn: "O man, in the name of the great Ahura-Mazda, be ever pure and faithful, and bright in good actions as the immortal Light. Be ever worthy of all praise and honor in the heart of this woman, now thy wife. May the spirits of fire, sun, and water give thee wisdom! May the peaceful earth, whose fragrance is excellent, whose breasts contain the heavenly drink, fill thee with the purity of the Pure and the benevolence of the great Yohoo mano (beneficent spirit) toward this woman thy wife!"

Then the chant is addressed to the bride: "O woman

of mysterious body, be thou immortal like Kosru (one of the fixed stars). Be full of understanding for thyself, thy husband, and the fruit of thy body, as a capacious vessel full of love, fervid as the sun by day, tender and pure as the moon by night; heavy laden as the cow (clouds) with moisture" (meaning heavy laden with kindness, as the clouds with moisture). "Be serene, be wise, be steady as the fixed stars. May Ahura-Mazda give you fire for brightness and purity, the sun for exalted rule! May the shadowless night give you the moon for increase and the sky for life everlasting!"

The instant the chanting—which was drawled out in monotone by the assembly of the Fire-priests—ceased the great white veil was withdrawn, and the young couple were man and wife.

The bride then, blushing scarlet and looking if possible still more lovely than before, received the eager and hearty congratulations of her friends and relatives, who pressed around her and embraced her. Her mother and aunts wept with joy and poured tender benedictions on her young head. It was a trying ordeal for the poor girl. I noted every shade of feeling that passed over her face. She wore a look of constraint, every now and then blushing crimson; she bit her lips in order to keep herself from giving way to her own conflicting emotions.

After this came the bridegroom's turn to salute and be saluted by his own and his wife's relatives. A knot of gay young Parsee gentlemen surrounded him with welcome sounds of greeting and laughter when the next important part of the ceremony began. A young Parsee lad, magnificently dressed, appeared, bringing in a large bowl of milk, and a charmingly dressed young maiden advanced, the younger sister of the bride, with a *choole*, or vest, belonging to the newly-made wife.

That "there is only one step from the sublime to the ridiculous" is only too true, for this rare and unique ceremony was absolutely concluded by the Fire-priests washing the toes of the bridegroom in the milk, and then they rubbed his face all over with the cast-off garment of his wife. As far as I could understand, the one was a sign of the great future happiness in store for the husband, and the other that he was no longer his own master, but henceforth under petticoat government. It is but just to add that most of the Parsee gentlemen present seemed to have outgrown this ridiculous custom, but the ladies smirked and giggled and seemed to enjoy it immensely.

After this came the end. The happy but confused-looking young couple retired (dripping with rose and jessamine waters showered over them) to their new abode, which in most cases is in the paternal home of the husband.

The Parsees have but few festivals; the birthday of Zoroaster and their New Year's Day are the most important. The former is held in the month of October, and it is a sight worth seeing. The men, women, and children, magnificently dressed in gold-wrought silks and flashing jewels, crowd the Fire-temples with offerings of fruit and flowers. Long processions of priests robed in pure white take turns in officiating, and chant after chant ascends from the temples to the shining Ahura-Mazda, accompanied with invocations to the spirits of the righteous dead, and to the seven high angels around the throne. The beautiful half-veiled women, the lovely children, the noble-looking fathers of families with their numberless sons standing at their right hand, and the priests magnifying and feeding the sacred flame from sunrise to sunset, form a sight as inspiring as it is novel.

Their Noow Rooz, or New Year's Day, is observed very

Parsee Lady and Child.

much as we do ours. The poor and destitute of all castes and creeds have alms, food, and clothes distributed to them by the rich and great, poor relations receive presents, and among friends kindly visits and gifts are exchanged.

The costume of this peculiar people is exceedingly simple, and said to be made obligatory on them by the rajah of Sajan on their first landing on Indian soil. That of the man consists of a long seamless muslin or silk shirt or tunic reaching to the knees, a woollen girdle with tassels, and a pair of silk trousers; when going out he puts on a sort of tunic, with a short silk vest over it; the modern Parsee gentlemen has also adopted shoes and stockings. The cap or turban by which a Parsee is distinguished is bound round a frame in the form of a little round tower, slightly higher on the right side. The stuff of which it is constructed is a peculiar manufacture made at Surat expressly for the Parsee turban. It is a sort of stiff paper-muslin, figured, and generally of a dark-red or chocolate color, bound round the frame smoothly, till it is made to assume this one particular form of a conical tower (typical of their earliest Fire-temple), around which emeralds and rubies are arranged on great festal occasions.

The Parsee women that I met and visited in Bombay were, on the whole, remarkably good-looking as girls; before they conceal their fine curly hair they are really beautiful, and the children among the loveliest and happiest to be found in the East.

The women are fair-complexioned, with a delicate brunette tinge, with large eyes and regular features, often exquisitely formed, owing to their dress being freed from anything like pressure on the body; but they rob themselves of a part of their beauty by the custom of concealing their beautiful hair under white linen bands bound around the brow. They wear very wide silk trousers, gathered and fastened at the ankles, over this a silk tunic, often descending in graceful folds to the feet and bound at the waist, while a deep, wide scarf of silk or some other light texture gracefully drapes the whole person and serves at once the double purpose of a head-dress and a veil.

They occupy in their homes a much more honorable position than either the Hindoo or Moslem women. They enjoy almost as much freedom as European women. I used to meet them in the streets and bazaars, driving in their open carriages, surrounded by their bright, happy-looking children.

So careful are the Parsees of their national honor that in the whole island of Bombay there exists neither paupers nor prostitutes among the followers of this religion. Polygamy is unknown among them. A wife can only be put away for immoral conduct. She is tried by the Punchayet or Parsee court, and if found guilty repudiated amid the whole assembly; formerly she was put to death.

The ceremonies attending the death of a Parsee are very singular. When a person is about to die he is conveyed to the ground-floor, washed in consecrated water, and his face anointed with holy oil. A lamp or lamps lighted from the sacred fire in the temple are placed by the dying man's bed, and priests stand before him with folded arms crossed on their breasts, and pray for him in a most earnest and beautiful chant. When life becomes quite extinct the body is clothed in a new white cotton shirt of nine seams and a sort of apron, which is thrown over the face. This is bound by a new and sacred girdle of seventy-two threads. The body is then placed on an oblong stone on the floor.

But the most curious part of all is, that along with the Fire-priests the house-dog is brought in, and after they have offered up prayer and praise in the presence of the assembled family, the dog is taken up to the dead body of his friend and master and exhorted to conduct him safely into paradise. If the dog should lick affectionately, as heretofore, the face, or even hands or feet, of his dead friend, it is held as a most auspicious sign of the dead man's ready admittance into heaven. It is but just to add here that the more refined and intelligent Parsees have outgrown this absurd custom and superstition; but the more ignorant certainly believe that every dog has an angel spirit residing in some star, whence it issues forth to convey the souls of the good safely into heaven.*

When the time for the removal of the body approaches, lamps lighted from the sacred fires burn around the corpse. The priests stand face to face with the dead, singing praises to the immortal Light; finally, their last prayer or exhortation to the dead soul is chanted. This done, the body, covered with white garments, the hands crossed on the breast, is laid on a long open bier. A number of priests robed in pure white carry the bier to the dohkma or tower of silence, and there the long procession of friends and relatives stand in a circle praying with arms folded, heads bowed, and lips moving silently, while the Fire-priests place the dead body on a long slide and slip it on the iron gratings of this strange circular tomb, to be devoured by birds of prey.

On the third day they pray again in the Fire-temple that the soul of the dead may ascend to heaven, for, according to their sacred books, on the third day "he reaches Mithra (Sun-god), rising above the mountains resplendent in his own spotless purity;" then he comes to the bridge of the "*Gatherer*," where he is asked as to the conduct of

* The dog is also brought in to be looked at by the dying man when at his last gasp.

his soul while living in the world. If he is pure, a beautiful, tall, swift spirit, called Serosh, comes thither with a dog, a nine-knotted hook, and the twigs of the "Barsom;" these things are considered efficacious for keeping off evil spirits and guiding him over the heavenly bridge (Chinvat). Here a most exquisite form meets him, lovely and smiling, and when he questions the beautiful maiden, "Who art thou shining so brightly on the wide shore?" she replies, "I am all thy good works, pure thoughts, and pure words, O man." She then takes his hand, leads him smiling and joyous to the archangel Yohoo mano, who rises from his golden throne and speaks thus to the soul: "How happy it is that you have come here to us from mortality to immortality!" Then the soul goes joyfully to Ahura-Mazda, and resides for ever with the immortal saints, praising the unbegotten, self-created Light.

Though the Fire-worshippers believe in the resurrection, they do not hold that it is to be made in the same body; their reverence therefore follows the soul, and not the body deserted by its spiritual tenant, while their reverence for the earth, water, and fire is so profound that they hold burial, cremation, or even casting the ashes into the waters, a sacrilege against the elements. The original idea in exposing the body to the weather was Brahmanic—that of absorption by the elements. The dead body was restored to the sun, air, and sky, to be reunited and launched on the bosom of that "*vast Illimitable*" whence it had sprung.

The Parsees also hold all birds sacred, as a sort of spiritual agent of universal purification, through whose agency all gross, unclean substances pass into healthy conditions. For these reasons the towers of silence which receive the dead spoil are open to the sky, and by means of the bird of prey it re-enters almost immediately into the domain of life and health and purity.

From the universal testimony of pagan or Christian travellers we find that the Fire-worshippers of India are thought to be more honorable in their dealings with one another, and even with strangers, than the generality of Asiatics, and even than those peoples professing Christianity. They rarely resort to written contracts, as their word is the best bond. Benevolence is said to flow in their veins, so conspicuous have they become for their love of charity. The Rev. Mr. Avington, during his stay at Surat so early as 1698, bore testimony to the fact that the Parsees there were ever more ready to provide for the comfort and support of the poor and suffering than even the Christians; and this reputation they bear to this day in India. The Bombay government voted thanks so far back as 1790 to Sorabjee Muncherjee, who during the scarcity that prevailed at that time daily fed at his own expense two thousand people, comprising Jews, Christians, Mohammedans, and Hindoos. Mrs. Graham, in her journal of a residence in India, declares that she was enraptured with the simplicity, purity, and never-ceasing kindliness of the Parsee community; and every one in India is familiar with the name of that very prince of benevolence and kindliness, the venerable Parsee baronet Sir Jamsetjee Jeeboy, knighted by the queen of England for his unbounded charities, which are not only unsurpassed, but without a parallel, in ancient or modern times. He has done more in his lifetime for Western India, in feeding the poor, releasing unhappy prisoners for debt, building causeways, founding schools and colleges for the education of all castes and conditions of men and women, erecting hospitals for the relief of the suffering poor, benevolent institutions for the deformed, spacious resting-places, or dhurrum-salas, for weary travellers in all parts of India, stupendous aqueducts, wells, and tanks, than any other single individual, or even the East India Company, for the benefit of mankind. Connected with the Grant Medical College of Bombay is the noble hospital, the gift of this Parsee baronet; and only a few years ago his family erected a hospital for incurables near it. An ophthalmic hospital has been opened and endowed by another liberal Parsee, Cowasjee Jehangheer.

The late Sir Jamsetjee commenced life in Bombay at the early age of twelve as a street peddler, selling old bottles, and was called "Bottle-wallah" to the day of his death.

In the short space of two centuries of undisturbed industry the Parsees have placed themselves in competition with the foremost of the Europeans in India. In liberality and enterprise they rank with the merchant-princes of England, and may be justly compared to the most famous merchants that America has produced in the last century, and yet no question has ever been raised as to the commercial integrity of the Parsees. In the Indian banks and various other stock companies the Parsees are prime movers. They are almost the exclusive owners of all the trading-steamers that now navigate the Indian and China seas. They are great landholders, and many of the finest residences in the island of Bombay are owned by Parsees. They have shared largely in introducing railways into India. Jamsetjee Dorabjee is now considered the foremost railroad contractor in India. The most difficult passes extending from the Thull Ghauts to the Kustsarah Mountains, covered with wild jungles, full of trap hills, mountain-torrents at one season of the year, and devoid of water at another, were laid open and made as easy of travel by railroad as the most finished roads in England or America. Many English officers of the engineer department have declared the building of this railroad across the Thull Ghauts and Kustsarah a more arduous undertaking than that of the great Pacific Railroad across the American continent.

Europe, during the great American War deprived suddenly of one of the chief products so necessary to her industries, resorted to India for cotton, and all at once the island of Bombay became not only the great centre of trade, but soon attracted to herself merchants and traders in cotton from the four quarters of the globe, each and all eagerly competing for the same prize, the monopoly of the cotton-market. Enormous fortunes were amassed in an incredibly short space of time, and for a brief period the whole commerce of the great East and West seemed to flow into the port of the small island of Bombay. Misinformed by the English press, and seemingly unwilling to investigate for themselves the true nature of the almost superhuman struggle carried on between kinsmen for the preservation of State rights and the suppression of slavery on the American continent, this eager crowd only foresaw what seemed the most natural, the utter destruction of the great republic of the United States and the magnificent future for themselves springing from the very ashes of this ruin. Thus assured, and blinded to every other consideration, even the wise and hitherto prudent merchants of Bombay became dazzled with the prospects in view, and launched forth into the most gigantic enterprises and into rash schemes for the utmost development of one and all the various resources of the country. Everywhere this feverish, insatiable thirst to profit by a great nation's approaching destruction displayed itself. Men and women who had never dreamed of speculating in stocks, the rich with his hundreds of thousands and the poor with hardly a few rupees to his name, master and servant, were alike seized with the distemper called by the few who looked calmly on "Rupea-Dewana," "the rupee-mad." How changed was the once happy population! What anxious faces, revealing lines of thought and care, of midnight toil, of mingled fear and hope! Still, the great drama went on, and for a short period immense fortunes were made in a day. But no sooner had the whole island gained sufficient encouragement to set on foot her gigantic schemes and rash enterprises, no sooner had she at one final throw staked all on the ruin of the Northern States, than came the appalling intelligence of General Lee's defeat. A fearful revulsion followed: sudden panic seized the busy world enclosed in the small compass of the Bombay "Commercial Square." Like a flock of birds, the business population took wing and vanished out of sight. The banks were closed, flourishing houses collapsed, firms disappeared, and an almost universal ruin stared every one in the face. The very atmosphere was filled with the despair of men who had so rashly staked all and lost all.

Painful as the lesson has been, it was a wholesome one, not only for all classes of merchants in British India, but for Old England herself. The merchants of Bombay are once more in their counting-rooms and warehouses, the banks are as firmly established as ever, with a richer experience and a more profound insight into the laws which govern the moral as well as the business world; they yet bid fair to render the beautiful island of Bambâ Dèvi the heart and centre of all the commerce of the East, even as she is now, owing to her remarkable sanitary conditions, the healthiest city in India. She is the second city in the British empire in point of numbers, having a population of six hundred thousand, and an average to the square mile exceeding that of London; nevertheless, the average death-rate for the past five years has been the same as that of London.

CHAPTER VII.

Hindoo Treatment of the Sick.—Pundit's House Defiled.—Its Purification.—Short Sketch of the Different Races and of the Origin of Castes and Creeds among the Peoples of Hindostan.

THE Hindoo treatment of the sick is quite peculiar, and I once had an opportunity to witness some of its curious features during the illness of my Sanskrit teacher, the pundit Govind. I was fortunate in this, since only exceptional circumstances permit a European to pollute with his presence the dwelling of a high-caste Brahman. Every one knows that caste still holds the Hindoos under an iron rule, but it is difficult for us of the Western World to realize, without actual experience, the tenacity with which its mandates are obeyed even in an extremity.

For several days Govind had not presented himself to give his usual morning lesson at the "Aviary." I feared he was ill, but did not venture to visit him, lest my very shadow might pollute his dwelling and place him in an unpleasant dilemma with the rest of his high-caste friends. I began to be alarmed, however, on the third morning of Govind's absence, and was on the point of starting off to his house, when I observed a native woman coming toward the "Aviary," her scarlet saree fluttering in the breeze and making quite a pretty picture in the distance.

I hastened to the doorstep to meet the stranger. She salââmed to me, but positively declined to enter the house. As she did so she flung back her scarf or covering, and from the sectarian mark on her forehead I knew that she was a high-caste Brahmanee. She stood for a few minutes breathless and silent, and I do not remember ever having seen a more delicate and sensitive-looking girl. The saree, which was a scarlet muslin cloth of Indian manufacture, and decorated with a handsome border, covered her person from head to foot, leaving the left arm and shoulder bare. I noticed that she had sandals on her feet and a number of bangles round her arms and ankles. Her shining black hair was tied in a massive knot behind and fastened by a gold pin, which also served to secure the end of her saree as a veil and covering for her head. Her features, form, arms, hands, and feet were of the most exquisite type, and her complexion of a rich chocolate-brown.

She at length lifted her dark eyes brimming with tears, and with a slightly quivering voice said, "Beebee saihib torâ douva daoh kuda ka wasta; Govind ka jahu jata hai" ("Lady, for God's sake give me a little medicine; Govind's life is passing away").

I inquired the nature of his complaint, but all I could learn from the young woman was that Govind's stomach and legs had gone away, and that his head was fast following his heels, which is the Oriental phraseology for extreme prostration.

I seized a small bottle of brandy, a physician's mixture at hand for cholera morbus, and some quinine, and started with the Brahmanee for the home of Govind the pundit. In less than half an hour we stood before a mean, wretched-looking bamboo dwelling, the walls of which were plastered with mud and covered over with an attap* roof. It stood in the middle of a small patch of ground neatly smeared over with cowordure. In the centre of

* A species of palm-leaf dried and stitched together, much used all over Hindostan in roofing houses and sheds.

this yard was a flourishing plant growing out of a large earthen pot buried in the ground—the Indian "mehndee"* (sacred to the goddess Bhawanee), called *Lawsonia* by English botanists. It was in full blossom, with small delicate, fragrant flowers resembling the clematis.

The sky was very much overcast, portending soon a shower or thunderstorm; the air was hot and sultry. I stood for a moment or two before the half-open door of the little hut, whence proceeded a low, faint, tremulous sound which I recognized as the voice of Govind, my teacher, enfeebled by his illness. As I stood there hesitating to enter, the pretty little Brahmanee dropped on her knees before the door, and, having saluted the presiding genius of the dwelling three times, advanced, creeping softly in on her knees. At length I summoned courage enough to walk in, but I did so in my stockings, leaving my shoes on the doorsill. Even this was, as I afterward learned, desecration to the Brahman's household.

On a low charpie, or native cot, standing apart within an enclosure formed by a mud wall a few inches in height, lay the pundit, his eyes closed, his features shrunk and wasted. The little woman, who I divined was his wife, had already taken her place at his feet, which she kept rubbing in a listless way, the sad expression deepening on her dark but beautiful face, the great tears brimming her eyes and coursing one after another all unheeded down her cheeks.

The dwelling consisted of two apartments. Through a

* Most of the high-caste Hindoo women cultivate this plant for the purpose of dyeing their nails and finger-tips. The dye is prepared by bruising the leaves and moistening them with a little lime-water. This mixture is then applied to the nails, tips of the fingers, palms of the hands, and sometimes even to the soles of the feet, which in a short time become dyed of a reddish-orange color. The stain remains on the skin until it wears off.

doorway to which there was no door I saw an old woman seated by a rude fire on the floor in the adjoining room cooking some rice in an earthen pot, and before her on the floor were a board and a rolling-pin, with which she had been rolling out some wheaten cakes, piled, already baked, in a copper platter by the fire. The moment I entered the hut she turned her shrivelled features, and, seeing a white woman, she gave a shrill cry; then, stretching out her bare, bony arms, implored me in piteous tones to begone. "But, lady," said I, trying to appease her, "I cannot go away. Govind is very ill, and I have some medicine here that may cure him."

Hearing her still entreating me to begone, Bhawanee begged her to let me stay and give the medicine to Govind; at which the poor old woman, shuddering, retreated to the inner apartment, resumed for a time her cries, uttering them in a loud voice and in a tone at once piercing and imperious, "You dare not come in here! you dare not! What reason have you for daring to give my son medicine? I want you hateful Inrage (English) to know that I would rather have him die, rather have him die, than be polluted by your vile drinks, made of devils' blood and pig's flesh; I would rather have him die." Rocking herself to and fro, she kept her strange glittering, dark eyes fixed upon me, and repeated, lowering her voice more and more gradually, "I would rather have him die," till she seemed to be talking to herself. I really thought she was delirious or perhaps out of her mind; but Bhawanee whispered to me, "She is very old and very cross, and sometimes possessed of a devil."

All the noise made by the old woman did not seem to disturb her son, who was in a deep sleep, his respiration so heavy and labored, and his pallor so death-like, that I almost feared he was dying. But at the end of half an hour he stirred and made a vain attempt to turn on his side; failing, he gave a look toward the foot of the bed, where his sorrow-stricken wife sat still and mute. Meeting his gaze, she crept to the head of the bed, and, taking his hand tenderly in hers, sobbed out in broken accents, "Govind duva piuh, tora duva piuh" ("Govind, drink some medicine—just a little of the medicine").

The pundit opened wide his half-closed eyes, looked full and inquiringly into his wife's face, and then turned them upon me. If I had been the very lowest wretch on the face of the earth, he could not have been more startled and horrified than he seemed at my presence. He almost sprang up, but in another second fell back on the bed, and, putting his hands before his face, cried feebly to his wife, "Wife, wife, what have you done?"

There was deep sympathy in the voice of the poor young woman as she exclaimed, "Oh, Govind, I thought you were dying. I did not know what else to do, and Doorah has been gone since morning, and is not yet returned. Oh, please take the lady's medicine. Never mind about caste; we can do 'puja' for it, and be restored;" and the poor woman began to sob as if her heart would break.

"What are my sufferings and death, that you should create so much disturbance about them?" feebly moaned Govind. "Let me die, oh, let me die quietly!" and again the deadly pallor overspread his face.

"Govind," said I in a very energetic tone, "drink this." I had already poured out a little brandy into an earthen lota or cup, which his wife handed me, and giving it back to her said, "Put it to his lips; he will be better as soon as he has swallowed a little of it."

Poor Bhawanee, nervous and trembling from head to foot, tried, and tried in vain, to persuade her husband to take even a mouthful of the medicine. Each time that she presented the lota to his lips he would put it aside, and turn away his face, muttering, "Better to die than pollute myself with what I am forbidden to touch."

The old woman, who had never taken her eyes off me, hearing his voice, began to moan, "Oh, beloved son, die, die, but do not touch their unholy drinks."

I did not know what to do, but, inspired by poor Bhawanee's entreating look, which, though she said not a word, plainly urged me to persevere, I once more endeavored to get the patient to swallow a little of the brandy. "Govind," said I, "do get over your scruples, which are well enough in health, but absurd in your fast-failing condition. Drink a mouthful of this; it will help to revive you until your doctor comes. No one need ever know that you have tasted brandy; I promise you to keep it a profound secret."

"Do, oh do!" urged his wife—"eke gutta piuh—take only one gulp."

"Much or little, a drop or a whole bottle, are all the same to me," groaned the poor pundit. "You may not speak of it, lady, and no one, no one may know it, but how can I conceal the fact from myself?"

I felt it was useless to persuade the patient to try the remedies I had brought with me.

At this moment we not only heard the sound of approaching feet, but a sudden clap of thunder, preceded by a flash of lightning, almost blinded us as we sat in the hut, and down came a deluging rain. Bhawanee rose, and in a state of great agitation begged me to retire by the back door; but, casting her eyes on my stocking feet, and apprehending that my European shoes on the threshold of her dwelling had already betrayed my presence to her friends, she begged me to keep my place, when in

A BRAHMAN GURU AT PRAYER.

walked, all dripping, three strange-looking men, accompanied by Doorah, her sister, who had been despatched in the early morning in search of a doctor, a priest, and a soothsayer.

Bhawanee rose and bowed before them, and so did the old woman from her place in the inner room. It was comforting to see the poor woman's expression, which till now had been full of despair, replaced by a look of child-like confidence and trust, though I doubted whether the Hindoo priest, doctor, or soothsayer could do much toward helping the sick man.

The doctor, who was a tall, dark, and rather handsome high-caste Hindoo, placed himself near the bedside of Govind and proceeded to feel his skin, pulse, and chest and to examine the condition of his tongue, eyes, and nails.

Meanwhile, the Brahman priest requested a pitcher of water and an empty bowl. Furnished with these by Doorah, Bhawanee's sister, he sat himself down in the middle of the room and began to transfer the water from the jar into the empty bowl, drop by drop, repeating over each drop the "Gayatree," the holiest text of the Vèdas, the most sacred and effacious prayer of the Brahmans, and thought by them to be absolutely necessary to salvation, while the soothsayer sat apart waiting his turn to perform certain magical enchantments for the benefit of the poor sick man. The latter opened his eyes once more and looked at his Guru,* or priest, and said solemnly, "I am dying."

* A "Guru" is a spiritual guide, a Brahman ecclesiastic, invested with the power of attending births, deathbeds, marriages, and settling all such questions as effect Hindoo caste and all its duties and obligations. A Guru is generally an ascetic of peculiar sanctity, and is often worshipped as an incarnate deity. This office descends from father to son. The Gurus comprise a very large and influential body of men, occupying the chief cities of India, wielding a despotic power over the people, as their curse is dreaded by all ranks and conditions of people.

"Dying? you are not dying," said the doctor. "I will soon make you well," whereupon he opened a bag and drew out of it some pieces of iron, which he placed on a charcoal fire. While these were being heated he took out various roots and dried herbs and began to rub them on a small stone, occasionally moistening the stone with a little water. Having compounded several queer, dark-looking doses, he, to my utter astonishment, deliberately began pinching, thumping, and slapping poor Govind—now on his back, anon on the soles of his feet. His sides, palms, shoulders, elbows, knee-joints were all slapped and beaten. This done, he branded with the hot pieces of iron the poor patient on the pit of his stomach, the inside of his arms, and the calves of his legs; then administered his queer-looking doses, which the unhappy-looking Govind swallowed without a sign of remonstrance; and, finally covering him from head to foot with a thick quilt, the Hindoo physician beckoned to the soothsayer to complete the cure.

The soothsayer robed himself in a dress covered with strange designs of men exorcising fiends, put on a cap to which was attached two or three long cords, at the end of which hung little brooms made of kusah-grass (a grass sacred to the Hindoo gods). He then took up the pan of burning coals and scattered them over the quilt which covered the patient; these he brushed off as rapidly as possible with the sacred brooms hanging from his cap. This was to dispossess the sick man of some extraordinary but invisible devil, which he then drove out at the door, running after the spirit and howling terrific invectives on it for having dared to enter the "divine precincts occupied by the *liver* of a Brahman." All this while the Guru, or priest, prayed, chanting in a monotonous tone, over each drop of water that passed from the pitcher to the bowl, and each of which was supposed to carry off with it the cholera of the sick man.

Strange to say, violent and absurd as were the remedies administered to poor Govind, he not only bore them patiently, but seemed better; a profuse perspiration having broken out upon him, it was looked upon as a most hopeful sign and an especial interposition of Brahm.

In another hour the rain ceased; Govind had fallen into a peaceful sleep; Bhawanee's face was irradiated with smiles; the old woman was setting out their mid-day repast on a mat in the adjoining apartment. I returned home, promising to call and see Bhawanee on the following day. The next day, when I started off, I fully expected to hear that Govind had passed away; but when I reached the outer gate of the yard enclosing Govind's dwelling I found the pundit, although looking weak and feeble enough, seated on a small stone holding in his left hand three blades of kusah-grass. The old woman, who was in the act of tying up the lock of sacred hair on his head in some mystical form, shouted to me to keep off. I stood at a distance and looked on. He was evidently undergoing the purification ceremony. Bhawanee, who smiled sweetly at me, was holding before her husband a bowl of water, which he first sipped, then flung a little of it toward the horizon, and washed his hands, ears, breast, eyes, nose, shoulders, and feet, repeating over each member a prayer. His wife then brought him a stick of lighted wood from the household fire; he breathed over it, repeating the mystic word "Aum," "O divine Spirit, resplendent Fire, purify me from all uncleanliness." He then placed the sacred grass on his right ear (Gunga, the sacred river, is supposed to have its source in the right ear of Brahm, the sacrificial fire (or life) in Brahm's nostrils, so that when the pundit touched these members of his person with fire and water all the impurity entailed by my visit to his house on the previous day passed away). Finally he took some sacred mud out of a pot which was handed to him by his wife, and made the holy mark, the circle and the cross of his caste and race, on his brow.

Meanwhile, Doorah, the sister, had been purifying the hut. First it was sprinkled all over with holy water, smeared with cow-ordure, and lastly fumigated with certain gums—a very sensible proceeding in a hot, moist climate like that of Bombay.

And at length the poor pundit, restored to his normal condition of holiness, was once more assisted into his bed by his tender and loving wife. I smiled at them from a distance, and went my way regretting more keenly than ever we were *so* separated from one another that the simplest act of kind interest on my part should entail on the whole household a series of purificatory rites to last for seven days.

As long as there exist in social life certain laws, manners, and customs by which the civilized man is distinguished from the savage, the gentleman from the cowherd, the high-born dame from her lowly maid, so long will caste, which is nothing more or less than social grades, complicate the lives and destinies not only of the races of the East, but of the West. The three great problems which yet remain to be solved by the British in India are to do away with the degradation of man by caste, the bondage of woman by custom, and the deterioration of childhood through the influence of the one and the other.

Caste on Indian soil was not in its beginning an entirely arbitrary institution; it was at first the natural expression of a high-bred and highly-sensitive race toward an inferior and savage population among which they had settled. It took centuries before caste was established on Indian soil, and nearly a thousand years before it became incorporated in the sacred books of the Brahmans in its present form. But the moment that divine authority was claimed for it, that moment it became to the God-fearing races of the East a law so subtle, so intricate, and yet so absolute, that the most daring as well as the most abject could not hope to escape its iron rule.

From the remotest times there has been a ceaseless march of tribes and races into the vast peninsula called Hindostan, from which there is no easy outlet, east or west, north or south; all points are equally difficult and impassable—mountain-barriers on the north, with ranges of mountains and circling seas on every other side. Nevertheless, pouring across the Indus and straggling down the narrow defiles and passes of the Himálayas, came wave after wave of immigration, pushing the earlier populations farther and farther into the hills and forest-boundaries of the occupied land. Each wave, borne down by the later arrival, disappeared or retreated deeper and deeper into the heart of the country till the whole of India was overflooded by the great Aryan invasion.

In no part of the world are there found so many remains of distinct tribes and races of men as in Hindostan proper. Everywhere in the forests, in the most inaccessible mountain-regions of the peninsula, and all along the sea-coast, are tribes and races who seem to have been hemmed in where we now find them. The vast plains of the regions of the Indus and the Ganges afforded no place of refuge to the retreating barbarians. Hence, with the exception of some few who were absorbed into the population of Lower Bengal, the Aryans drove all before them, even the Tamuls, a partly-civilized people, who, having swept the earlier inhabitants southward, were in their turn forced south.

From the latitude of the Vindhyan chain down to Cape Comorin, and in the forests of Ceylon, the aboriginal populations of India are still to be met with, living in detached communities, distinct in physical appearance, manners, customs, and religions, not only from the Hindoos, Tamuls, Moslems, and Parsees, but from one another.

Nothing annoyed our pundit so much as when he heard me call my bhistee, or water-man, "a Hindoo:" "Hindoo nay, maim sahib, whoo jungly-wallah hai" ("Not Hindoo-man, but a savage of the forest"). And, to tell the truth, one could not fail to notice between the Hindoo pundit and the coolie-bhistee as marked a difference as one sees between a high-bred American gentleman of the Anglo-Saxon race and the newly-emancipated American negro.

In crossing the Indus one comes upon the relics of ancient races in the dark-complexioned, diminutive, but powerfully athletic natives of Guzerat, many of whom are now the coolies or porters of Bombay. Again, scattered over the Vindhyan and Satpurah mountains and the banks of the Nerbudda and Tapti are other tribes of a very peculiar race called Bheels or Bhils, probably from the Sanskrit word "bhil," which signifies "separate" or "outcasts." The legends of these tribes, one and all, trace their origin to the union of the god Mahadèo with a beautiful woman met by him in a forest. From this union sprang a sort of giant distinguished by his ugliness and vice, who, after having perpetrated a series of horrible crimes, killed the sacred Brahmanic bull of the god, and was banished to the wilderness of Jodhpoor. The history of the Rajpoot princes of Jodhpoor and Odhpoor corroborates this account of the Bhil emigration. The Bhats,* or minstrels, of the Bhils still reside in Raj-

* The Bhats and Charans, the bards and genealogists of these tribes,

Bhistees or Water Carriers.

pootana, and make yearly visits to the countries of the various Bhil tribes to celebrate festal seasons with music and song. The celebrated Nádir Singh, a Bhilahah (that is, one sprung from the marriage of a Rajpoot with a Bhil woman), was one of the most formidable freebooters of his time until the establishment of an English settlement at Mhau,* when he was compelled to discharge his foreign adherents and renounce plundering.†

The Bhils are short in stature, thick-set, almost black, with wiry hair and beard, but extraordinarily active and capable of enduring great fatigue, delighting in flesh of all kinds and intoxicating drinks, with which no Brahman will ever pollute his sacred lips. The chiefs of the Bhils are called Bhomiyahs, and are generally of the Bhilalah or mixed race. They exercise the most absolute power over their subjects; each chief is styled a "dhani," or lord, and the most atrocious crimes are often committed at his bidding. In order to limit this absolute power, however,

are remarkable for their power of reciting from memory whole epics describing the birth, exploits, and death of the various Bhil chiefs. They will also devote themselves to death or to receive the most cruel mutilations in order to keep a promise, accomplish a vow, recover a debt, or to obtain any end which might be secured by inspiring others with superstitious reverence and dread. A Bhat of Viramghaw in 1806 put his little daughter, a beautiful girl of seven years old, to death by decapitation, and with her blood, which he carried in an earthen vessel, he sprinkled the gate of the Malliah Rajah's castle, and thus compelled him to pay a debt to the Gaikwar for which he had become security.

* The British established in 1825 a Bhil agency in Central India, and organized a Bhil corps in order to utilize the warlike instincts of the various Bhil tribes. This brave body of men, who have distinguished themselves in war, have recently done good service in aiding to put down the predatory habits of their countrymen. They are slowly becoming cultivators of the soil, though still unwilling to rent land and thus bind themselves to fixed habits for any length of time.

† A remarkable account of a residence with Nádir, and of some of his murderous exploits, will be found in the *Autobiography of Lutfullah.*

there are certain religious officers called "tarwis," or heads of tribes, whose counsel must be attended to by the chiefs. The worship of the Bhils is paid to Mahadèo, the high god, and Dèvi his consort, the goddess of small-pox. A great number of infernal deities are also propitiated by yearly offerings and pilgrimages to their respective shrines.

While the Bhil men are brutal, cruel, and drunken, it is a remarkable fact that the Bhil women are chaste, gentle, and almost always very good-looking.*

Driven southward by the conquering Rajpoots, numbers of the Bhils adopted the savage life of freebooters and robbers, which they still retain, and the more wealthy settled in Guzerat and Candeish, where most richly-ornamented temples and rock-shrines are to be found to-day, and such as remained with the Rajpoots became hardy cultivators of the soil or the bravest of watchmen when employed as guards.

In character they are sensitive on points of honor among themselves, but desperate foes, revenging themselves, sometimes years after, for any grievance perpetrated against one of their tribe. I remember an incident related to me by my mother which is characteristic of the Bhil freebooters and robbers. My stepfather was appointed to survey the public road newly opened from Cambay to the confines of the great and then almost unknown province of Guzerat. She had decided to accompany him on his long and hazardous journey. Having acquired a fair knowledge of the Guzerati language, she proved, as he had hoped, an invaluable aid in settling disputes about payments of money for work done, and in

* The great reforms which have been effected in many of these tribes have been very materially assisted by the influence of the Bhil women.

directing and instructing such of the Bhils, Khands, and other tribes as were employed on the roads. Furnished with a sepoy guard and a large amount of government money to defray the expenses of the road repairs, they travelled for some time unmolested through the strange country. On one occasion, however, they had pitched their tents in the village of Balmere, and had retired for the night. My stepfather, fatigued with a hard day's ride over the roads, slept soundly. The guards patrolled the little encampment, which consisted of three tents, two for the servants and sepoys on duty, and the other, a double-poled tent, consisting of two rooms with a double wall of canvas around it, for the family. The tumbril which conveyed the government money from place to place stood in the corner of the room, near the cot on which my mother slept. My stepfather occupied the adjoining room. A small lamp stood burning on the tumbril, and the key had been carelessly left in the treasure-box.

About midnight my mother was suddenly aroused by a slight shuffling noise. She raised her head, and, looking toward the spot whence the sound proceeded, was horrified at seeing the shadows of the nude figures of several men passing between the outer and inner walls of the tent. Presently a gang of Bhil robbers opened the tent-door and stood before her, confronting her, armed with bows and poisoned arrows. There were six men in all, with nothing on their persons but *langoutis** of straw round their loins, and their bodies highly greased, so as to slip away from the grasp of any person who attempted to seize and hold them.

Divining that their object was to rob the tumbril, the brave lady, without uttering a single cry, sprang to her

* A strip of cloth worn by the lower population of India around the loins.

feet, standing erect and seemingly fearless, and gazed defiantly at them. For a moment or two the foremost robbers seemed to hesitate. Then the one of the gang nearest her addressed her in Guzerati, and said, "Woman, we do not desire to hurt you; we only mean to possess ourselves of what we need, the money in that cart there;" saying which, he attempted to advance toward the tumbril. To scream for help would imperil her own and her husband's life, for these freebooters would at once use their poisoned arrows; but to permit them quietly to rob the government treasury would be almost as fatal, entailing on them endless delay, trouble, and perhaps even unjust suspicion at head-quarters. The intrepid wife suddenly remembered that the Bhils had a superstitious reverence for the person of woman, and before they had time to reach the tumbril she flung herself on her face and hands across their path, and said solemnly in Guzerati, "Only by stepping over a woman's body can you obtain possession of what is entrusted to the care of her husband." There she lay, not daring to utter another word, trembling from head to foot, and anticipating momentary death from their cruel arrows.

Minute after minute passed away, but she still did not dare to open her eyes or even turn her head toward them. After lying there for nearly half an hour, which seemed almost an eternity of agonizing suspense, and unable to endure it any longer, she ventured timidly to glance in the direction of the robbers, and, lo! their places were empty; the tent-door was closed. The Bhil freebooters, hearing this strange being address them in their own language, hurling at them one of their most formidable threats, had vanished as softly as they had entered the tent, vanquished by the presence of mind shown by a delicate woman.

On another occasion the military chaplain at Desa, a British station in Guzerat, was on his way to seek change of air at Mount Aboo. At dusk one evening he found himself surrounded by a gang of Bhil robbers; his travelling-wagon was stopped, his driver took to his heels and fled; his servants too had gone on ahead. Not knowing what to do, he addressed them in Guzerati, and said, "I am not a rich man; I am a poor servant of God, a Christian priest in search of health." Immediately the chief of the gang gave orders that he should not be hurt. They stripped him, however, and divided among themselves whatever they could find. Two of the gang, presenting their short daggers to the poor clergyman, made him march before them in his shirt for some distance. Every time that he turned to remonstrate with the robbers they pricked him slightly with their pointed daggers, till at length he resolved to take no further notice of them. On and on he went. A great darkness had overtaken him; almost fainting from fatigue, he sank to the ground unable to take another step, when, to his surprise, he found that the robbers had departed, leaving him to pursue his way through a wild jungle. He spent an anxious night in the forest, retraced his steps to the village, and by complaining to the headman was at once furnished with a guard and every facility to pursue his journey, the law here being that if robbery or murder is perpetrated in the vicinity of a village, the headman is obliged to make ample restitution; and he has the power to levy a fine on the community to indemnify himself for all the expenses that such acts entail on him as patèl, or governor, of the village. The reverend clergyman always maintained that his escape from death on this occasion was owing to the fact of his being able to address the robbers in their own tongue.

South of the Nerbudda, and in the very heart of the Vindhyan chain, are the Gonds,* so called from their habitual nudity—a race of the lowest type, jet-black skin, stunted, thick-lipped, and with small, deep-set eyes. This race is often called by the Hindoos Angorees—*i. e.* cannibals. They live in miserable huts, surrounded by swine, poultry, buffaloes, and dogs, without any industries, literature, or priesthood, and with few ceremonials of any kind whatever—worshippers of serpents, demons, or anything, in fact, that inspires them with dread, to whom they sometimes sacrifice their children or captives taken in war. Such religious rites as prevail among them are conducted by the aged and honored members of their tribe, both male and female.

Verging on the Gondwana † are the hilly provinces of Orissa, inhabited by the Khands, no doubt a tribe slightly in advance in physical type and civilization of their neighbors, the Gonds, the Thugs, and Sourahs. They regard the earth-spirit as in rebellion against the Supreme Deity. To the earth-spirit they direct their prayers, and seek to propitiate her by human sacrifices.

* The Gonds are supposed to be the aborigines of the Sagar and Nagpoor provinces, and have much in common with the Khandsor Khands, another tribe of North Sarkar. They have dialects peculiar to themselves, and which have no affinity whatever with the Sanskrit, but probably are akin to that of the Dravidian stock. They kept up their old religious custom of human sacrifice until 1835-45, when the strong arm of the English interfered and has almost put a stop to it.

† Gondwana has been thought by some Oriental scholars to be the ancient Chĕdi, which was ruled by the great Sisupal, who is said to have governed India about the time of the appearance of Krishna (the last of the incarnations of Brahm) on earth. They identify Chanderi, his ancient capital, with the modern Chanda, a city in British India in the Nagpoor division of the Central Provinces, and abounding in fine remains of huge reservoirs for water, cave-temples, and the curious tombs of the aboriginal Gond kings.

Their victims are called "Meriah"* by the Oriyahs, and Kudatee by the Khands. These victims must not belong to their tribes nor to the Brahman caste. They are purchased, or more generally kidnapped, from the surrounding districts by persons called Panwhas, who are attached to their villages for these and other peculiar offices. They may be either male or female, and as consecrated persons are treated with great kindness. To the "Meriah" youth or maiden a portion of land is assigned, with farming stock. He or she is also permitted to marry and bear children, who in turn become victims. If a "Meriah" youth form an attachment to the daughter or even wife of a Khand, the relatives indulge him in his wishes, regarding it as an especial favor. These sacrifices take place annually, when the sun is in his highest point in the heavens. The victim is selected by casting of lots. The ceremony lasts three days, and is always attended by a large concourse of people of both sexes. The first day of the approaching sacrifice is spent in feasting, merriment, and prayers, which go hand in hand with wild revelry of all kinds. On the second morning the victim who is to propitiate the earth-goddess is washed, attired in a flowing white robe, and conducted, with music, beating of drums, blowing of horns and rude reed instruments, to the sacred groves preserved for these rites. Here the assembled community implore the earth-goddess Tari (called Pennu by the Shanars and Davee by the Rajpoots, who have in great measure been tainted by their contact with these hill-tribes) to accept the sacrifice about to be offered, and to bless their land with increase of corn, wine, cattle, and so forth. After the offering up of prayer the victim, whether male or female, stands up before the assembly,

* Meriah means "death-doomed," and Kudatee, "dedicated to the god."

draws forth his glittering knife, and passes his hand three times over its sharp edge. He then deliberately steps up to the rude altar of Tari, lays down his knife upon it, and, bowing his head, worships the insatiable earth-goddess; then snatching up the knife, he cries, "Drink of my blood and be appeased, O Tari," etc., etc. He waves it aloft three times and plunges it into his side. Leaning toward the earth, which he desires to propitiate in behalf of his fellow-men, he slowly draws out the knife, pours his life-blood out upon her parched and thirsty soil, and expires at the foot of the dreaded altar raised to her name. Honored as no other creature in the land, reared for death, the "Meriah," or doomed one, exults in the performance of this self-sacrifice with a consciousness of being a savior of the country, and has never been known to evade or escape the doom in store for him.

After this horrible sacrifice the human victim is cut into small pieces, and each head of a Khand or Gond family obtains a shred or infinitesimal portion of the body, which he buries in his field to please the spirit of the earth. This is believed to aid not a little in rendering the soil rich and fertile.

The Thugs, or "stranglers," are not unlike the Gonds in physical appearance and natural characteristics. They live by robbery and murder, and are banded together by certain vows which they religiously follow. One sect of Thugs are called Phansigars, or "throttlers." It is their practice to strangle wayfarers, whence their name, and appropriate such spoils as may fall to their lot in these onslaughts. Efforts have been made, through the British government, to put a stop to both these religious atrocities of the Meriah and the Thugs, and in some parts of the country with great success.

The Jadejas are a branch of the great Samma tribe once

so powerful in Sindh; they assumed this title from a celebrated chief named Jada. Their arrival in Guzerat dates from 800 A. D. The remarkable characteristic of this tribe is their systematic murder of all their female children. Another branch of the Jadejas settled in Kach, or Cutch. These differ materially from their brethren in Guzerat. They are half Musulmans and half Hindoos, believe in the Kuran, worship Mohammedan saints, swear by Allah, eat, drink, and smoke with the followers of the Prophet. But, on the other hand, they do not undergo circumcision, and adore all kinds of images of wood and stone. In appearance they are fine, tall men, light-complexioned, handsome-featured, and have singularly long whiskers, which are often allowed to come down to the breast. They owe their good looks to their mothers, who are either bought or kidnapped from other tribes; no females of their own are ever reared.

The Kalhis (another curious tribe) are evidently a northern race; they are tall, well-formed, with regular features, aquiline nose, blue or gray eyes, and soft dark-brown hair. The sun is their chief deity. On the Mandevan Hills, near Thau, is a temple to the sun, said to have been erected by the Kalhis on their first arrival in Guzerat. In this temple there is a huge image of the Sun-god with a halo round its head. The symbol of the sun with the words, "Sri suryagni shakh" ("the witness of the holy sun") is affixed to all official documents and deeds of property.

A number of tribes may be found in the district of Bilaspoor, which forms the upper half of the basin of the river Maha-Nadi—the Gonds, already mentioned, the Kanwars, Bhumias, Bingwars, and Dhanwars—all differing among themselves in physical characteristics, customs, manners, and certain religious observances. Among the

Hindoos here are two tribes which deserve particular mention—the Chamars, or Chamar-wallahs, and the Pankhas. The former take their name from their dealing in "chamar," or "leather." They are the shoemaker and leather-trading castes of the Hindoo communities, and have always been held in great contempt by the high-class Brahmans and Hindoos. About sixty years ago a religious movement was inaugurated by one of the Chamars named Ghasi-Dhas. He represented himself as a messenger from God sent to teach men the unity of God and the equality of men. He was the means of liberating his tribe from the trammels of caste; he prohibited the worship of idols or images, and enjoined that prayers should be offered up to the Supreme Being, whose spirit should be ever present to their minds without any visible sign or representation. The followers of the new faith call themselves "Satmanes" or the "worshippers of Satyan, the truth." Ghasi-Dhas was their first high priest; he died 1850. His son succeeded him, but was assassinated by some Hindoo fanatic, but his grandson is the present high priest of the Chamars.

The "Pankhas," or weavers, are also deists of a very high order; they are the followers of a religious reformer named Kahbir, who flourished about the fifteenth century. There is very little difference between the Kahbir-Pankhas and the Satmanes-Chamars in their worship and religion. The province of Sindh derives its name from the Sanskrit word "Sindhu," "ocean or flood," which name the Aryans of the Vèdic period who were settled about the sixth century B. C. in the Panjaub and along the Indus gave to that river. In the third "Ashtaka" and the sixth "Adhyáya" there appears to be a distinct mention of the Indus River in the twelfth verse, which runs as follows: "Thou hast spread abroad upon the earth by thy power the swollen Sindhu when arrested (on its course)." * The Indus is still called Sindhu throughout its course from Kalabágh to Atâk; it is sometimes locally termed Atâk. From Kalabágh to Bâhkhar is the upper Indus, and from Bâhkhar to the sea the lower Indus. It begins to rise in March and falls in September, but, unlike the Ganges and the Mississippi, it does not submerge its delta or inundate the valley through which it passes to any great extent. Its floods are irregular and partial, pouring sometimes for years on the right bank, and then on the left, so that even at the height of the freshets the Persian wheel may be seen at work watering the fields on either bank.

The principal tribes of Sindh are the Beluchis and the Jâts, or Sindhis, once Hindoos, but converted to Islam under the Khalifs † of the house Ommayyah. The Sindhis are taller, stronger, more robust, and muscular than the natives of India; they belong chiefly to the Hanifah sect of Mohammedans. Their language is a strange mixture of Arabic and Sanskrit words, the noun being borrowed from the Sanskrit, and the verb from the Persian or Arabic grammar. The Beluchis are a mountain-tribe; they are superior to the Jâts or Sindhs, fairer, more powerfully formed, very hardy, not deficient in courage under brave leaders, and extremely temperate. The Beluchi women are remarkably faithful and devoted as wives, and those of the Mari tribe often follow their husbands to battle.

One of the peculiarities of the Hindoos of Sindh is that they have no outcast tribes among them, like the Parwaris, or Pariahs, Pasis, and Khandalas of Hindostan;

* See *Introduction to the Second Book of the Rig-Veda*, by H. H. Wilson, p. xvii.

† Khalif, or Caliph, successor or vicar of Mohammed, from Khalifah, an Arabic title given to the acknowledged successors of Mohammed, who were regarded as invested with supreme dignity and power in all matters relating to religion and civil polity.

and many of the Musulmans of Sindh are followers of Nanak * and Govind his disciple.

Farther north, in the Afghan districts, numerous warlike tribes are found. Afghans, properly so called, distinguish themselves from the aboriginal populations. The chief clans or tribes of the Afghans are the Duranis, south-west of the Afghan plateau; the Ghilzais, the strongest and most warlike of the Afghans, occupying the highlands north of Kandhar (this tribe is noted for its deep-rooted hostility to foreigners, and especially to the British); the Yusufzais, north of Peshwar; and the Khakars, who are chiefly the highlanders of this region. Of the non-Afghan tribes very little is known; those that have come under the notice of the British officers are no doubt mostly a mixed race, descendants of the Aryans and Turanians. The purest of these are the Parsivans, the Kizibashes, the Hindikis, and the Jâts, all more or less closely allied to the Persians and Hindoos in language, manners, and customs. The Eimâk, the Hazaras, Tajiks, and the Khohistans are semi-nomadic tribes—Mohammedans; some are of the Shiah † and others of the Sunni sect.

As a race, the Afghans are a very handsome, athletic

* A Mohammedan reformer and founder of the Sikh religion. He preached about the fourteenth century against the abuses of the Mohammedan religion, and inaugurated the spiritual worship of God alone. One day, when Nanak lay on the ground absorbed in devotion, with his feet toward Mecca, a Moslem priest, seeing him, cried, "Base infidel! how darest thou turn thy feet toward the house of Allah?" Nanak answered, "And thou, turn them if thou canst toward any spot where the awful house of God is not."

† The Shiahs and Sunnis are the two most important Mohammedan sects. The Sunnis hold the "Sunnat," or traditions of Mohammed, as of nearly equal authority to the Kuran, and they revere equally the four successors of the Prophet, Abu-Bahkr, Omar, Usman, and Ali. The Shiahs, on the other hand, reject the traditions, and do not acknowledge the successors of the Prophet as Khalifahs.

NATIVE NOBLEMEN OF HINDOSTAN.

people, with fair complexion, aquiline nose, and flowing black, brown, and sometimes even red, hair, which the men wear long, falling in soft curls over the shoulders. The women are beautiful, and often of fair rosy complexion, dark eyes and hair, which they wear under a skull-cap, with two long braids falling to the waist behind, finished off with silk tassels. Since the Mohammedan conquest the custom of excluding women from the society of the male members of the family has been introduced into Afghanistan, and is now rigidly enforced.

In the very apex of India, the hilly districts of Southern Madras, are numerous early races and tribes, distinct and peculiar to themselves, of whom the Tudas and Cholas are most worthy of notice. The former is as superior in type to the latter as the Caucasian is to the Mongolian. The Tudas are chiefly found in the Nilgherry Hills; they are tall, athletic, and well-formed. Their women, though dark, are singularly pleasing when young. The comparatively treeless character of these hills indicates that in former times large spaces were cleared and cultivated, though at present the Tudas seem to prefer roaming about the hills and leading a nomadic life.

In the Dhendigal and neighboring Wynadd Hills appear other tribes, apparently the oldest of all the primitive races of India, and of the lowest type of humanity. They are called Shanars, and are clothed, if at all, with the bark of trees, using bows and arrows, and subsisting chiefly on roots, wild honey, and reptiles. Short in stature and agile as monkeys, living without habitations among trees, they penetrate the jungle with marvellous speed, and seem only a step removed from the orang-outang of Borneo and Sumatra. There is no doubt that these wild people, if not indigenous to the soil, occupied at one time a large portion of this country, and are the remains of that "monkey race" whom the first Aryan invaders met with, and who, with their leader Hanuman, figure so largely in the old poems as the allies of Rama in his conquest of Ceylon.

Among these numerous but isolated relics of aboriginal populations there is another and superior race, divided into several distinct nationalities, such as the Tamuls, Telingus, and Canarese, who people the greater part of Southern India. Nevertheless, between them and those still later Aryans the difference, both mental and physical, is plainly seen.

There are still current in Southern India a number of languages and dialects, which, though largely intermixed with Sanskrit terms in consequence of Aryan conquest and civilization, belong to distinct families of languages. The most comprehensive of these are the Tamul, Telingu, and Carnatic, showing the existence of separate nations at the time of the Aryan conquest. The Tamul language has no inconsiderable literature of its own.

The Mahrattas, whose chief seat is in the Deccan, belong to still another race, although there is now among them a larger infusion of Aryan blood than is to be found farther south in India.

In the van of Aryan imigration settling along the plains of the Ganges from Hurdwar down to the eastern frontier of Oude and the Raj-Mahal Hills were the Brahmans, founders of the great cities Hastinapoora ("abode of elephants"), Indraspatha, Delhi, Canouge on the Doab, Ayodhya (Oude), Benares, and Palibothra (Patna). They concentrated themselves in the upper part of the Ganges valley, but did not attempt to pass into Lower Bengal, as may be seen to-day by the physical and mental inferiority of the Bengalees to the populations of Northern Hindostan.

All travellers and historians agree in stating that the

early Aryan settlers in the valley of the Ganges closely resembled the Hellenic race in Greece in almost every feature of their military, domestic, and social life. They were split up into a number of small states or communities. The Kshatryas, though originating in their military profession, and not in a single family, were not unlike the Heraclidæ, who became the royal race of the Peloponnesus. But in process of time these Kshatryas were absorbed into the Rajpoots, who are supposed to have arrived in India about the time of Alexander's invasion of the Panjaub. They settled where we find them to-day, in the neighborhood of Rohilcund and Bundelcund, and shortly after them came the Jâts, another branch of the Indo-European or Aryan family, thus completing the four great waves of the so-named Pandya, or white-faced, immigration—the Brahmans, Kshatryas, the Rajpoots, and the Jâts. It was the Brahmans who founded the celebrated Pandhya kingdom, so called from their white skins, and established the "Meerassee" system—*i. e.* an aristocracy of equality among the four conquering races. They shared the land equally among themselves, and regarded all others as servants or subjects.

In this primitive village-system the Brahman, or priest and poet, the Pundit, or schoolmaster, the Vakeel, or pleader, were as essential as food and drink to the community. Priest, teacher, and pleader by virtue of their high functions enjoyed peculiar and unquestioned privileges: land free of all tax was religiously assigned to them, and servants to cultivate it for their use were attached to the grant.

In each and every Hindoo village or town which has retained its old form the children even to-day are able to read, write, and cipher. But wherever the village-system has been swept away by foreign and other influences there the village school has also disappeared with it. A trial by jury, called "punchayet," was also a part of the primitive system of self-government instituted by the early Brahmans: each party named two or more arbitrators, and the judge one; the jury could not in any case be composed of less than five persons, whence the name "punchayet"—five just ones. In difficult cases the influence of the heads and elders of the village was brought to bear upon the contending parties, and the administration of justice was so pure in those days that the saying "In the punchayet is God" became proverbial.

Out of these marked mental and physical differences grew up the monstrous and extraordinary system of caste in India. Not that caste does not exist in some degree everywhere throughout the world. In the British Isles it is as fixed and absolute as a Medo-Persic law, and even among Americans a marked social inequality exists. Caste naturally sprang up with the first mingling of the conquering and conquered races on Indian soil. At first the distinctions of class and rank were no more marked than that of an English peasant and the lord of a domain, or that of the negro girl and her mistress in the United States to-day. But the proud, white-skinned Brahmans, in order to guard the purity of their own "blue blood," and to rivet their own ascendency, invented at length a distinct and most binding code of laws, and then claimed for them the divine authority of the Vèdas.

Of the four great castes that we read so much about, three only were fixed—Brahmans, Kshatryas, and the Vaisyas. This last was the common Aryan people, and they were not separated from their superiors by any harsh distinctions. But the Sudras, "the threefold black men," among whom the Aryan population established themselves, all the non-Aryan races and tribes of the peninsula

BORAHS, OR NATIVE MERCHANTS.

of Hindostan, were kept off by a wide gulf and the most galling marks of inferiority. The Sudra could not read the Vèdas nor join in their religious meetings. He could not cook their food, or even serve in their houses; he was unclean, gross, sensual, irreligious, and therefore an abomination to the noble white-faced Aryan.

The code of Manu, with all its "unparalleled arrogance" toward the Sudra, was founded rather upon what a high-bred Brahman ought to be than with any deliberate intent to degrade the Sudra. But with its practice came that inevitable deterioration to the moral character of the Brahmans themselves, who forgot that the humblest man has a right to the same sanctity of life and character as the highest. The lower the Brahman sank in his spiritual and moral nature, the more he tried to hedge himself about with artificial claims to the reverence of the peoples around him, until finally the code of Manu swelled into minute details. Reaching the unborn child of Aryan parents, it directed its nursing in the cradle, it shaped the training of the youth, and regulated the actions of his perfect manhood as son, husband, and father. Food, raiment, exercise, religious and social duties, must be brought into subjection to its sovereign voice, and in the course of time it was inseparably interwoven with every domestic usage, every personal and social habit. From the cradle to the grave it undertakes to regulate and control every desire, every inclination, every movement, of the inner and outer man. Such is the code of Manu.

In spite of these laws, however, there flourished Sudra kings and Sudra communities, influenced though not absorbed by the Aryan population. Sudra kings were invited to the court of the great *Yudishthira** and treated with

* One of the greatest of Aryan kings mentioned in the Mahabharata.

marked respect and courtesy; indeed, this word "Kiriya" or "Kritya" (courtesy) was held to be the distinguishing mark of a high-bred Brahman. The Sudras in their turn soon caught the infection of caste feeling, and were not slow in adopting the same distinctions among themselves.

From being at first a sign of superiority of race, it gradually took form and extended to every branch and profession. Priest, teacher, soldier, sailor, tinker, tailor, robber, murderer, and beggar, was each one fixed immovably and for ever in his place and grade, and no earthly power could draw him into any other. Every one piqued himself on his particular caste; each man confined himself sternly to his own perfect circle. There was hope for every man who belonged to a caste, so that even those fallen from caste bound themselves together in a brotherhood and called themselves Pariahs, "outcasts," which in time became a large and distinct caste. "Even in the lowest depths they found a lower still."

So monstrous and deteriorating was this system that in the course of time, losing sight of its original purpose, it separated the Aryans themselves, for whose especial preservation and union it was designed, by distinctions and restrictions almost as galling as those it had formerly imposed only on the Sudras.

Nevertheless, it had its noble features, and did good work for a time. The high advancement to which the Indo-European art, literature, painting, music, and architecture attained was due to the leadership of the Brahman civilization. It was an aristocracy to rule and educate the masses, which everywhere exhibited a uniform inferiority. But even with all the help of caste and the inflexible code of Manu to preserve them on every side, the proud white-faced Aryans did not long escape the deteriorating influences both of the climate in which they had settled and the debasing usages of the non-Aryan populations around them.

The most degrading practice that sprang up in time on Indian soil was asceticism. The amount and the terrible nature of this self-imposed penance practised by the Hindoos exceed anything known in the world, and are almost inconceivable to any ordinary European, whose first instinct is self-preservation. Ablutions and commands of personal cleanliness, which formed a part of the code of Manu, have increased in number, and also the penalties attached to their violation to such a degree that now-a-days a Brahman or Hindoo is defiled by the most trifling accident of place or touch. To eat with the left hand, to sneeze when he is praying, to gape in the presence of the sacrificial fire, to touch one of a low caste, are all pollutions. In fact, the very shadow of an Englishman or a Sudra falling on his cooking-pot renders it obligatory on him to bury his meal in the earth and to throw away his pot if earthen; if not, it must undergo seven purifications before it is in a sufficiently holy condition to boil the rice sacred to the Brahman. The simple contact with pig's fat in the cartridges made the sepoys, who believed they were thus lost to caste and to heaven, willing and terrible tools in the hands of the arch-enemy of British power in the East. Nana Sahib, or, more properly speaking, Dundoo Punt, who, in order to revenge a private wrong—the lapse to the East Indian Company, on the death of his uncle and royal father by adoption, of a large territory bequeathed to him—worked upon the caste-prejudices of the sepoys until he maddened them into committing the most fiendish acts ever recorded in Indian history. But the original code does not so regard the eating of pork. If a Brahman purposely eat pork he shall be degraded, but if he has partaken of it involuntarily or through another's connivance, a penance and purification are sufficient for full atonement.

Thus, injunctions originally designed as rules of pure living and high-breeding, cleanliness, abstinence, kindliness, charity, and courtesy, have been so multiplied and distorted that it is now difficult even for the most precise and devout Brahman to carry them all faithfully into practice. And if Christian teachers and reformers were seriously minded to overthrow this vast system of caste in India, they could successfully do so by quoting the Vèdas and the code of Manu, which prescribe no such arbitrary rules of life as now exist in India. It is our want of knowledge, and that of most of the modern Brahmans, which still holds them in their old fetters, rendering the efforts to free them of little avail, for we know not how nor where to begin the attack on such a strong fortress as caste and custom are to these blind followers of law and order.

Centuries after the consolidation of the Brahman power and system of caste there arose a strong-souled Aryan, a prince by birth, a republican at heart, and a reformer by nature, called Sakya Suddarthà, who no sooner became of age than he suddenly began to deny the inspiration of the Vèdas, the divine right of Brahmans to the priesthood, and the obligations of caste. He offered equality of birthright and of spiritual office alike to all men and women. Sudra, Pariah, Khandala, bond or free, were of one and the same great family. He went about declaring all men brothers. This was the strong point of Buddhism. The new religion spread at once. It ravished the hearts and kindled the imaginations of many Aryans, but chiefly the non-Aryan nations. Everywhere it was received with enthusiasm. Brahmanism and caste received their first great shock, from which they have never wholly recovered.

Monastic orders first arose among the Buddhists, and as caste was abolished the monasteries were open to all men, and even to women, who were bound over to celibacy and self-renunciation. These Buddhist priests went about preaching their new religion to the common people, and found ready acceptance with them. Barefooted, with shaven heads, eyebrows, and chins, wearing a yellow dress instead of the pure white robes of the Brahmans, they seemed indeed lower than the lowest Pariahs. They built lowly chapels, and had regular services in them, chanting a prescribed liturgy, offering harmless sacrifices of incense, lighted tapers, rice, wine, oil, and flowers, and taking the lily instead of the Brahmanic lotos as the emblem of the purity of their faith.

Buddhism spread with amazing rapidity, and flourished for some time on Indian soil. During the reign of the celebrated Indian king Asoka, three centuries more or less before Christ, it was the dominant religion of India, about which time it was also introduced by Buddhist missionaries into Ceylon, China, and the Japanese Archipelago. At length, the Brahmans, recovering from the lethargy that seemed to have overtaken them, joined all their forces, and, rising *en masse* everywhere against these dissenters from the Vèdas and from the old code of Manu, drove out of Hindostan proper those whom they could not put to death. The Buddhists finally found refuge in Guzerat and ready acceptance among the early primitive races; and here the new religion reached its highest prosperity, but began to decline in the eighth or ninth century after Christ. At this juncture a new sect arose under the leadership of one Jaina, or saint, a man of great purity of character, who undertook to correct the many errors which had crept into Buddhism. Veneration and worship of deified men, confined by the Buddhists some to five and others to seven saints, were extended by the Jains to twenty-four, of whom colossal statues in black or white marble were set up in their temples. Tenderness and respect for animal life they carried to an extreme point, which has led to the establishment of the hospitals for infirm aged animals in different parts of India. In its essence Jainism agrees with Buddhism. It rejects the inspiration of the Vèdas, has no animal sacrifices, pays no respect to fire. But in order to escape the unremitting persecution of the Brahman priesthood it admits *caste*, and even the worship of the chief Hindoo gods. Thus Jainism secured that toleration on Indian soil which was never extended to Buddhism, the very birthplace of Buddha having been rendered a wilderness and untenanted by man through the rage and fury of Brahmanic persecution.

Brahmanism, finding itself once more in the ascendency, proceeded with great tact to incorporate into its ritual all the divinities, the rites, and the ceremonies peculiar to the non-Aryan populations. In Southern India Vishnoo is worshipped under the name and character of Jaggernath (or Juggernaut), "Lord of the universe;" but in Northern Hindostan this worship is mingled with that of Rama and Krishna, two Aryan heroes, whom the Brahmans with great political adroitness represent as later incarnations of both Vishnoo and Jaggernath. The pre-Aryan Mahrattas and Marwhars were brought to believe their supreme deities, Cando-ba, and Virabudra, as incarnations of Siva, and so on, until at length every god, hero, or saint belonging to the pre-historic inhabitants of Asia found a place in the Brahmanic calendar of incarnations of gods and goddesses.

Monotheism and polytheism exist side by side; purity and vice are only different expressions of a system as complex as life itself. Through all manners, acts, and usages, the most trivial or the most momentous, the Brahman religion flows in perpetual symbolism and stamps everything with its seal and mark. The pure Hindoos live in a network of observances, the smallest infraction of which involves the most terrible social degradation and loss of caste. They are bound by observances for rising, for sitting, for eating, drinking, sleeping, bathing; for birth, marriage, and death; for the sites of their homes and even the positions of their doors and windows.

The dwellings of Hindoos vary according to their means. The poorer have only one apartment, which must be smeared over once a week with a solution of the ordure of the cow. The better classes always have a courtyard and a verandah, where strangers, and even Europeans, may be received without risk of contamination. Very often the walls of the dwellings are covered with frescoes and paintings. The entrance to the dwelling is always placed, out of respect to the sun, facing the east, but a little to one side. Every morning at an early hour the Hindoo wife or mother of the home may be seen cleansing her house and her utensils for cooking, eating, and drinking. This done, she will wash or smear with cow-ordure the space about her dwelling. After this purification the wife will proceed to ornament the front of the door, which in itself is held sacred to the Brahman, with the form of a lotos-flower. This she makes out of a solution of lime or chalk, and imprints it on the door and on the space in front of it. This flower is emblematic of the name of God, too pure to be uttered, but supposed to bestow a magical charm on the dwelling on which it is inscribed.*

* The sectarian marks of the Hindoos vary with their caste and the deity to whom they attach themselves. The high-caste Brahman makes

No one is so scrupulous with regard to personal neatness, purity, and cleanliness as the true Hindoo woman. The Hindoo sacraments are ten in number, with five daily duties that are as obligatory on the Brahman as are the sacraments in the Roman Catholic Church. The first sacrament begins with the unborn babe; it is the conceptional sacrament. Attended by the mother of a large family, the young wife repairs to a temple with a peculiar cake made of rice, sugar, and ghee (clarified butter), and with a fresh cocoanut. The goddess invoked on such occasions is Lakshina, the consort of Indra. They first offer up a prayer before her shrine, meditate on her glorious progeny of gods and heroes, then implore her kindly interposition in behalf of the young woman who is to become a mother; after which the elder matron breaks the cocoanut and pours the liquid out as an offering to the goddess, and part of the cake and cocoanut is brought home and distributed among the members of the family.

The next ceremony is a very profound one, and has an especial reference to the quickening of life in the babe.

only a circular mark with a little sacred mud of the Ganges, and mixed with water, on his forehead. This is symbolic of the mystic word "Aum." The followers of Vishnoo, a second grade of Brahmans, use a species of clay brought from a pool, Dhwaiaka, in which the seven shepherdesses, who are always represented with Krishna, are supposed to have drowned themselves on hearing of the death of their favorite hero. This mark is a circle with a straight line passing through, symbolizing the regenerative powers of nature. The Mahadèo sect wear two straight lines on the brow; the one on the right stands for God, the one on the left for man, a transverse streak of red lime: a preparation of turmeric and lime is used; it means God and man united. A great many wear the mark of Vishnoo's weapon with which he is supposed to have killed the sea-monster to rescue from destruction the three Vèdas. The followers of Siva, one of the four great sects of Hindoos, wear a complex mark of circle and cross combined, made with the ashes of burnt cow-ordure, symbolizing the destruction of all sin and the beatitude in store for the pure and holy.

The mother, shrouded in pure white from head to foot, accompanied by an elder female and mother of a large family, with her husband and father repair to the temple. One or more Brahman priests are invited to preside on this occasion. Oil, flowers, and lighted tapers are offered to Mahadèo the Great God. The priest pours the oil presented on a lighted lamp, then performs a wave-offering over the head of the expectant mother, praying, "O thou who art light, thou art also life and seed. Accept our sacrifice and make the new life thou hast created in secret visible in beauty and strength and power of intellect." After which offerings according to the wealth of the parties are made to the priests. There is one more important ceremony, similar in character to the others. All these sacraments are performed only in the case of the first child.

The birth ceremony takes place on the birth of every child. On this occasion a Brahman priest and an astrologer are invited. The mother of a large family and the grandmother are generally present. Before dividing the umbilical cord fire is waved over the child, a drop of honey and butter out of a golden spoon is put on his lips, after which the cord is severed. This is a very sacred ceremony, called "Jahu Karan" ("introduction to life"), and is performed with prayer, indicating that as the child's life is now severed from the parent life, so is all life at some time or other parted from the Central Life, but yet dependent on that as the infant is on the tender care of a mother. The father then draws near and looks upon the face of his son or daughter for the first time, at which he must take a piece of gold in his hand, offer a sacrifice to Brahma, and anoint the forehead of the child with ghee which has first been presented to Brahma. A string of nine threads of cotton, with five blades of durbagrass, must be bound by the father round the wrist of the child, indicating that the life matured by nine months is to be made perfect by the five daily sacraments or duties. This done, the astrologer casts the horoscope of the child, which is carefully written down, whether good or evil, and is confided to the father. This paper is generally burned with the person at death.

When the infant is a month old, and the new moon is first seen, he is presented to it as his progenitor with a solemn prayer. After which the naming takes place. The child's nearest relatives are invited. A Brahman priest waves over it a lamp, then sprinkles holy water, and calls aloud its name as he anoints the ears, eyes, nose, and breast of the child with clarified butter. This done, a little dress prepared for the child is put on for the first time.

When the teeth begin to appear a grand religious service takes place, and its first food of milk and rice is given to it after it has been consecrated by the priest. At three years of age the prescribed religious ceremony connected with the shaving off of the boy's hair takes place, and the consecration of the single lock left on the top of the head. Next comes the investiture of the sacred thread, performed only in the case of the male child.

Between the ages of fourteen and sixteen the youth formally presents himself before the temple to be admitted to the order to which he belongs. He is placed on a stone near a sacred tank in the precincts of a Hindoo temple; he is then washed in pure water by the priests robed in spotless white garments; the holy "Gayatri" is repeated in his right ear by one priest, while the other breathes over him the mystic trisyllable of "Aum, Aum, Aum," after which he is invested with a new sacred thread.

Marriage is also a sacrament. The male may be married at any time after the "mung," or investiture of the sacred thread; the time for this ceremony varies among the different castes. The female, however, must not be under ten years of age, and as she is obliged to be several years younger than the male, he is generally from sixteen to eighteen at the time of marriage.

Particular rules are laid down to be observed in the choice of a wife. She must not have any physical or moral defects; she must have an agreeable voice, sweet-sounding name, graceful proportions, elegant movements, fine teeth, hair, and eyes. Deformity inherited or constitutional delicacy, or disease of any kind, weak eyes, imperfect digestion, an inauspicious name, or lack of respectable lineage, always operate as strong impediments to marriage. Once the choice is made by the parents, then the particular months and junctions of the planets are consulted by the joshis or Hindoo astrologers: the birth-papers of both parties are first examined, followed by a profound study of the stars, which sometimes takes a year to be completed, after which a writing called the Lagan-patrika is prepared, in which the day, the hour, the names of the parties, and the position of the planets are put down, and one of the eight different kinds of marriages mentioned in the Shastras prescribed as the most fitting in view of the astral relations of husband and wife. These eight different kinds of marriages, however, are more or less similar, and vary only when the different castes intermarry one with the other. This intermarriage is always attended with loss of caste. The ceremony observed by the Brahmanic caste is the most interesting, and is called "*Brahma,*" from the sacredness attached to the rite. The bridegroom is obliged to prepare himself by certain prayers and ablutions before he can be presented to his future wife, whom he often sees for the first time, but of whose charms, graces of person, and character he is fully informed beforehand. Robed in pure white, anointed with holy oil, and wearing garlands of fresh flowers around his neck, he goes in procession, accompanied by his friends and relatives, to the bride's house, where he and his friends are welcomed as guests by the bride's father. The future wife is allowed to appear, and is generally veiled, so that even then the young couple do not see very much of each other.

On the afternoon of the day appointed for the wedding company to assemble at the house of the bride's father a raised platform is placed at one end of the hall; here the bridegroom takes his place, surrounded by the priests. Presently the bride enters the room accompanied by her father, who does homage to his future son and places his daughter at his right hand. After this a young priest enters bearing a large censer containing a charcoal fire, which is placed at their feet, and is emblematic of their warm affection. Two priests stand before them holding each a lighted torch in his hands, reciting some very beautiful prayers; meanwhile the bride rises and treads three times on a stone and *muller** placed beside her, and which is meant to indicate that the cares and duties she is now about to assume as a married woman will be carefully observed. The bridegroom then makes an oblation of oil and frankincense to the fire, as typical of his gratitude to the gods for the blessing which is now about to crown his life; this done, the priest hands him a torch, which he takes and waves three times around the person of his bride, signifying that his love will always surround and brighten her existence; he then drops it into the pan or censer at their feet. The bride now scatters a handful of

* A mill or grinder, used for grinding rice and wheat.

rice and a little oil as an oblation to the gods. The chant having ceased, the father steps up, and, taking a new upper and a lower garment, clothes the person of his daughter; he then fastens the end of her dress to the skirts of her lover's robe, and, taking the bride's hand, he places it in that of the bridegroom, binding them together with a mystic cord which is made of their sacred grass, typifying the delicacy of the marriage-tie, the strength and solidity of which depends not so much on the fragile cord which binds them, as on the individual will and resolution not to break it asunder. Then, conducted by the bridegroom, the young bride steps seven times around the sacred fire, repeating the marriage vows, the priests chant the nuptial hymn, and the marriage is consummated.

Every act of the Brahmanic ritual is symbolic. Thus in the evening of the same day, after sunset, the bridegroom sees his blushing little bride alone for the first time; he takes her by the hand, seats her on a bull's hide, which in its turn is symbolic of several spiritual and physical facts, one of which points to his power to support and protect her. Seated side by side, they quietly watch the rising of the polar star; pointing it out to her, he repeats, "Let us be steady, stable, serene, for ever abiding in each other's love, as that immovable and deathless star." Having sat in silent contemplation, they partake of their first meal together. The bridegroom remains three days at the house of the bride's father; on the fourth day he conducts his wife to his own, or, as it sometimes happens, to his father's house, in solemn procession. The Hindoo women are remarkably devoted as wives and mothers: instances of conjugal infidelity among the high caste are unknown, and extremely rare even among the lower castes of the Hindoo women.

The ceremonies attending the dead are worthy of brief

notice here. The last moments of a Brahman are generally made very impressive by the prayers and recitations that take place around his dying pillow, the chief aim of which is to concentrate the thoughts of the departing soul on the fact that life is the *master* of death. "The sun rises out of life and sets into life; so does the soul of a pure Brahman. Life sways to-day, and it will sway tomorrow, O Brahman! Life is immortal; death but conceals the fact as the garment covers the body. Hasten, O soul, to the Unseen, for unseen he sees, unheard he hears, unknown he knows. As by footprints one finds cattle, so may thy soul, O Sadhwan (pure one), find the indestructible Soul," etc., etc.

The moment life is fled the high priest bends over the corpse with his hands folded on his breast and repeats a prayer. After which the near female relatives indulge in the most dismal howls and shrieks as expressions of their grief and lamentation. The body is then bathed by the priests, perfumed, decked with flowers, and placed on a temporary bier or litter. This is borne along through the chief thoroughfares, preceded by men who carpet with certain pieces of cloth the entire way; women follow, howling and weeping and casting dust on their heads. The funeral pyre, formed of dried wood, is three or four feet high and over six feet long; the corpse is laid on it, and over it is poured oil, clarified butter, and flowers made of fragrant woods. The priests stand around, sprinkle the body with holy water, and repeat a number of prayers which very clearly point to the mystery which enfolds all animate and inanimate life, within and without, and express earnest hopes that the body now about to be consumed may not draw down the soul to enter another body again. The nearest relative then applies the fire and the body is consumed. They who watch the fire repeat to themselves long passages from the Shastras and the Puranas on the vanity of human life and the deathless nature of the soul, after which they purify themselves before returning home. Eleven days after death the Shrada, or purificatory ceremonies, are performed by the heir, and in his absence the next nearest relative; then every month for a year, and lastly on the anniversary of his death.

Brahmans are held unclean for ten days after the death of a relative, the military caste for twelve, the mercantile for fifteen, and the Sudra for thirty. Among the Hindoos the body is burnt, except only in case of infants under two years, when it is buried. The "Shrada" is a ceremony very much like mass performed in the Roman Catholic Church for the souls of the dead who are in purgatory. Prayers are offered by the high priest and the nearest relatives, accompanied with gifts and offerings of rice, flowers, oil, and water, in order to free the deceased soul from a purificatory abode in which it is held, and to enable it to ascend to the heaven where its progenitors are thought to be united to the universal Soul.

The worship of the Brahmans and the high-caste Hindoos, though complicated by trivialities, is in its essence very simple and pure. The Brahmans do not themselves worship the idols in the temples, although they encourage the inferior castes and races to do so. Every act of a Brahman's life is stamped with a religious character, even as every breath that he draws is held to be a part of that "Divine Soul" that exists in the heart of all beings.

As the Brahman priests accommodated their religious beliefs to suit the popular mind, so have the Roman Catholic missionaries and priests effected a compromise between Hindooism and Christianity in India, and Eastern Christianity has assumed features as foreign to the sublime teachings of Christ as demon- and serpent-worship are foreign to the pure and natural religion of the Vèdas.

It is only by examining the existences of all the different races and layers of populations, and the mingling of so many and such conflicting religions, that we can rightly understand the India of to-day with her hydra-headed creeds, dogmas, and castes.

CHAPTER VIII.

A Visit to the House of Baboo Ram Chunder.—His Wife.—Rajpoot Wrestlers.—Nautchnees, or Hindoo Ballet-Girls.—A Hindoo Drama.—Visit to a Nautchnees' School.—Bayahdiers, or Dancing-Girls, attached to the Hindoo Temples.—Profession, Education, Dress, Character, Fate in Old Age and after Death.—Cusbans, or Common Women.—Marked Differences between these three Classes of Public Women.

AMONG the most interesting of the rich Hindoos whose acquaintance we made during our long residence in Bombay was one Baboo Ram Chunder. A wealthy gentleman, educated in all the learning of the East as well as in English, possessing quite an appreciative intelligence on most English topics, but nevertheless a pure Hindoo in mind and character, clinging with peculiar affection to the manners, customs, and religion of his forefathers, and struggling to the last degree to counteract the vulgar and popular superstitions of modern Brahmanism, though not a member of the Brahmo-Somaj,* he left nothing undone

* A new school of the Brahmanic order—"Brahmo-Somaj," meaning an assembly in the name of God. This Church has connected itself with every progressive movement in India. The originator of this social and religious movement was Rajah Rammahun Roy, a very learned man. In 1818 he published, for the benefit of his own countrymen, selections from the teachings of Jesus, taken from the Gospels, in Sanskrit and Bengali, calling the book "The Precepts of Jesus, the Guide to Peace and Happiness." He died and was buried in England in 1833. Rammahun Roy built a church in Calcutta, where the Brahmo-Somaj still hold their worship. The members belonging to this new school of religious thought are estimated at

to revive the pure and simple teachings of the Vèdas. It was his custom to give every year a grand entertainment at his residence, to which he occasionally invited his European friends.

One morning Ram Chunder called in person at the "Aviary" to invite us to one of these to take place on the following evening, and promised me if I would be present not only a rare treat in the performance of a newly-arranged Hindoo drama from the poem of "Nalopakyanama," but also an introduction to his wife and child.

Ram Chunder's house, though not far from the vicinity of the Bhendee Bazaar, stood apart, surrounded by a well-built wall. The building was a large white-stuccoed dwelling decorated with rich carvings. There were two courts—an inner and outer court. We were received by a number of richly-attired attendants, and conducted through several dimly-lighted passages into a spacious apartment. It was a circular hall or pavilion with a fountain, and a garden with gravel-walks and a large area in the centre. The pavilion itself was decorated in the Oriental style, hung with kinkaub (or gold-wrought) curtains and peacocks' feathers; the floors were inlaid with mosaics of brilliant colors; the roof and pillars were decorated with rich gold mouldings; and the whole would have been very effective but for the mélange of European ornaments that were disposed around on the walls, tables, and shelves—clocks, antique pictures, statues, celestial and terrestrial globes, and a profusion of common glassware of the most brilliant colors.

ten thousand. The women have a separate prayer-meeting from the men. Their form of worship is very simple—singing of hymns adapted from the Vèdas or from the Brahmanasu, or Brahman Aspirations, the Christian Bible, and extempore prayer, followed by an exhortation on morality and purity of thought and character. The late Mr. Keshub Chunder Sen was everywhere recognized as their chief leader.

Ram Chunder, a young man not over thirty, with remarkably courteous manners, with that refinement and delicacy which are the distinguishing characteristics of a high-bred Hindoo, rose and bowed before us, touching his forehead with his folded hands, and then placed us on his right hand. In person he was rather stout, with peculiarly fine eyes and a benevolent expression of countenance, though he was darker in complexion than most of the Brahmans. His dress on this occasion was unusually rich and strikingly picturesque. He wore trousers of a deep crimson satin; over this a long white muslin "angraka," or tunic, reaching almost to the knees; over this again he wore a short vest of purple velvet embroidered with gold braid. A scarf of finest cashmere was bound around his waist, in the folds of which there shone the jewelled hilt of a dagger. On his head was a white turban of stupendous size encircled with a string of large pearls; on his feet were European stockings and a pair of antique Indian slippers embroidered with many-colored silks and fine seed-pearls.

Thus attired, he was a gorgeous figure, and, like a true high-born Hindoo, he sat quietly in his place, except that every now and then he rose and bowed with folded hands to each guest as he entered and pointed out their places, reseating himself quietly and simply. There was no sign of bustle or expectation, nor any conversation to speak of. In course of the evening about twenty native and two or three European gentlemen were assembled in the pavilion. The Europeans were on the right, the native gentlemen on the left, and Ram Chunder in the middle. No native ladies were visible, but from the sounds of female voices behind the curtain it was evident they were not far off.

Richly-dressed native pages, stationed at the back of

each guest, waved to and fro perfumed punkahs of peacock and ostrich feathers. After the usual ceremony of passing around to the guests sherbet in golden cups and "paun suparee," or betel-leaf and the areca-nut done up in gold-leaf, the performance began.

A herald dressed like a Hindoo angel, with wings, tail, and beak of a bird and the body of a young boy, announced with a peculiar cry, half natural and half bird-like, the presence of the Rajpoot athletes; and in stepped some ten men, their daggers gleaming in the dim light of the pavilion, which flickered on the gravelled space in front and barely lighted the surrounding garden, in the centre of which stood a fountain. The Rajpoots were in the prime of life, displaying great symmetry of form and development of muscular power. Their heads were closely shaven, with the exception of a long lock of hair bound in a knot at the top of their heads; their dress consisted of a pair of red silk drawers descending halfway to the knee and bound tightly around the waist with a scarf of many colors.

The wrestlers advanced, performing a sort of war-dance; they disposed of their daggers by putting them in their topknots; they then salââmed before the audience and began the contest. Each slapped violently the inside of his arms and thighs; then, at a given signal, each seized his opponent by the waist. One placed his forehead against the other's breast; they then struggled, twisted, and tossed each other about, showing great skill and adroitness in keeping their feet and warding off blows. Suddenly, with a peculiar jerk, one of the wrestlers almost at the same moment dashed his opponent to the ground, and drawing forth his dagger stood flourishing it over the fallen victim. At this juncture a strain of music wild but tender swept from the farther end of the pavilion, seemingly given forth to arrest the premeditated thrust of the exultant victor.

They listen with heads slightly turned to one side; presently their grim, bloodthirsty expressions give place to looks of delight and wonder. All at once their faces break into smiles; simultaneously they drop their uplifted daggers, release their knees from the breasts of their prostrate foes, stoop, and, taking a little earth from the gravelled walk, scatter it over their heads as a sign that the victor himself is vanquished, salââm to the spectators, and retire amid deafening shouts of applause.

After this the musicians struck up some lively Hindoo airs, and at length the heavy curtains from one side of the pavilion curled up like a lotus-flower at sunset, and there appeared a long line of girls advancing in a measured step and keeping time to the music. They stood on a platform almost facing us. Some of them were extraordinarily beautiful, one girl in particular. The face was of the purest oval, the features regular, the eyes large, dark, and almond-shaped, the complexion pale olive, with a slight blush of the most delicate pink on the cheeks, and the mouth was half pouting and almost infantile in its round curves, but with an expression of dejection and sorrow lingering about the corners which told better than words of weariness of the life to which she was doomed. For my part, it was difficult for me to remove my eyes from that pensive and beautiful face. Every now and then I found myself trying to picture her strange life, wondering who she was and how her parents could ever have had the heart to doom her to such a profession.

The Nautchnees, or dancing-girls, of whom there were no less than eighteen, were all dressed in that exquisite Oriental costume peculiar to them, each one in a different shade or in distinct colors, but so carefully chosen that this mass of color harmonized with wonderful effect. First, they wore bright-colored silk vests and drawers that fitted tightly to the body and revealed a part of the neck, arms, and legs; a full, transparent petticoat attached low down almost on the hips, leaving an uncovered margin all around the form from the waist of the bodice to where the skirt was secured on the hips; over this a saree of some gauze-like texture bound lightly over the whole person, the whole so draped as to encircle the figure like a halo at every point, and, finally, thrown over the head and drooping over the face in a most bewitching veil. The hair was combed smoothly back and tied in a knot behind, while on the forehead, ears, neck, arms, wrists, ankles, and toes were a profusion of dazzling ornaments.

With head modestly inclined, downcast eyes, and clasped hands they stood silent for some little time, in strong relief against a wall fretted with fantastic Oriental carvings. The herald again gave the signal for the music to strike up. A burst of wild Oriental melody flooded the pavilion, and all at once the Nautchnees started to their feet. Poised on tiptoe, with arms raised aloft over their heads, they began to whirl and float and glide about in a maze of rhythmic movement, fluttering and quivering and waving before us like aspen-leaves moved by a strong breeze. It must have cost them years of labor to have arrived at such ease and precision of movement. The dance was a miracle of art, and all the more fascinating because of the rare beauty of the performers.

Then came the cup-dance, which was performed by the lovely girl who had so captivated my fancy. She advanced with slow and solemn step to the centre of the platform, and, taking up a tier of four or five cups fitting close into one another, she placed this tier on her head and immediately began to move her arms, head, and feet

THE BEAUTIFUL NAUTCHNEE.

in such gently undulating waves that one imagined the cups, which were all the time balanced on her head, were floating about her person, and seemingly everywhere except where she so dextrously poised and maintained them. This dance was concluded by a cup being filled with sherbet and placed in the middle of the platform. Removing the cups from her head, the dancer, her eyes glowing, her breast heaving, swept toward the filled cup as if drawn to it by some spell, round and round, now approaching, now retreating, till finally, as if unable to resist the enchantment, she gave one long sweep around it, and, clasping her arms tightly behind her, lay full length on the pavement, and taking up with her lips the brimming cup drained its contents without spilling a drop. Then, putting it down empty, she rose with the utmost grace and bowed her head before us, her arms still firmly clasped behind her. The grace, beauty, and elegance of her movements were incomparable; the spectators were too deeply interested even to applaud her. She retired amid a profound and significant silence to her place.

Presently a tall, slim, graceful girl took her place on the platform with a gay smile on her face. An attendant fastened on her head a wicker wheel about three feet in diameter; it was bound firmly to the crown of her head, and all around it were cords placed at equal distances, each having a slipknot secured by means of a glass bead. In her left hand she held a basket of eggs. When the music struck up once more she took an egg, inserted it into a knot, and gave it a peculiarly energetic little jerk, which somehow fastened it firmly in its place. As soon as all the eggs were thus firmly bound in the slipknots round the wheel on her head, she gave a rapid whirl, sent them flying around, while she preserved the movement with her feet, keeping time to the music. Away she whirled, the eggs revolving round her. The slightest false movement would bring them together in a general crash. After continuing this about a quarter of an hour, she seized a cord with a swift but sure grasp, detached from it the inserted egg, managing the slipknot with marvellous dexterity, dancing all the while, till every egg was detached and placed in her basket; after which she advanced, and, kneeling before us, begged us to examine the eggs whether real or fictitious. Of course the eggs were real, and she was almost overwhelmed with shouts of "Khoup! khoup! Matjaka! matjaka!"—"Fine! fine! beautiful!" And then the Nautchnees vanished from the pavilion.

During the interval that followed the pages went round with goulab-dhanees, or bottles with rose-water, to sprinkle the guests.

Suddenly the cry of the herald announced a new scene. The heavy curtain slowly folded up and a long line of male actors, superbly attired as Oriental kings and princes from different parts of the East, entered and took their places on the divans ranged along the farther end of the pavilion. Ram Chunder approached us and informed me that the piece about to be represented was a pure Hindoo drama, a beautiful episode from the Sanskrit epic *Mahâbhârata*, called "Nalopakyanama, or, The Story of Nala."

After the kings and princes had seated themselves, in came a string of attendants arrayed in gold and gleaming armor, who took their places behind the royal personages on the divans. Then came twelve maidens attired in cloth of gold and fantastic head-gear, belonging to the ancient Vèdic period. Each of these girls had a cithara in her hands; they disposed themselves on seats to the left of the pavilion. After these a shrill cry of many voices announced the gods Indra, Agni, Varuna, and Yama, and in stalked four men splendidly robed, bearing gold wands, with serpents coiling around them, in their hands, and lotos-shaped crowns richly jewelled on their heads. Their raiment was one blaze of tinsel and glass jewels, made to shine with all the brilliancy of real gems.

Then came the hero Nala, with faded flowers on his tiara, dust on his garments, and looking picturesque enough with his bright scarf thrown across his shoulders, but travel-stained and very commonplace in the presence of so much gold and finery.

Nala was the hero to whom the matchless Damayanti, "whose beauty disturbed the souls of gods and men," had pledged her love, in spite of the proposition he brought her from the four gods to choose one of them and reign the unrivalled queen of the highest heaven. Damayanti, desirous of averting from her well-beloved Nala the vengeance of the gods, invites all her suitors to the "Swayamvara;" that is, a public choice of a husband by the lady, according to the custom of that age, assuring Nala that then there will be no cause of blame to him, as she will choose him in the presence of the gods themselves. Hence the presence of the four gods among the assembled princes suitors for the hand of the lovely Damayanti.

The herald once more gave the signal for the performance to begin. The musicians struck their citharas and recited in musical intonations the chief parts of the drama of Nala. At a certain part of the recitation the curtain descended, and in a few moments went up again. During this interval the gods were transformed into the likeness of Nala, presenting five Nalas instead of one; which the singers explained was a trick of the gods by which they hoped to bewilder poor Damayanti and perhaps induce her, in her ignorance of which were the gods and which Nala, to select one of their divine number as her future husband. The interest of the drama was centred among these four suitors of Damayanti, each the counterpart of the favored Nala.

The music at this point rose and fell, now vibrating in low tender accents, and anon rising in wild, startling emphasis of expression. At this moment the curtain parted and there stood the cup-dancer with her quiet yet entrancing beauty. Calmly she entered, looking down and meditating, as we were told, on the object of her affections. Her dress was exquisite of its kind and character; I never saw its counterpart on a Nautchnee before or after. It was a long gown without sleeves, falling from her shoulders to her feet, open at the throat, exposing a part of the neck and breast and the whole arm from the shoulder. It was very full, but of the most delicate texture, revealing the whole outline of a very lovely form. A bright border of variegated silk ran down the front and round the hem of this ancient Vèdic garment, and it was fastened at the waist by a rich silk scarf. Her hair fell back, flowing down to her feet; on her head was a curious crown of an antique pattern, and over it all was thrown a long veil that streamed on the floor, and was of such transparent texture that it looked like woven sunbeams.

Such was the impersonation of the Vèdic beauty Damayanti. When she reached the centre of the circular pavilion she lifted her eyes, and, seeing five Nalas instead of one, started backward, clasped her lovely arms on her bosom, and, rocking herself gently to and fro, moaned, "Alas! alas! there are five Nalas, all so like my own true sinless chief. How shall I discover the one to whom alone I have pledged my undying love?"

At this juncture the music ceased and a deep silence fell upon the audience. Every eye was riveted on that lovely creature seemingly overcome with the tide of sorrow and uncertainty that swept over her. Suddenly pausing in her moans, she turned up her fine eyes to the sky, and with some new inward light dawning as it were upon her troubled soul said audibly, "To the gods alone I will trust. If they are indeed gods, they will not deceive a poor mortal woman like me."

Then, quivering and trembling, with flushed cheeks and lustrous eyes, she folded her hands and knelt in reverence before the gods and prayed aloud, and said, "O ye gods, as in word or thought I swerve not from my love and faith to Nala, so I here adjure you to resume your immortal forms and reveal to me my Nala, that I may in your holy presence choose him for my pure and sinless husband."

Kneeling there with her face turned up, her hands folded, the outlines of her beautiful form made even more lovely by the half-softened halo of light shed over her from above, she seemed like some beautiful vision, and not a thing of flesh and blood. I never witnessed anything more truly exquisite and tender in its simple womanhood than this rendering of the beautiful Vèdic character of Damayanti.

Again the voices of the musicians were heard interpreting for us the thoughts and feelings of the gods: "We are filled with wonder at her steadfast love and peerless beauty," etc., etc. Once more the curtain is dropped, and presently it folds up again, revealing the forms of the four bright gods as at first in all the splendor of their robes, crowned and flashing with jewels, and fragrant with the garlands of fresh flowers that hang around their necks.

Damayanti rose from her bended knees. With pleased and childlike wonder she gazed at the gods one moment, then turned to her own true Nala, who stood before her in striking contrast to the gods, with moisture on his brow, dust on his garments, soiled head-dress and faded garland. But on recognizing him as the true Nala she folded her hands in sudden rapture and gave a cry of joy; then, removing from her own neck her garland of mohgree-flowers, moved with quiet grace toward her lover, knelt and kissed the hem of his dusty robe, arose and threw around his neck her own fresh, radiant wreath of flowers, saying, "So I choose for my lord and husband Nishádah's noble king." At this speech a sound of wild sorrow burst from the rejected suitors, but the gods shouted, "Well done! well done!" Then the happy Nala, turning to the blushing Damayanti, said, "Since, O maiden, you have chosen me for your husband in the presence of the gods, know this, that I will ever be your faithful lover, delight in your words, your looks, your thoughts, and so long as this soul inhabits this body, so long as the moon turns to the sun till the sun grows cold and ceases to shine, so long shall I be thine, and thine only."

One more loud shout from the herald, the curtain dropped, the play and the day were over, for it was just twelve o'clock.

The Oriental and European guests took their leave of their amiable host with much salââming and many expressions of delight, for the play had been arranged by Ram Chunder himself.

After a few minutes our host kindly conducted me to an inner apartment of his dwelling to introduce me, as he had promised, to his wife, who had already quitted her place behind the curtains, whence she and her maids had witnessed the performance, and had retired to her own rooms, which were (as in the case of all rich Hindoos or even Mohammedans) separate from those occupied by her husband. Traversing a long and narrow passage, we came to an arched doorway, with a dark silk curtain

A Hindoo Lady.

hanging before it, guarded by two women seated on either side. They rose and salââmed to us, and Ram Chunder, instead of walking in as any ordinary European husband would have done, inquired of them if the lady Kesinèh had retired.

"No, your lordship," replied the ceremonious Hindoo maid-servant; "she waits yours and the English lady's presence."

On which Ram Chunder drew aside the heavy drapery and bade me enter, saying, "I will return for you in a quarter of an hour or so."

Left alone, I stepped into a dimly-lighted but spacious room, at the farther end of which I saw seated a Hindoo lady surrounded by several female attendants.

As far as I could observe in the dim light, she was dark, but handsome and dressed like the generality of Hindoo women, only that her veil, instead of being drawn over her head, was thrown back, and trailed on the floor beside her. She did not rise to greet me, but salââmed to me from her place, and patted a cushion close by her as an invitation for me to be seated. This was, as I soon found, owing to the fact that her little daughter, lying half asleep in a little Hindoo cradle close by, was holding her hand, and she feared to disturb her. I sat down and looked over into the cradle; there lay a soft plump, brown child, a little girl of about two years of age, perfectly nude, with a string of gold coins around her neck and each of her arms. In the presence of such perfect innocence and trust the narrow distinctions of races and creeds seemed to fade away: I only felt here was another woman like myself, and she a mother; and, in truth, I could not have long felt otherwise, in spite of any prejudices I may have had; Kesinèh was too natural and simple a creature for one to feel anything but at home with her.

The first words that she said to me, after satisfying herself that little "Brownee" (as I always called her) was asleep, were, "How long have you been married?" Then, "What does your husband look like? How old are you? Where do you live?" etc., etc. My answers seemed to please her very much, for she patted my knee and laughed softly, and said, "Oh, heart! oh, heart! how happy you must be!"

We then talked about her own life. She told me that she had been married four years, that she had hoped "Brownee" was going to be a son, "but she turned out a daughter after all," said poor Kesinĕh with a sigh. "Do you love her less for that?" I inquired. "Oh no, indeed," said Kesinĕh quickly; "I think I love her more, but my lord would have been better pleased with me if she had been a son instead of a daughter." "But," said I, trying to comfort her for her disappointment, "it was not your fault that your child happened to be a daughter." "Oh yes," said the lady with great energy, "it was my own fault. I committed the sin of marrying my own brother in a former state of existence; thus I am now doomed to have a daughter for my first-born child in this." I did not know what to say to this odd explanation, and there was a pause, but at length I ventured to suggest that whether it was so or not she must admit that little "Brownee" was a treasure. "Oh yes," said Kesinĕh with joyful emphasis—"a lovely, bewildering little thing;" and she leaned lovingly over the little sleeper.

I noticed that in everything this Hindoo lady said or did there was no affectation of voice or manner, no effort to please or entertain me, but a simple and natural expression of herself.

When it was time for me to go I put her one question which I longed most to have answered: "Who is that very beautiful Nautchnee who danced the cup-dance and performed the part of Damayanti this evening?"

"I do not know," said the lady Kesinĕh with great interest in her manner. "Is she not beautiful? The Nautchnees were hired for this evening. I would like to know who she is too."

Then, turning to one of her attendants, who was listening to every word we said with a smile on her face, she inquired, "Ummah, do you know the owner of the Nautchnees who were here to-night?"

"Yes, my lady," replied the woman.

"If you hear anything about her you will let me know, for I have fallen in love with her," said I, half in jest and half in earnest. "Mah mi! mah mi!" laughed Kesinĕh—"so have I. She is a heart-distracting creature. Every one who saw her dance and act will dream of her to-night. Mah mi! mah mi! how proud she must feel!"

I wished her good-night in the strictest Hindoo fashion, taught me by the pundit.

"Ram, Ram," said I, "devâ Ram!" * Putting my folded hands to my brow and stooping, I lightly kissed the little sleeper in the cradle.

The very next moment Kesinĕh had sprung up, and, putting her arms around my neck, she laid her brow against mine and repeated that tender Hindoo farewell than which there is nothing more exquisite in human language: "The gods send that neither sun nor wind, neither rain nor any earthly sorrow, brush by thee too roughly, my friend."

Content and pleased with my new acquaintance, we parted, but not without my promise to visit her again.

The dancing-girls of India may be divided into three classes: the Nautchnees, who are actresses, or ballet-girls,

* "Rama, Rama, the god Rama, bless you!"

or both; the Bayahdiers, or Bhayadhyas, dedicated by their parents in childhood as votive offerings to certain temples, and consecrated to them at the age of womanhood; and the common "Cusban," a grade even lower than either of these, whose ranks are chiefly supplied from the abandoned Mohammedan women, the Purwarees, the lowest of all castes in Central India, as well as from the disaffected runaways of either of the two former and more reputable professions. The Cusban, therefore, is the scum and refuse of the lowest-caste females in India.

One day, accompanied by Kesinĕh, I visited a Nautchnee establishment of which the beautiful dancing-girl who so much attracted me was an inmate. It was kept by a native man and his wife, named respectively Dhanut and Saineh Bebee. We drove to it in a Hindoo carriage, a round seat for two or more persons placed on wheels, drawn by a pair of milk-white bullocks, and covered with a curious conical structure of wickerwork hung with crimson silk curtains. We took our places on two cushions cross-legged; the driver sat in front, and with a sharp crack of the whip started the bullocks at a brisk trot and sent us bumping up and down. On our way we caught glimpses of a population even more strange than those to be met daily in the parts of the island more frequented by Europeans. The dirtiness of a low-caste, poverty-stricken Oriental street is inconceivable. Filth reigned supreme in some of the lanes and alleys through which we passed. A rank vegetation clothed everything; trees hung with many-colored festoons of leaves and flowers formed thick tapestries of foliage on the right and on the left.

There is no country in the world (save the beautiful island of Ceylon) that is kinder to the sluggard. The poorest soil will grow certain qualities of fruit and cocoanut palms. The native population in some parts here seemed almost too indolent to move out of the way of our carriage-wheels, but they were peaceful enough. Stones, old broken bits of earthenware, wheels, broken litters, impeded the way, and cows, dogs, hens, chickens, pigs, ducks, and children less clad than any of these, roamed idly about in the streets and gutters or narrow lanes. As a rule, no refuse or rubbish of any kind whatever is removed, but is left to accident and the action of natural chemistry. Burnt-down huts covered over with the ever-ready parasitic plants, old wells and tanks filled with stagnant water abounding in frogs, water-snakes, and all kinds of reptiles, add to the sluggish appearance of the place. Gayly-dressed native women, idle men—among whom may be seen some poor depraved British tars—and male and female hucksters of fruit and sweetmeats, complete the picture.

The Nautchnees' establishment was a curious building surrounded by a high wall. We entered through a gate, and were at once conducted by a couple of old women across a paved courtyard planted all around with the mohgree, oleander, and tall red and white rose trees. Passing this, we were introduced into a great bare hall, with low seats ranged around the walls, curtained all along the farther end of the room, into which inner chambers seemed to open. Here we took our places. One of the old women stayed by us, while the other went off to announce our visit to the head lady of the establishment.

The great slave-markets which we have all read so much about, where tender young girls are bought and sold as if they were cattle, no longer exist in British India, but the amount of traffic of the kind that is still carried on everywhere is incredible, although the fact is vigorously denied by both the buyer and the seller. In many cases these Nautchnees are not bought, but hired for a term of years, for money paid not to the girls themselves, but to parents or friends. In the course of time the parents die or move away, and the girl, after having given her best days to her employers, finds herself without money, friends, or social ties, and is glad enough to spend the remainder of her life in instructing the younger members of the establishment of which, with the fidelity so natural to Oriental women, she considers herself a member, and therefore bound for life to promote its interests.

After a few moments Sainah Bebee came in to greet the lady Kesinèh. She salâămed most deferentially to us, and took her place on the floor. She was a woman about fifty and a native of Afghanistan, tall and finely formed. She spoke of difficulty in procuring respectable young girls to fill the places of those who ran away, were sold to certain rich admirers for wives or concubines, or died. It would appear that the lowest, or Cusban, class was largely increasing, whereas that of the Nautchnees was fast diminishing. On my questioning the old lady about the average life of the Nautchnees, she could give me no clear estimate, but intimated very decidedly that they generally died young.

At my especial request we were shown into the exercising-room and almost over the entire establishment. There were over a hundred girls, of all ages, and all shades of complexion from dark-brown to a pale delicate olive, going through their exercises at the time. The hall was composed of bamboo trellis-work, and was light, spacious, and airy enough. From the roof hung all sorts of gymnastic apparatus, rude but curious—ropes to which the girls clung as they whirled round on tiptoe; wheels on which they were made to walk in order to learn a peculiar circular dance called "chakrance" (from "chak," a wheel); slipknots into which they fastened one arm or one leg, thus holding it motionless while they exercised the other; cups, revolving balls, which they sprang up to catch; and heaps of fragile cords, with which they spin round and round, and if any one of these snap under too great a pressure, they are punished, though never very severely.

Altogether, it was a strange sight. Most of the girls from ten to fourteen had nothing on but a short tight pair of drawers; the older ones had tight short-sleeved bodices in addition to the drawers; and those under ten were naked. They were all good-looking; a few here and there were beautiful. The delicate and refined outline of their features, the soft tint of their rich complexions, the dreamy expression of their large, dark, quiet eyes, added to great symmetry of form, made them strangely fascinating.

The teachers were all middle-aged women, some of whom looked prematurely old. The girls are taught to repeat poems and plays, but no books are used.

The dormitories in this establishment were bare rooms; the girls all slept on mats or cushions on the floor. Each had a *lota*, or drinking-cup, a little mirror, and a native box in which to keep her clothes. The more finished and accomplished Nautchnees had rooms to themselves. I went into one of these. It was matted, and was very simply furnished. A tier of boxes in which her jewels and robes were kept, a cot, a few brass lotas, fans, cojas, or water-holders, with some tiny looking-glasses ranged along the wall,—and this was all.

I inquired for the beautiful Nautchnee who had interested me. Her name was Khangee; she was a Soodahnee by birth. The Soodahs are a military race or tribe inhabiting parts of the province of Cutch; they find their chief wealth in the beauty of their daughters, and for one of the Soodahnees a rich Mohammedan will pay from a thousand to ten thousand rupees.* Rajahs, wealthy Mohammedan merchants, and proprietors of dancing-girls often despatch their emissaries to Cutch, Cabool, Cashmere, and Rajpootana in search of beautiful women. The fame of the Cashmerian and Soodah women has spread far and wide, and often some beautiful creature is picked up out of the hovels of Thur, Booly, or Cashmere and transplanted to the gorgeous pomp of a royal harem. The Rajpoots intermarry with the Soodah and Cashmerian women, and, being naturally a handsome race, they have preserved by this means that physical beauty of which they are so justly proud.

Very little was known of Khangee's history beyond the fact that she was a Soodahnee by birth. She was bought at an early age from her parents, who were poor and occupied a hovel in the village of Thur in Cutch, and sold to this establishment when in her seventh year, and was almost as ignorant of her parentage as a newly-born babe. At the time of our visit she had been hired with a party of Nautchnees to assist in the marriage-celebration which was to take place at the house of a rich Bunyâh, or Hindoo grain-merchant.

These Nautchnees often marry well, and become chaste wives and mothers of large families. The four requisites for a Nautchnee are bright eyes, fine teeth, long hair, and a perfect symmetry of form and feature. A small black mole between the eyebrows or on either cheek will enhance her value to an extraordinary degree.

The utter friendlessness, the quiet submission, expressed in the actions and faces of the young girls, and even of the little children, we had seen exercising and acquiring

* The value of a rupee is about forty-five American cents.

their different parts that morning, were very pathetic. There was none of the impetuosity of youth nor of the joyousness of childhood. It is a sad and dreary picture, these parentless children of the East living for some rich man's pleasure, and dying as they live, often unloved and uncared for by any relative or friend.

"Bayahdier" is the name generally applied by the French and Portuguese to the dancing-girls attached to temples.* They are distinct from the Nautchnees, and are held sacred as priestesses. In case of sickness, famine, or other individual or social calamity Hindoo parents will repair to the temple and there vow to dedicate a daughter, sometimes yet unborn, to the service of Siva, provided the gods avert the threatened danger. Such vows are also made by barren women, who promise, if the curse of barrenness be removed, to dedicate to Siva their first-born daughter; and all such vows are religiously performed. When the child thus consecrated is born, the first thing that is necessary is for the father to repair to the temple and register her name as a devotee of the temple, break a cocoanut at the shrine of Siva, and take from the hand of the Brahman priest a little holy oil, shaindoor, a sort of red paint, and mud obtained from the Ganges; with which he returns to mark the newly-born child. From this moment she is looked upon as a priestess, and is exempt from all household or any other employment. At the age of five she attends the temple daily, where she is taught by the priests to read, chant, sing, and dance in the schools attached to it. When the girl has reached womanhood she undergoes certain puri-

* Their names vary with the language. I have heard them called "Khoo mattees" in parts of Guzerat; also "Dhayahtees" in the Deccan, and Bhaladhya in parts of Western India, from Sanskrit "bala," youth, and "dhya," tenderness.

fications. Holy oil and grated sandal-wood are rubbed over her person; she is then bathed, perfumed, fumigated, dressed in a robe peculiar to these priestesses—a full petticoat with a handsome border, short enough to show her feet and ankles, which are covered with jewels; a very short boddice, and over this is thrown a spotted muslin veil; the hair is ornamented with jewels of gold and silver, as are the neck, arms, and throat. She then enters the temple, takes her place near the stone image of Siva; generally her right hand is bound to that of the holy image, her forehead is marked with his sign, and she confirms the vow made by her parents to dedicate her body to the service and maintenance of the temple. With some few advantages of education, this temple-service may be regarded as one of the most corrupt and depraving institutions of the Hindoos—injurious alike to the moral and physical welfare of the community at large, and moreover debasing to the character of the Brahman priests themselves in their open recognition and encouragement of vice. These poor devotees often accept their fate with that stolid indifference peculiar to the Orientals, and are taught to believe that their immoralities are sacred to the god to whom they are dedicated.

The services on the death of one of these priestesses are peculiar. When at the point of death a mud idol of Siva is placed in her arms. Her mouth, eyes, nose, and ears are rubbed with holy oil, and then touched with flame obtained from a sacrificial fire, to purify from the taint of her impure life; in her hands are placed the *toolsi* *

* Ocymum or sweet basil. This plant has a very dark-blue flower, and hence, like the large bluish-black bees of India, is held sacred to Krishna and his amours. A fable, however, is told in the Purânas concerning the metamorphosis of the nymph Toolasi (by Krishna) into the shrub which has since borne her name, because he could not return her love.

flowers, and her body is robed in pure white; after which she is made to repeat a hymn praying that as she has consecrated her body to the service of the gods, so may her soul be freed from rebirth and reunited to the Infinite Soul. If she is too feeble to repeat this prayer, the priests chant it in her dying ear. When life becomes extinct she is carried to a quiet spot in the vicinity of the temple, burned, and her ashes buried then and there. Sometimes a fellow-sister will plant a toolsi or moghree tree on the site, but no monument ever marks the spot where these poor priestesses of passion are cremated.

These devotees are never taken in marriage; they are looked upon as the brides of their various deities; they are generally childless. If a woman happens to have a child, however, she is sole arbitress of its fate, and in no instance has she ever been known to dedicate it to the life to which she has been doomed. She generally hands it over to her parents or nearest relatives as a substitute for herself.

There are hospitals and asylums for the sick, infirm, and aged of this class of women, though from all I could learn very few arrive at old age.

The Cusban, or lowest class of dancing-women, is very largely recruited from runaways from these Hindoo temples, and it is said that in course of time they become the most abandoned and desperate of the native community.

Even the most intelligent people, unless they have made a special study of India, can have no idea of the marked differences that exist between the Brahmans and these different classes of women. The pure Brahman, with the three other Aryan castes in so far as they have not intermarried with the aborigines, are of Caucasian type. In the northern provinces they are not brown, but of a complexion almost as fair as that of many dark Europeans.

Both the men and women are distinguished by symmetry of form, fine soft hair, and beautiful eyes. Their ideal of beauty is similar to ours, with this exception: that they have adhered more closely in matters of dress to the original simplicity of form than Europeans have done.

Theatrical representations, such as that of Ram Chunder, are much in vogue. The dramatic art in Hindostan about the period of the Christian era was of a high and lofty character. It was the great school wherein kings, warriors, and soldiers were taught the purest ideals of chivalry and manly and womanly purity of character; but at the present time it has greatly degenerated, although in many parts of India the more enlightened Hindoos are trying to restore it once more to its true and original place among the high arts. Everywhere theatrical exhibitions are held, often in the open air or under temporary sheds. The actresses are the Nautchnees, and a respectable Hindoo woman will rarely attend these public places. The native Roman Catholics in Southern India and Ceylon have also religious dramas, in no way superior to those of the Hindoos; the overshadowing of the Virgin, the birth of Christ, the crucifixion, and so forth, are very similar to the scenes represented of Krishna and the Hindoo incarnation.

Social dancing does not exist among the nations of the East, and it is considered highly indecorous for a Hindoo woman of pure character to dance. Even the Nautchnees, if they become wives or even concubines to rich men, as often happens, abandon all such practices; and their children are never allowed to know their mother's early profession, so deep is the national sentiment with regard to the domestic relations of a wife and mother.

Public reading of popular poems, histories, and dramas

as a source of amusement is very common all through Northern and Southern Hindostan. The reading is always performed in parts. A wealthy Hindoo will engage a number of professional readers to perform the task, and every one who wishes to hear may do so. The readers always take their places in an open verandah, and the people in large numbers seat themselves around within hearing distance. The recitation is given; each person performs his or her part in the prescribed order with a musical cadence. The expositor gives a free translation for the benefit of the people, who are thus made acquainted with the most celebrated Hindoo works.

Chess is a favorite game among the Hindoos, and it is one of the most ancient, alluded to even in their earliest productions, and quite common among all classes and grades of society. This game is peculiarly adapted to the Hindoo mind, in which quiet thought, perspicacity, and shrewdness are so strongly marked. Cards with the figures of their gods and goddesses are a source of great amusement; the women are much given to this indoor recreation. The Ashta-Kasti is a game played on a board of twenty-five squares with sixteen cowries or small shells. It is played by four persons, and is finished when one of the pieces, traversing the length and breadth of the board, enters first into the central square. Mohgali * Patan is a favorite game among the superior classes of Hindoo women. It is a representation of a battle between the *Mohgals* and Patans. The battle-field is accurately drawn; on one side is the *Mohgal* army, and on the other the Patan. Hindoo ladies play it with great skill. Another military game, the Pàshà, played on ninety-six squares and with sixteen pieces, is played with great vigor and amid peals of laughter. The moves are regulated by the throws of dice. Among

* This word is generally pronounced *Mohgul* by the natives of India.

the outdoor sports are kite-flying, throwing the sling, bat-and-ball, croquet on horseback, wrestling, running, boating, boxing, and hunting. Itinerant jugglers are everywhere patronized.

Musical recreations are most popular of all, and not only from the temples and palaces, but from the humblest hut of the poorest peasant, sweet sounds everywhere greet the ear. When an instrument cannot be had the voice is substituted; men seated in clusters under trees by the wayside beguile the evening hours with song after song. The common bhistee at the water's edge, the farmer at the plough, the cart-driver, the boatman, the shepherd, the warrior, the spinner at her wheel, and the mother beside the cradle, all delight in song, giving great effect to tender or spiritual sentiments by the measured or animated tones of chant, psalm, or song as it may happen to be.

Instrumental, and even vocal music, though held among the fine arts, has not attained great eminence, yet no people are more susceptible to its peculiar charms than the Hindoos. The word "sang-gheeta," or symphony, implies not only the union of voices and instruments, but suitable action.

Musical treatises always combine "gána," the measure of poetry, "vadya," instrumental sound, and "uritya," dancing. The most remarkable of their musical compositions are The Ragar Navah, "The Sea of Passion;" Sabha-Vinodah, "The Delight of the Assemblies;" Sang-gheeta-Derpana, "The Mirror of Song;" Raga Nibhoda, "The Doctrine of Musical Modes." All these works explain more or less the laws of harmony, the division of musical sounds into scales, etc., enunciation, cadence, rising and falling variations, long and short accentuations, and rules for playing the vina and other musical instruments. The vina is the most common; it is not unlike a guitar, five or six feet long, with seven or more strings, and a large gourd at each end of the finger-board.

Music, like almost everything else in India, is thought to be of divine origin. The gamut is called swaragrama, and is uttered as *Sa, ri, ga, ma, pa, dha, ne.* Little circles, ellipses, crescents, chains, curves, lines, straight, horizontal, or perpendicular, are employed as notes. The close of each strain is always marked by a flower, especially the rose and lotus.

The mode of dress of the Hindoo is both simple and suitable to the climate. The men wear a cloth called dhotee bound round the loins, with an upper vest, of cotton or silk according to the wealth of the wearer, over it. This angraka, or coat, is very graceful, generally of pure white, and descending to the ankles; it is bound around the waist by a colored shawl or scarf called cumberbund. A white muslin turban artistically wound around the head and sandals complete the attire. On festive occasions a gay handkerchief is thrown over the right shoulder, which adds very much to the picturesqueness of the dress.

The women wear a cloth, or saree, some yards in length, often edged with a rich and delicate embroidery of gold or silver, descending to the feet. They gather this into a point in front, and fasten it around their waists with or without belts, as the case may be. They then twist the rest most gracefully around the entire person, after which it is thrown over the head and made to serve both as a bonnet and a veil. It is very becoming, and, wrought over with delicate Oriental devices of fine texture, lends a peculiar charm to the most ordinary features. A bright silk boddice is worn under the saree, and the whole dress accords well with the sweet, modest grace and beauty which characterize the pure Hindoo woman.

They also wear a profusion of jewels, and ears, nose,

arms, wrists, ankles, toes, and fingers are often bedecked with them. In some instances all their wealth is thus preserved. The hair, which is often very luxuriant, is combed back in the ordinary European style, and is tied in a knot behind. Rich women often fasten it with a band of gold bound around the entire head and very expensive ornamental gold pins. The Hindoo women possess in a far greater degree than Europeans an eye for color. The most ignorant of them have the peculiar art of selecting strong and brilliant contrasts in color, and so disposing them on their persons as to make a perfect harmony.

There is a marked difference between the moral and social character of the Hindoo and the Mohammedan women of India. The Hindoo woman does not occupy that position in society which she is so eminently fitted to grace, and which is accorded to women in Europe and America; but she is by no means as degraded as is so frequently represented by travellers, who are apt to mistake the common street-women with whom they are brought into contact for the wife and mother of an ordinary Hindoo home. It is difficult for a stranger to find out what an Indian woman is at home, though he may have encountered many a bedizened female in the streets which he takes for her.

The influence of the Hindoo woman is seen and felt all through the history of India, and is very marked in the annals of British rule. Though the political changes, the invasion, and despotism of Mohammedan rule may have forced upon them the seclusion now so general, it is evident that they once occupied a very different position in society, from the testimony of their earliest writers and the dramatic representations of domestic life and manners still extant.

One of the most startling facts is, that among the Asiatic rulers of India who have heroically resisted foreign invasion the women of Hindostan have distinguished themselves almost as much as the men. Lakshmi Baiee, the queen of Jahnsee, held the entire British army in check for the space of twenty-four hours by her wonderful generalship, and she would probably have come off victorious if she had not been shot down by the enemy. After the battle Sir Hugh Rose, the English commander, declared that the best *man* on the enemy's side was the brave queen Lakshmi Baiee. Another courageous and noble woman, Aus Khoor, was placed by the British government on the throne of Pattiala, an utterly disorganized and revolted state in the Panjaub. In less than one year she had by her wise and effective administration changed the whole condition of the country, subjugated the rebellious cities and villages, increased the revenues, and established order, security, and peace everywhere. Alleah Baiee, the Mahratta queen of Malwah, devoted herself for the space of twenty years with unremitting assiduity to the happiness and welfare of her people, so that Hindoos, Buddhists, Jains, Parsees, and Mohammedans united in blessing her beneficent rule; and of so rare a modesty was this woman that she ordered a book which extolled her virtues to be destroyed, saying, "Could I have been so infamous as to neglect the welfare and happiness of my subjects?"

In the historical notices of the rule of Hindóstanee women nothing is more conspicuous than their fine, intuitive sense of honor and justice. Clive, Hastings, Wellesley, and other governors-general of India, have all acknowledged their high appreciation of the character of the Hindoo women they have known, declaring that in many instances, under the administration of Ranees and

Begums, India has been more prosperous and better governed than under the rule of the native rajahs.

The present ruler of Bhopal is a lady of high moral and intellectual attainments; both she and her mother, who preceded her as head of the state, have displayed the highest capacity for administration. Both have been appointed knights of the Star of India by the empress of India, Queen Victoria, and their territory is the best governed native state in India.

Very recently the queen of England created her Asiatic sisters, the queens of Oude and Pattiala, knights of the Star of India in appreciation of their wise and beneficent rule over their respective kingdoms.

During the dreadful ravages of the French and English, or the Carnatic War, the Hindoo women administered to the wounded and suffering European soldiers of both nations with equal tenderness and impartiality, causing one of the English generals to report to head-quarters, "But for the Indian women, who better understand the qualities of love and tenderness than we Europeans, I should have left half of my wounded soldiers to die on the battle-field. They washed the toiling feet of the poor tired soldiers, stanched their flowing wounds, and bore them in their united arms from the strife of the battle-field to the quiet and shelter of their own little huts."

In that interesting narrative of occurrences at Benares during the latter days of the month of June, 1857, furnished by a soldier of the Seventy-eighth Highlanders, are several incidents characteristic of the devotion and self-abnegation of the Hindoo women. This regiment or company of soldiers, in its work of retaliation upon the Indian mutineers, often set fire to whole villages in order to punish the rebel sepoys sheltered by them. On one of these occasions a humane Highlander, after having rescued several persons from the fire, rushed into the flames to save a young woman seated calmly by a dying man, whose lips she was wetting with some siste* while the fire was raging around her. No inducement of self-preservation could prevail with her to quit his side till they were both carried out.

Tenderness and self-devotion, as I said before, are the chief characteristics of the pure Hindoo woman. Her love for her offspring amounts to a passion, and she is rarely known to speak hastily, much less to strike or ill use her child. Her devotion as a wife has no parallel in the history of the world. Marriage is a sacred, indissoluble bond, which even death itself cannot destroy, and the patient, much-enduring women of India took the terrible yoke of sutteeism upon them in becoming wives as calmly as the young English or American girl puts on her bridal veil, and have gone to the funeral pile for centuries without a murmur.

In the purer and more ancient period of Indian civilization it was not customary to force a widow upon the funeral pyre of her husband. But the fearful prospects of Hindoo widowhood, which made her future existence appear to her a long, wearisome, and distasteful series of sad duties, made her gladly choose death rather than life. Besides which, she died honored and happy, having by her death redeemed her husband from a thousand years of penance. By degrees, this fearful practice, fostered by the priests and poets of India, became a sacred tradition carefully handed down from mother to daughter, and at last came to be regarded as a sublime sacrifice on the marriage altar. The practice of sutteeism has been virtually abolished by the British government on British-Indian

* A peculiar little seed from which a cooling drink is prepared. A preparation of rice and water, when cooled, is often called "siste."

soil, but to this day women will perform painful journeys to places still governed by native princes in order to burn themselves alive.

In 1834, while Dr. Burnes was residing at Cutch, a very remarkable case of sutteeism took place in that province. The only wife of Bhooj-Rhai, a wealthy and intimate friend of the rao or king, had, during her husband's illness, declared her intention of performing suttee at his death. When the time arrived the rao, at the instance of the British resident, expostulated with her, but all in vain. Protection was also offered her in the name of the British government, but her determination remained firm and unshaken. On the morning appointed for the burning of Bhooj-Rhai's body a funeral pyre was erected immediately in front of Rao Lakka's tomb. A spot was enclosed with a circle of bamboos, the tops of which were bound together in the form of a beehive, covered with dried grass and thorns; the entrance was a small aperture on the left side. Crowds of gayly-dressed people flocked to the spot. The moment the victim, a remarkably handsome woman about thirty, and most superbly dressed, appeared, accompanied by the Brahman priests, her relatives, and the dead body of her husband, the people greeted her with loud exclamations of praise and delight, poured forth benedictions on her head for her constancy and virtue, and showered flowers on her path as she was borne along; women pressed to touch the hem of her garments, hoping thereby to be absolved from all sin and preserved from all evil influences.

Dr. Burnes addressed the woman, desiring to know whether the act she was about to perform was voluntary or enforced by the priests, and offered her again, on the part of the British government, a guarantee for the protection of her life and property. Her answer was calmly heroic, and she could not be dissuaded from her purpose: "I die of my own free will," said she; "give me back my husband and I will consent to live." Seeing that nothing could move her from her resolution, Dr. Burnes despatched a message to the rao requesting his interference. He returned answer that it was beyond his power to arrest the ceremony. Everything was done, but in vain, to save the life of this infatuated woman, and at length the ceremony began. Accompanied by the officiating Brahmans, the widow walked seven times round the pyre, repeating the usual mantras or prayers, strewing rice and cowries (small shells) on the ground, sprinkling holy water over her friends and relatives and on the bystanders. She then removed her jewels and presented them to her nearest relations with a glad smile. The Brahman priest then presented her with a lighted torch; taking it from his hand, she stepped through the fatal entrance and calmly seated herself within the pile. The body of her husband, wrappped in rich *kinkaub* (gold cloth), was then carried seven times round the pile, and finally laid across her knees. The door was left unclosed, in the hope that the deluded woman might yet repent and escape. Not a sigh, not a whisper, broke the death-like silence of the crowd. The intrepid woman held up her torch and ignited the pile. Presently a slight smoke, curling from the summit of the pyre, gave notice that the fiery ordeal had begun; then came a tongue of flame darting with lightning rapidity toward the clear blue sky, announcing that the sacrifice was completed, though not a sound betrayed that a living victim was within holding a dead corpse in her arms. So far as courage and silent, resolute determination went, she was more immovable than the dead clay she held in her last fiery embrace. At the sight of the ascending crackling flames wild shouts of exultation rent the air, the drums beat, the people clapped their hands in delighted applause, while the English spectators of the scene withdrew, bearing deep compassion in their hearts.

After the fiery consummation had taken place, on the ground where the sadhwee, or "pure one," had expired three chatties, or earthen vessels, full of consecrated balls of rice, were placed as offerings to the gods.

The Bombay government notified the rao at once that the repetition of such inhuman atrocities would not again be overlooked.* This had no doubt some effect on His Highness, but nevertheless some time after this sacrifice the beautiful mother of the rao suddenly fell ill and died, and one of her female attendants voluntarily buried herself alive near her mistress, in order that she should be in readiness to attend her in a future state.

It is very difficult for the Western mind to comprehend this utter self-abnegation on the part of Hindoos, and it can only be accounted for by their deep faith in the universal metamorphosis of life and the unreality of form. *Maya* † is illusion, the evanescent dream of life, which is only a "sleep between a sleep," the constant flow of form into form, of thought into thought, of life into other life. Even Brahm does not recognize himself in the second person: "I know when I am I, but who am I when I am thou?" It renders individuality illusive, intangible, and uncertain, so that to the Hindoos life and possession assume a meaning entirely different from that with which we are disposed to regard them. It is true that life loses half its charms, but death is robbed of its terrors. Life is valued only in so far as they are prepared to lay it aside, or rather to change it for some other form; for life and

* See *Cutch*, chapter vi., by Mr. Postans, 1839.

† The illusion or unreality of all created things, according to Brahman mystics.

death are but the perpetual ebb and flow, the advance or retrograde, of soul toward "the Soul." Under this ardent faith, that everything above, below, beyond, God himself, is illusion, change, metamorphosis, is hidden the secret that helps them to endure suffering not only without a murmur, but with joy, and to count death itself a positive gain in the presence of the eternal, immutable, and solid fact of life to be found at last in the final reunion of the human with the divine life. This faith so potent, so absorbing, so far reaching, has stamped a character hereditary and almost ineffaceable on the Hindoo mind.

To-day Brahmanism is so expansive in character that it takes in every form and peculiarity of religious sentiment. The more earnest and spiritual have grand and magnificent theories of God that supply ample food for the imagination; the tender have laws that reach down almost to vegetable life; the ignorant and vulgar have attractive festivals and endless ceremonials suited to engage their attention; the vicious and degraded have the loves and frivolities of the gods and heroes, whose lives encourage pursuit of sensual gratifications; the devotee who abandons all that is sensual for spiritual insight has text upon text and example upon example, taken from the Puranas * and from the actual lives of saints, to support him in the effort of finding God at last. The self-sacrificing only quits an illusion for a reality, and the idolater who bows down before wood and stone believes that he sees before him only the form of a divine life hidden everywhere in matter. Thus highest religious thought and life and lowest sensual indulgence meet together in the theology of the Brahmans.

* The "Puranas," or Hindoo Antiquities, are by no means as ancient as they are named. They are eighteen volumes in all, but consisting of no less than one million six hundred thousand sacred lines treating of creation, mythology, tradition, and legend.

CHAPTER IX.

From Bombay to Poonah, the capital of the Maha Rashtra, or the great Indian kings.—Campooly.—The Ascent of the Bhor Ghauts.*—Khandala.—Caves of Carlee or Karli.—"Puja Chakra," or the famous Wheel-worship of the Brahmans.—Poonah.—Kirki.—A Visit to the Peishwa's Palace.—Temple of Parvati.—The Pundit and the Brahman Priest at Prayer.—Sanskrit and English Colleges at Poonah.—Suttee Monuments at Sangam.—Hindoo Bankers, etc.

FROM the island of the ancient goddess Bamba Dèvi to Poonah, the capital of the great Indian kings, one passes through the most extravagant contrasts of sights and scenes to be found anywhere in the wide world—gorgeous temples of gods and squallid dwellings of men; fertile plains and arid wastes; towering hills crowned with ancient forts and temples, now lonely or deserted; deep cave-structures in the hearts of isolated mountains, where still lie written in stone the romantic culture of a long-past age.

Our dâhk, which was simply a native carriage furnished with horses instead of bullocks, trotted briskly along the magnificent "Lion Causeway." Passing rapidly the eastern side of the island of Salsette to Thannah, and crossing the great viaduct and round the promontory of Parsek, we turned to the south, and emerged on a striking plain whose attractiveness increased at every mile of the road until we began the descent of the Bhor Ghauts on the other side.

* *Bhor*, a Mahratta word for the jujube tree, *Zizyphus jujuba*, which is found among these mountains. The *Ghauts*, or "Landing-Stairs," are the two ranges of mountains extending along the eastern and western shores of the peninsula of Hindostan. The highest peaks in the northwestern part are found in the Mahablashwar Mountains, the summer retreat of the Europeans of Bombay.

NATIVE CARTS WITH TROTTING BULLOCKS.

In some parts our road lay over a great green floor soft as velvet, intersected with innumerable river-like channels, made in the lowlands by the ever-encroaching sea. Palm trees fringed these salt-water streams, dotted with hundreds of the fanciful sails of fishing-smacks, bunder-boats, and brightly painted canoes, all moving to and fro swiftly and silently under the shadows of the hills, which rise in fantastic broken forms on one side. There is no sound far or near to break the spell; the silent, forest-clad Ghauts and the whole sea-begirt valley lie asleep in that enchanted atmosphere.

At sunset we reached the village of Campooly, at the foot of the Ghauts—a mean, dirty, and terribly unhealthy spot, situated immediately under the lofty barrier-wall of rock called the Bhor Ghauts, which props up the great table-land of the Deccan *—an immense plateau, with large rivers, innumerable hills covered with forts, magnificent towns, cities, villages, and many millions of inhabitants.

This enormous mountain-chain of the Deccan, the first of the steps that rise one above the other till they terminate in the great plateau of Thibet, the highest land of the Himâlayas, starts up almost perpendicularly from the Konkan, or lowlands, and is securely fastened together by huge buttresses of primeval granite, naked and frightful to look upon in some places, and again singularly beautiful in others. A railroad and a tunnel have since been built across this once almost inaccessible barrier, and is said to be "a noble piece of engineering," for the Ghauts extend over thirteen degrees of latitude and rise in some parts to a height of five thousand five hundred feet above the level of the sea.

There was a fine bungalow, built by Bala Roa Angria for the accommodation of European travellers, at Cam-

* From *Dakshina* (Sanskrit), "South Country."

pooly, where we passed the first hours of the night to await some palanquins with their bearers that had already started up the Ghauts. This bungalow is only occupied by chance wayfarers. Here we took up our abode, and only a tribe of monkeys showed the least inclination to prevent our doing so. There were sixteen in all; they were evidently enjoying themselves running in and out of the half-deserted building. A number on the roof were throwing down into the verandah the peculiar nut-like fruit of the large and graceful peepul trees that overshadowed the house. Some were peeping in at the doors and windows, and some were swinging themselves from the rafters. The moment we appeared they showed regular fight, screamed, chattered, and no doubt swore at us hard and fast in monkey fashion; but, what seemed to me most curious, there was not a man in our service who would perform the unkind office of dispersing them from the bungalow. We had to send for our driver, who, being a Musulman, had no scruples of early ancestry or primitive divinities. He took off his cumberbund, or scarf, twisted it into a whip with a knot at the end, and despatched the bulk of the tribe back into the forest whence they had come. Only one great black-bearded male monkey remained on the roof in spite of the brandished rag; when we were at supper this huge creature suddenly suspended himself downward by the tail, looked in upon us, and, opening his hideous jaws, uttered some fierce imprecations, which, as our pundit would say, "were perfectly intelligible, but not translatable," and, having done this, he vanished, and we saw nothing more of him for that evening.

There is here a Hindoo temple, and a fine reservoir which occupies a quarter of a mile of ground. This reservoir and the adjoining temple, dedicated to Maha Dèo, were built by that most subtle of Mahratta ministers, the

Travelling in Palanquins.

famous Nana Furnaveez, whose real name was Balaji Jahnardhan. It is exceedingly well built; the sides are lined and the banks paved with fine stone; steps lead everywhere to the edge of the water; a magnificent banyan tree overshadows the artificial lake, and near it flourishes a fine grove of mango trees.

On the opposite side of us men, women, and children were bathing, swimming and disporting themselves in the water. Some of the young women were symmetry itself, with exquisitely-proportioned, slender forms, delicate hands and feet, finely-poised heads and necks. Their long hair streamed behind them in the water as they swam merrily about. Others were just stepping out of the tank arrayed in their graceful but dripping sarees, which they allow to dry on their persons while they proceed to fill their water-jars, and, piling them one above the other on their heads, depart to their respective homes. These women seemed very innocent and child-like, and a closer acquaintance with several high-bred and true Hindoos proved that these were their distinguishing characteristics.

At three o'clock next morning we began the ascent of the Ghauts in palanquins, or, as they are commonly called, palkees, with coolies to transport our baggage and provisions. About sunrise we reached a very remarkable point in these mountains, a deep and frightful-looking chasm. We alighted from our palkees and went over this part of the Ghauts on foot. At length we were directed as near as we dared to approach the spot where the mountain was split in two.* Not a sound was heard anywhere. As we stood there the shadows of the crags brightened every

* This chain is now bridged over by a viaduct which once crumbled down and disappeared into the depths below in the presence of a brave English engine-driver, who had the good fortune to arrest the train, that was speeding on its way toward it, just in time to save many valuable lives.

moment, now shimmered along the sides, and shed flickering shafts of light far down upon the midnight darkness below. It was a glorious picture—the depth below and the height above, on whose summits the plumes of the palm trees waved their branches to the rising sun.

The atmosphere was remarkably clear, and this helped us to see a great distance with the naked eye. On one side gently-falling slopes gave place to abrupt precipices and innumerable peaks, and on the other far below were smiling plains, each more beautiful than the other in form and color, affording now and then most magical glimpses of green fields dotted with great reservoirs that looked like silvery spots, and cozy little Hindoo villages nestling amid charming groves and palm-plantations.

As the story goes, the duke of Wellington, then a simple colonel, cast all his guns into one of these reservoirs when he found no means of conveying them any farther, lest they should fall into the hands of the enemy, as he marched over the same road to Poonah and there quelled the famous Mahratta rebellion of 1802.

Now on foot and now in palkees we at length ascended these Ghauts, sweeping round and round, now ascending, now descending, passing by dreadful precipices, drawing breath under quaint natural bowers, following winding paths, and coming suddenly upon foaming cascades leaping from rock to rock. So we went from beauty to ever-increasing beauty, till we reached the village of Khandala, on the very top of the mountain, near which a travellers' bungalow stands with open arms—or verandahs—to receive us. And here was opened to us the full enchantments of the fairyland through which we had been passing upward. All of a sudden from this high peak we beheld a most beautiful and varied picture—sharp peaks of every form and shape and size, tremendous ravines, towering mountains, leaping waterfalls, sloping hillsides, and waving palms and mountain-forests, clearly outlined against a deep-blue sky, and over all these varied forms of nature the sunlight floats and melts, a sea of gold. No artist, however gifted, no pencil, however matchless, can catch and transfer to canvas the entrancing beauties of the views as seen from the top of the Bohr Ghauts and at such a moment.

This lovely spot has for more than twenty years been the favorite retreat of the wealthy and change-seeking inhabitants of Bombay, and now that the railway is opened it is much more easily reached.

The ravines in this neighborhood harbor many wild beasts, and it is said that at night tigers, leopards, and bears are often seen prowling about in search of prey. The natives raise wild shouts when they think they hear or see them, and thus frighten them away.

The travellers' bungalow at Khandala is most picturesquely situated on the edge of a deep ravine. On the right is a small lake or reservoir adjoining the residence of the late Parsee knight, Sir Jamsetjee Jeeboy. To the east is a magnificent hill, called the Duke's Nose, from its supposed likeness to that of Wellington. From this point there are splendid views. The pretty little mountain-village of Khandala is close by, and as we pass on to Karli we skirt the beautiful woods of Lanauli,* so often quoted in Mahratta song, once the hunting-grounds of the rulers of the Deccan, and still abounding in wild boars and other game.

We spent four days at the bungalow here, and, what was more, saw every sun that rose and set on these mountains. Each day was a counterpart of the preceding one, clear and bright. We traversed some miles of the sur-

* A small village on the Khandala Hills.

rounding country to visit hill-forts, caves, and viharas, which abound in this neighborhood.

Our next halting-place was at the village of Karli, a cluster of Hindoo houses hid amidst a fine grove of trees. There was a nice bungalow here, and even barracks to hold about two hundred men.

The most famous cave is that of Karli. It far surpassed those we had visited on the islands of Salsette and Elephanta, and took us very much by surprise. The caves are on a hill about two miles or more from the travellers' bungalow. We entered seemingly into the heart of the mountain, and found ourselves in the body of the temple or cave, which is separated from the side-aisles by fifteen columns of magnificent design and workmanship; on each side, on the upper part of each of these columns, are two kneeling elephants, and on each elephant are two seated human figures, sometimes a male and female, with their arms around each other's shoulders sometimes the figures are both female. The effect is remarkably striking. The *chaitya* * is plain and very solid, and behind it are seven plain octagonal pillars without any ornamentation. The interior of the temple seems to have been lined with woodwork. Right in front of the arched roof or hall is a second screen, as at the great cave at Salsette. It is composed of plain octagonal columns with pilasters. Over these is a mass of wall crowned with a superstructure of four dwarf pillars; the whole of this appears to have been covered with wooden ornaments.† These are thought to have been a broad balcony in front of the plain wall, supported by two bold wooden brackets

* An immense hemispherical altar of stone with a kind of wooden umbrella spreading above, beneath which lies interred some relic of the god to whom the temple is dedicated.

† See Fergusson's *Rock-cut Temples of India*, p. 27.

PRINCIPAL NAVE AND CHAITYA OF K

from the two piers. This balcony is thought to have served the purpose of a music-gallery or nagara khánah, as are still found in the Jain temples to-day. Everything here is executed in the finest style; the bas-reliefs, the windows, the doors, the halls, roofs, vestibules, and figures are each, one and all, beautifully executed. The colossal figure of the Buddha perched on a lotos throne, with angels hovering around him, his hands folded in everlasting repose resting on his knees, is grand and imposing. On the walls are carved many a beautiful flower, some not unlike those we passed in our morning's ride, with strange characters and symbol after symbol replete with the wisdom of the Buddhists. Rows of half-nude gigantic women, elephants, lions, birds, and beasts relate in solid stone the triumphs of Buddhism over Brahmanism. Dr. Stevenson dates the building of this temple at seventy years before Christ; executed, according to him, by the emperor Devabhute, under the care of Xenocrates or Dhennuka-Kati.. There has been, however, much doubt thrown by recent explorers on the dates given by Dr. Stevenson. The inscriptions under the gateway are thought to place beyond dispute the dates of these scattered excavations, so similar in point of architecture, at the second century before Christ and not long after the great Buddhist dispersion from North-western Hindostan by the Brahmans.

A number of queer-looking Brahman priests of the Sivite* sect, who take care of these caves and encourage pilgrims to them, came out to see us, and, finding our pundit to be a countryman, though he was not of their sect, invited us to witness their worship in a vihara adjoining.

It was difficult to believe that the quiet, dark, handsome men who spoke to us could be such dupes as they seemed

* Followers of the god Siva or Shiva.

while at worship. In the largest of the caves was a huge, rude machine very like a common wheel, in the centre of which was a round place for a fire, and another and smaller fireplace on each of the seven spokes of the wheel. To the wheel was attached a long pole, and to this pole was tied a large-eyed, patient-looking Brahmanee cow with bells around her neck. To the cord which fastened these bells was tied a long rope, and this rope was held by a Yoghee, a sort of mystic Brahman priest, who had nothing on but a wisp of straw around his loins, and a half-starved-looking dog at his heels.

The moment the sun sank behind the mountains a white-robed priest issued from one of the smaller caves and placed a little earthen lamp, containing a long wick and some cocoanut oil, in each one of the receptacles for the fires. This done, the deafening sounds of multitudinous drums were heard from the secret recesses of the intermediate caves. At this, away went the Yoghee, the dog, the cow, and the wheel, with the seven tiny lamps revolving around the larger one in the centre. This furious dance continued, the dog barking, the cow lowing, and the drums beating, for an hour, and then another Yoghee stepped forward and relieved the first one. There were twelve priests, or rather ascetics, for the twelve hours of the night, and this was the celebrated "puja chakra," or wheel-worship, of the ancient Brahmans.

We could not wait, of course, to see the end of this strange, wild, deafening performance. I nearly fainted from the oppressive heat and disagreeable odors of the cave, and was obliged to seek relief in the open air. Here we found the Yoghee who had begun the dance seated on a stone clothed in a long dusky mantle and evidently enjoying the evening breeze. He answered me in pure Hindostanee, and told me that the central fire or lamp represented the Surya, or the Sun, the smaller ones the seven planets, naming each one—Soma, the Moon; Mangala, Mars; Buddh, Mercury; Virhaspati, Jupiter; Sukra, Venus; Sani, Saturn; Deva Bheemi, the Earth. The cow stood for Providence, or, as he termed it, the All-giver; he himself for mankind; while the dog was the emblem of the human family; his dance was in honor of the solar system.

A look of supreme satisfaction overspread his face as he informed me that the deep spiritual meaning which was conveyed to his heart was not in the wheel or in the fires, but in himself as he thought of the efficacy of the daily sacrifice which he offered to the gods, which convinced me that he at least firmly believed that the return of the sun-god to his place in the heavens every morning was due to his efforts and that of his brethren in performing from one end of the year to the other this self-imposed mystic night-dance in honor of the solar system.

The moon had risen as we put our little tattoos'* faces Khandala-ward and trotted away from the Karli village and the Hindoo ascetics. We had a very amusing half-broken and half-rattling talk with our pundit, who insisted that there was nothing more holy in the way of worship than the "puja chakra," which we had just seen. When my husband irreverently inquired, "If the wheel-worship was not a gentle hint to the sun to be up and about his business every morning," our good guide and teacher became suddenly grave and silent, and not another word would he say to us on the subject of this curious worship.

Next day we climbed a hill to see the old fort of Lokgarha, which was twice captured from the Mahrattas by the East India Company's generals. It occupies a com-

* The Mahratta horses.

manding position, and we enjoyed the view from it. This grand old Mahratta fortress is full of historical interest. It was here that the beautiful and astute widow of Nana Furnaveez, the most famous of the Mahratta ministers, took refuge, and the killadhar, or commander of the fort, obtained for her from General Wellesley not only a guarantee of safety, but an annual pension of twelve thousand rupees. On our return ride we passed through a wild but beautiful part of the hills. We saw and heard the stately pea-fowl that are found in this neighborhood; they added very much to the wild, luxuriant beauty of the woods.

On the following morning we bade adieu to the beautiful Bohr Ghauts. There was a great deal more of loveliness to be seen for many a mile until we reached the slope of the mountains, which is gradual rather than abrupt, as it is on the opposite side, and after that it was of no consequence at all where we looked. We were riding down a bleak, rugged, desolate country, slightly inclined; this was that immense triangular plateau between the Ghaut districts on the east and west and the great Vindhiya chain on the north. As we approached Poonah we found the views more interesting—fields of wheat, maize, orchards of fruit trees, plantain-groves, and the peepul, tamarind, and palm waving above them all. When we reached the bridge that spans the Moota River, it was near sunset. A flood of light poured from the sky over hill and dale and valley, gilding with unusual brilliancy the venerable roofs of Parbuttee and the half-ruined turretted walls of the Peishwa's palace.

Poonah, with the adjoining military station at Kirkee, where the scenery, owing to the junction of the Moota and Moola Rivers, is very picturesque, has a very respectable English population. But the majority of the natives are almost exclusively Brahmans of the Deccan and Hindoos from various parts of Hindostan.

This spot is famous in Mahratta annals. In 1599 Poonah and Supah were made over to Mahlaji Bhonsli, grandfather of the renowned Sivaji, by the government of the Nizam. In 1750 it was made the capital of the Maharashtra empire under Balaji Baji Rao. It was once more seized and destroyed by the Nizam's forces, by Alih Shah, who had established the Mohgul empire at Haiderabâd in the Deccan. And here again another battle took place in 1802, when Jeshwant Rao Holkar defeated the combined armies of the Peishwa and Scindhia.

With our usual good-fortune we procured a house at Kirkee to stay in during our visit to this neighborhood. It was the residence of a moolah, a Mohammedan bishop, and must have been built many years ago. It is a beautiful spot. A British cavalry regiment is stationed here, and here was fought the battle in which the English gained one of their most remarkable Indian victories over the last Peishwa.

The native city is divided into seven quarters and dedicated to the seven high angels or planets after whom the days of the week are named.

The streets of the city of Poonah are more picturesque and far more Oriental than even those of Bombay. The principal street is long, wide, and furnished with sidewalks, with shops of all sizes and all kinds of merchandise, having open fronts, and the goods are exposed on inclined platforms. The lanes and thoroughfares are thronged with people of all nationalities—the sedate and white-robed Brahman; the handsome Hindoo; the refined and delicate-looking Hindoo woman in her flowing graceful saree and pretty red sandals (for in this city Mohammedan influence has not yet reached the point which it has in other parts of India, and the women are not cooped up in harems, but are met everywhere in the streets, temples, and bazaars); the pompously-dressed Musulman, Arab, and Mahratta horsemen completely armed, prancing along on their splendid chargers; Mahratta foot-soldiers with their lordly swagger, equipped with sword and shield and buckler; emaciated devotees, fakeers, and mendicants of all denominations, some wholly nude, others clothed in the skins of wild beasts, and yet others covered with dust and paint and ashes of cow-ordure; fat, lazy-looking Brahmanee bulls; Jews, Parsees, native Portuguese Christians, and occasionally a British Mahratta sepoy in his neat undress uniform. This moving picture, so strange and incongruous, had the additional fascination of state elephants; splendid cavalcades of the Peishwa's troops decked out in brilliant colors and accompanied by richly-caparisoned led horses; camels trotting along at a quick pace to the sound of merry little tinkling bells suspended from their necks; fighting rams, kept for combats, one of the favorite Mahratta pastimes, parading the streets in long rows, now leaping and butting at dreamy Brahmanee cows. Add to all this that almost every day in the week there are crowded markets, religious processions, passing funerals with gayly-dressed corpses seated on the biers, looking ghastly enough on this dancing bubbling current of human life, and some idea may be formed of the sights and scenes to be met with in the capital of the Mahratta empire.

At my first arrival at Poonah I remember seeing some Hindoo children at play in the square. They were playing at marbles in all respects like the English game, save that the boys had nothing in the world on but a sacred cord round their shoulders and some gold and silver ornaments. New-born infants could not have been more unconscious than they were. The boy who won, a lad about eight or nine, seemed the least elated of the party. The one who lost had a better time; he clapped the winner on the back and cheered him all the way across the square, crying, "Khoop! khoop!" ("Fine! fine!"). There were thirty or more nude little fellows watching the play with intense interest, and evidently having the most enjoyment out of it, to judge from the wild shouts of applause with which they hailed the victor, screaming at the very top of their lungs, "Marliah! marliah!" ("Beaten! beaten!"). How many English or American boys would behave so well?

It would be simply impossible to enumerate all the places of historical interest to be found here. The hill-sides are everywhere crowned with forts and religious and military strongholds, where many a battle has been fought and won, and many a treaty formed only to be broken, both by the servants of the East India Company and the contending Mahratta and Mohgul forces, on this debatable land of the Hindoos, Mohguls, and English conquerors.

There are Bambura, or Bampoora, whence in former times an enormous gun, the Mahratta curfew, boomed sunset warnings to honest men to betake themselves home; and Dapooree, where Colonel Ford, C. B., built a palatial residence, and raised and commanded a brigade of magnificent Mahratta troops after the European fashion for the service of the Peishwa Baji Rao.

At Chinchore, near by, a boy is still worshipped as God by the credulous natives. The originator of this curious deception was one Marâbo, who is said to have restored sight to a blind girl, and who effected a like miraculous cure for the great Sivaji.* In order to prove his divinity,

* Founder of the Mahratta empire, born at Junir, about fifty miles from Poonah, in the year 1627.

this Marâbo caused himself to be buried alive in a sitting posture with a holy book in his hands. His son succeeded him as God. For several miracles performed by the latter, especially the feat of transforming a piece of cow's flesh into roses, the emperor of Delhi, Alamghir, presented to this man-god Narayana eight villages in perpetuity.

Then there is another curious old fort, Chakhan,* with its ramparts and parapets constructed, according to Hindoo story, by an Abyssian chief named Palighar, A. D. 1295. In 1818 it was captured by the troops of the East India Company. And last, but not least, there is the famous Sing-garh, "the lion's den," a vast triangular-shaped fortress, where the brave Mahwalee soldiers, headed by the braver Tanaji Mahisreh, Sivaji's general, fought against the Rajpoots. The latter lost his life after he had captured from the Rajpoots this stronghold of the Mahrattas, causing Sivaji to exclaim, "The den is taken, but the lion, alas! is slain."

This fortress was finally captured by the English during the Mahratta and English war. The ascent is made by palanquins. Splendid trees and many a wild flower crown the hillsides, creeping over gate and tower and moat, spreading beauty and gladness where once was heard the perpetual war-cry of deadly combatants.

We visited the Peishwa's palace. Our syce, or groom, looked like a bedizened prince as he led the way with his gay turban and brilliant sash. We kept close to his horse's heels, and the pundit, whose long white robe gave him the appearance of a lady on horseback, brought up the rear.

The palace, temples, and pavilions of the late Peishwa

* This fort is reputed to be of great antiquity, and was constructed by Palighar, but as to who he was, or how he got there, they do not pretend to know.

all cluster about a most beautiful hill called Parbuttee, a corruption of the Sanskrit word Pharvati, "Sacred Mountain." A magnificent garden called "Hira Bâgh" ("the gem or diamond garden"), and a fine reservoir with an old pavilion on its bank, are some of the features of this sacred spot. The palace is in no way worthy of notice, and is fast crumbling away, but it is approached by a magnificent staircase of stone steps cut out of the mountain, and so gradual that we rode up it on horseback. The hill is covered with temples. The view is very fine; seen over the lake with its pretty little tree-covered islands and wide fields studded with palm- and mango-plantations, it was one vast beautiful picture.

Our syce pointed out to us the spot where a young Mahratta prince dashed himself headlong from his pavilion because he was publicly reprimanded for some breach of etiquette by his prime minister, Nana Furnaveez.

There was much to interest us, however, in the temples, that are still kept in good repair, filled with the monstrous idols of the Hindoos; and here are held great annual festivals in their honor. Over two hundred Brahman priests worship here, and are supported by the voluntary contributions made to their shrines.

We went into the temple of Parvati. Our pundit led the way, accompanied by a singularly interesting Mahratta Brahman priest, but I noticed that the sectarian marks on his forehead and those on the pundit's were very different. The former wore the marks of Siva, two straight lines crossed, and the pundit those of Mahā Dēo, two concentric circles with a straight line. Before our eyes had become accustomed to "the dim religious light" of this temple, the power of which the Hindoos so well understand, I looked and saw right in front of me, and immediately at the foot of the altar, the prostrate figure of the pundit, and the Brahman priest beside him, their arms and hands stretched out, their faces hidden on the pavement, their limbs stiff and rigid, and their long white robes clinging to their persons.

Within full sight and hearing of the beauty of Christianity, with all the wonders and marvels of scientific discoveries taught hard by in the public native school and in the Sanskrit college, here were these men, neither of whom lacked intellectual training, bowing down to idols of wood and stone. Surely, the more earnest and spiritual of these lowly worshippers see something of the truth, beauty, and goodness of God, denied to less ardent natures, and only discernible with closed eyes and in moments of deep, silent emotion.

There is a massive silver statue of Siva seated on the altar, holding on his knees his wife Parvati and their son Ganesa. These smaller idols, it is said, are of pure gold; a princely fortune in precious gems adorns their head-dresses, their necks, and gleams out of their eyes. There were dusky arches and dingy, time-stained columns and all kinds of figures on the walls, and over them all a smoky atmosphere and an odor of incense mingled with that of burnt-offerings.

We went out almost faster than we had gone in. Pundit and his guru, or spiritual guide, were still going through some genuflexions. A Brahman is a Brahman indeed, but are Christians always the followers of Jesus? We sat down on the steps of the temple, and by and by the pundit came out with his spiritual guide, looking calm and serene.

We visited the English school for the natives in the Budhwar * portion of the city, also the Sanskrit college,

* The city of Poonah is divided into seven quarters, corresponding

and saw there hundreds of handsome, eager-looking students, and we were assured that it produced men of very great learning, who could hold their own in Sanskrit, Mahratta, Hindostanee, and English even, with some of the greatest scholars in England, France, or Germany.

A spot is shown at Sangam, not far from where we took up our abode, where the devoted Hindoo widows formerly underwent cremation with the dead bodies of their husbands. These monuments can only be seen when the water at Sangam (the spot where the Moola and Moota Rivers meet) is at its lowest ebb. They consist of flat stones or slabs laid in the river-bed, with two female feet engraved on each of them. Even in this, the most hideous and barbaric of Hindoo customs, is found lingering a beautiful and tender sentiment. The feet engraved on the slabs prove the willingness with which these unknown women followed their loved ones through the ordeal of a fiery death into the world beyond, and the meeting of the two rivers typifies the final reunion of their souls.

We visited a banker's office in the native city of Poonah. This bank, in which large sums are deposited and extensive business transacted, was nothing but a mud house plastered over within and without. The counter was an inclined platform reaching from the front to nearly the whole length of the building; on it squatted, cross-legged, surrounded with bags of all kinds of money, a Mahratta banker with his handsome countenance and keen piercing black eyes, talking to his customers, discounting bills, and counting money with astonishing rapidity and ease.

The bank where our pundit obtained his "hoondee," or money-order, was managed, in the absence of his father,

to the days of the week. Budhwar, therefore, is the Wednesday quarter of the city.

by a young Hindoo boy who could not have been over twelve years of age. This youthful cashier astonished us with his accuracy and quickness in counting and discounting money. His only account-book, as far as I could see, was a flat board covered with fine white sand. On this primitive slate he made all his calculations, writing them down with his forefinger. When he had finished he blew away the sand and handed over the amount due to pundit, with interest for odd days, etc., all calculated with the nicest accuracy down to the smallest fraction. We wondered very much to see these banking establishments left in the charge of such young lads, who sit there demurely—and, what is more strange, securely—until late at night, often amid heaps of gold, silver, and other coin left temptingly in full view; but one rarely hears of any attempt to rob them.

The bankers' checks are written on a thick country-made paper; every check has a secret mark or sign that renders forgery difficult. It is rolled up and fastened with gum-water, and thus laks * upon laks of rupees are circulated with ease and safety throughout the country.

The European portion of the city of Poonah stands on a fine open plain. There are here wide fields, handsome barracks for the European soldiers, bungalows for their commanding officers, a hospital, a lunatic asylum, a pretty little church with reading-room and library adjoining. In fact, there is everything here to render the European comfortable and happy, except the temper of the people, who still cling to the recollections of old times, when Poonah was the capital of their own great kings and warriors, filled with all the pomp and parade of Oriental splendor.

The late Sir Jamsetjee Jeeboy has erected a fine residence

* A *lak* is one hundred thousand rupees.

here; near it is a simple and unpretending Fire-temple for the benefit of the Parsees in this vicinity.

The last of the many bright hours spent here we drove about the native town and enjoyed Poonah at night. Every house, fort, temple, palace, and hut was illuminated, those of the poor by a dim light, those of the temples and palaces by innumerable tiny flames that flickered and gleamed in thousands of colors on the marbles and frescoes of the walls, floors, and verandahs. It seemed like passing through some fairy scene filled with the thousand and one pictures of the Arabian Nights.

CHAPTER X.

The beautiful Hindoo village of Wye.—The Mahabaleshwar Hills.—The Temple of the Gods.—The Couch of Krishna.—The Stone Image of the Cow from whose mouth the Five Rivers of this Region are said to Spring.—The Holy Tank.—Satarah, the Star City of the Mahratta Empire.—The Fort.—The Palace of Sivaji.—Jejureh, the famous Hill-temples where the Dancing-girls of the Country are recruited.—The Mad Gossain, and the Story of his Ill-fated Love.—The Dancing-girl Krayâhnee.

WE made a journey from Poonah to the Mahabaleshwar Hills in a common bullock-cart, but through a country of unrivalled beauty. We spent a night and a day at the rural village of Wye. I have never seen any place where the charm of Oriental grace working through the pure Hindoo imagination has more forcibly stamped itself. The soil, the climate, the temples, the river, the wide-spreading trees, the sportive figures of the gods and goddesses, are all calculated to bring out in strong relief the characteristics of the adjoining mountains, which here assume a multitude of beautiful shapes, rising heavenward like innumerable battlemented towers, pinnacles, or spires, each loftier than the last and endowed with a certain air of individuality peculiar to these hills. One isolated rock near the village rears its flat-topped brow, crowned with an old Mahratta fort, more than a hundred feet high, sharp and abrupt, lending a singular picturesqueness to the smallest object under it.

Wye stands on the left bank of the river Krishna, which is shaded by fine peepul and mango trees; handsome stone steps lead down to the edge of the swift-flowing waters, and are crowded all day long with figures of graceful men, women, and children sporting, bathing, drawing water, or lounging idly around. There was an irresistible freshness and quiet beauty about the gay, careless life of the people, which was passed absolutely on the banks of the river.

We had no sooner taken up our abode in the travellers' bungalow, which here commands a fine view, than the patel, or chief of the city, accompanied by several Brahmans, paid us a visit, bringing us presents of fruit and flowers. I was much struck with the genial kindliness and courtesy of these men.

We rose at dawn next morning to see this Hindoo community perform in one body, on the banks of the Krishna, the peculiar ceremony of worshipping the sun. The people literally lined the banks of the river; their faces were turned up to the sky, and as they stood in rows on the steps leading to the water's edge the effect was very impressive. They then simultaneously filled their palms with water, snuffed it up through their nostrils, and flung it toward the north-east, repeating certain prayers. After this they all proceeded to stand on one foot, then on the other, each holding in his hand an earthen bowl filled with clarified butter, with a lighted wick in the centre. Then they all together saluted the mighty luminary with folded hands raised to their foreheads, and then marched toward the west in imitation of his path through the heavens; which terminated their sun-worship* for the day.

We also visited the garden and palace of the Rastias. Mohti Bagh, or "pearl garden," as the entire palace and grounds are called, is only a little distance from the village

* Hindoos also worship the sun every evening.

of Wye. The approach to the palace is through an enchanting road formed of tall bamboos, mangoes, and tamarind trees. Wye is a spot famed in Hindoo literature. Here the heroes of the Mahâbharata spent their years of exile and expiation, and here they are said to have built many wonderful temples. The river is almost gemmed with beautiful temples in the finest style of Hindoo architecture, owing to this historic fact or fiction, whichever it may be. The temples are filled with idols of heroes and heroines, and the city with Hindoo men and women of the finest type and utmost purity of character.

We visited an old Brahman college here, which was once famous for the clever pundits it furnished to the country around. There were some students in one of the rooms; they were all young and good-looking, but had about them an air of decorous restraint and an expression of old age that were depressing to one's spirits.

Passing through a luxuriant country full of venerable trees, groves, gardens, and wide fields, we stopped at the little village of Dhoom to see a famous temple. It was of fine stone, artistically built, but full of strange gods. An arched door led to one of the shrines, where there was an image of Siva. Vessels containing rice and flowers were before him, and the basin in front of the temple is something peculiarly beautiful. It is unique in form—like a huge tulip-shaped cup, of pure white marble, with its rim most delicately carved into the petals of the lotos-flower. It is impossible to give any adequate idea of this exquisite bit of Hindoo sculpture. A pillar of white marble with five heads of Siva, and the cobra de capello twisted round them, adds another charming attraction to this insignificant Brahman village.

The ride up the Tai Ghauts was one of great beauty. Here and there in the dells and hollows were little patches of grass which looked at a distance very like a green velvet carpet. Low-growing wild plants, tall trees, and creepers were matted together in one network of green, yellow, red, blue, and purple. The views looking back were lovely. The noise of mountain-torrent and trickling waters in the midday heat was most refreshing.

The ancient village of Mahabaleshwar is perched on a high table-land, and is said to be the most elevated portion of that interminable western range of Ghauts forming some of the highest ground between the Southern Ghauts and the Himâlayas. The temple of Maha Dèo stands close under a projecting rock on the very spot where, according to Brahmans here, the five sacred rivers of this region take their rise—the Krishna, the Koina, and the Yena, which flow toward the Deccan, and the beautiful Savitri and Gaiutri, which, after leaping down the mountain-sides in many picturesque cascades and waterfalls, unite with other small streams to form quite a large river, at whose mouth stands Fort Victoria. There are no lovelier scenes than some of those formed by these two rivers, and especially remarkable is the spot where they unite, flowing between deep and wooded banks till they lose themselves in a broad, quiet, placid stream.

A large reservoir is excavated in front of the temple to receive the waters of the Krishna and Koina, and in front is a huge stone cow, through whose mouth the waters flow into it. All around this reservoir is a fine stone walk, and farther on are several cells where saints who have long abandoned the world still reside unseen, but not unheard, for night after night their voices, like the feeble wail of infants, are borne on the night air, imploring the gods in behalf of the lost, erring human race. Fiends, angels, heroes, demons, and gods are all worshipped here.

The Brahman ascetics who have charge of these temples

ring a bell to give notice that the deified beings have taken up their abode in their respective cells. Krishna, the last incarnation of the Hindoos, has also a couch prepared for him here. When the sound of this bell is heard all the inhabitants of this mountain-village betake themselves to a few moments' meditation. We saw some remarkably pretty women who were attached to this temple filling the lamps with oil and gathering flowers and fruit to lay before the shrines; but they seemed to be shy of Europeans, and would not notice us.

The discoverer of this spot, so far as the English are concerned, for it has long been inhabited by the Brahmans, was Colonel P. Lodwick, who, when stationed with his regiment at Satarah, undertook the exploration of these hills, and, pushing through forest, brushwood, and jungle, found himself at the edge of a high projecting rock, when a sudden turn brought him to the brink of a grand promontory formerly called "Sidney Point," but now after the true discoverer. No sooner was the discovery of this delightful and most accessible mountain-region made known than Sir James Malcolm, then governor of Bombay, hastened to establish here a convalescent hospital for European soldiers. In course of time good roads were constructed, partly by the British government and partly by the rajah of Satarah. Parsee shopkeepers soon made their appearance, and in a few years a little British colony was transplanted here. There are now a little Protestant church, reading-room, library, hotel, barracks, handsome European villas and bungalows, with bridle-paths all along the most picturesque points. There is no more beautiful and healthful sanitarium to be found anywhere in the East. We spent two delightful months, November and December, at the travellers' bungalow. The weather was perfect—clear, cold, and with-

Elephant Hunting in India.

out any rain. With all the beauty with which a tropical climate surrounds the hillsides the temperature varied from 62° to 45° in the open air. The elevation, four thousand seven hundred feet above the level of the sea, places it beyond the influence of cholera and malaria, which are so deadly in many parts of India. The soil is scanty in some parts, but in many portions a rich mould of great depth is found, admirably adapted to agricultural purposes. The finest strawberries I ever saw in India were brought me one morning by the pundit, cultivated by the Brahmans on these hills as offerings to their gods. The hills are also covered with fine trees—the willow, the jambul with its dazzling green foliage, the iron-wood, and the arrowroot plant. There are here several kinds of jessamines—one, the night-blooming jessamine, a large and beautiful flower and peculiarly fragrant after sunset. Ferns abound: one called by the natives pryha khud, or "the lover's leap," is extraordinarily beautiful, but not very abundant. A plant resembling the yellow broom is also found here, but it far surpasses the latter in size and beauty of flowers. Bulbous and parasitical plants abound, and their flowers are much larger and far more beautiful than those found on the plains, and each plant has its season.

To the sportsman the Mahabaleshwar Hills are a treasure-trove. The shikarees, or native hunters, are always at hand to lead the adventurous into the very lairs of tigers, panthers, bears, wolves, and to the resorts of all kinds of jungle-fowl. The monkeys in this neighborhood are generally the first to give notice of the vicinity of a tiger by their loud and reiterated cries resounding from tree to tree. The wild bison, for which this region was once famous, is now found only occasionally. A spot is shown where Lieutenant Hinds, a fine, athletic, noble-looking young English officer, over six feet in stature, was killed by one of these beasts. He and his shikaree had pursued the bison for some distance. Lieutenant Hinds had just taken his aim, when, in the twinkling of an eye, the infuriated beast suddenly turned upon him, with one bound caught him upon his horns, and bore him thus wildly along through the forest, and finally dashed him headlong over some rocks. His mutilated body was found, and lies in the little Christian burial-ground here.

In returning from the Mahabaleshwar Hills we took the Satarah road, the most picturesque of the three roads which lead up to the hills. It commands extensive and diversified views of all the country around—the wild tangle of the forests, the towering peaks of the mountains, the bristling forts of the rock-bound city of the "Northern Star," the ample fields dotting the landscape like huge green emeralds, and the Savitri and the Gaintri struggling through brake and forest dingle and many a deep shade to find each the other, till they meet at last just over the wide brow of a sharp cliff, and leap together in gladness and beauty down five hundred feet, dashing and tumbling over masses of rock, till they gain the low-lying lands, then move on in quiet, dreamy irregularity to lose each the other once more—one amid the waters of the famous Krishna, and the other at Karar afar off.

We turned off the road to visit a formidable towering rock on which stands the old Mahratta fort of Pratapgarh. In the centre of it are found two lovely Hindoo temples—one to Maha Dèo, the high god, and the other to Bhawanee, who is at once the goddess of love and hatred —with the attending Brahman priests officiating there. Somewhere under this fortress lies the head of the simple-hearted Afzal Khan, the renowned Bijapoor general. Here was enacted by the hand of Sivaji, the founder of the great Mahratta empire, one of the darkest of the many tragedies with which the history of India abounds. Having induced, through false pretences, Afzal Khan to visit him unarmed and attended by one sole follower, Sivaji met the trusting foe with open arms and slew him when in the act of embracing him. Sayid Bunder, the faithful follower of the general, refused to surrender even on condition of having his life granted to him, and suffered the same fate as his master. There and then the signals agreed upon boomed forth from this old fort. The Mhawalis rushed from their places of concealment all along the hillside on the khan's retinue, stationed at the foot of the hill, and slaughtered and dispersed them. Thus Sivaji defeated the enemy and acquired at the same time great amount of treasure as well as reputation as a warrior.

Satarah, or "the Star City," is full of antiquities and historical associations; every rock and hill and fortress has its own deadly secret—sometimes more than one—of murder, bloodshed, treachery, and triumph on the part of the Mohguls, Mahrattas, or British, besides other local interests. The town lies on a high slope or plain between two ranges of hills, one on the east and one on the west. The western hills have been occupied for many hundred years by the descendants of the early Mahratta Brahmans. They are covered with temples, huge, ancient, and solemn; gods and goddesses in ivory and stone, admirably wrought, sit enshrined in each of these. The priests worship them merely for the sake of their age and number. Tall, gray-bearded monkeys abound on these hills, and while we stood gazing at one of the temples a troop of these creatures assembled on the roof and showed signs and symptoms of great excitement or displeasure.

The Satarah bazaar is peculiar and well worth visiting. The Mahratta women are as free and as unconfined in their movements almost as the English. They are darker and less good-looking than those at Wye and on the hills.

The flat-topped hills around absolutely bristle with forts that the "Mountain Rats," as Aurungzebe called the Mahratta warriors, loved to build everywhere. A zigzag pathway leads from the city up to the western gate of "Azim Tarah," the most renowned of these strongholds. If individual energy and vehement self-assertion indicate character, the Mahratta soldiers possess it to an extraordinary degree, over and over again proving themselves grandly capable of confronting the very dangers they had brought down upon themselves. This fort is full of stories of Mahratta exploits against their threefold enemies. It has been captured, lost, and recaptured over and over again. It was built by a King Panalah in 1192, and was once the state-prison of the great Sivaji. It was defended against the emperor Aurungzebe by Phryaji Phrabu, a brave *hawaldar*,* who had learned the art of war under Sivaji. When the Mohguls attempted to enter the "Star City" huge stones were rolled down the mountain-sides, and were as destructive as the discharge of artillery. Tarbhyat Khan, a Mohgul in the service of Aurungzebe, undertook to destroy it by mining the north-east angle, one of its strongest points. The mine was completed after months of severe labor; a storming-party was formed on the brow of the hill. Aurungzebe, confident of success, marshalled his men in brilliant array to see the attack. The first explosion crushed many of the Mahratta garrison to death, and was followed by another that rolled down great rocks upon the Mohguls, destroying, it is said, two thousand men at once. Animated by this disaster to the enemy, the garrison would have continued to

* A Mahratta officer, but not of very high rank.

hold out, but their supplies failed and they were obliged to capitulate.

After the well-known rupture with Baji Row, the English troops marched into Satarah, took possession of the fort, and installed as king Pra Thap Singh, the eldest son of Shah Hoo the Second. He was deposed, however, on account of a series of intrigues against the East India government, and was imprisoned at Benares. Apa Saihib, the last of the descendants in a direct line of the great Sivaji, was then placed on the throne, but on his death the province, much to the indignation of the princes and people of Western India, was annexed to the possessions of the East India Company. It is but just to say that there were men among the court of directors who remembered, with Sir George Clark, then governor of Bombay, the treaty of 1819, and knew that the East India Company had agreed to cede in perpetual sovereignty, to the rajah of Satarah and his heirs and successors, the territories which he held, and they protested, but all in vain, against the annexation of Satarah, calling it "an act of unrighteous usurpation." Here, alas! was laid the first seed of the "Sepoy mutiny," that terrible retribution which ten years after overtook not the guilty, but the innocent and faithful servants of the Company.

On the west of the fort are a number of Hindoo temples dedicated chiefly to Siva and to Bhawanee, the Indian Venus, who seems ever to have been a favorite with these hardy mountaineers. The view from the fort is one of the most charming in the world. The forms of the different hills are quaint, and crowned with barbaric fortresses and temples that are fast crumbling away to give place to a rich and tropical vegetation; the great plain below, dotted with the houses and gardens of the European and native residents; the lakes, the bazaars, the busy thoroughfares, and, far away for many a mile, a road, leaf-canopied and cool in the hottest midday sun, lined on each side with thousands of magnificent mango trees. These mango trees were planted by one of the native rulers in expiation of the murder of a noble Hindoo statesman, an envoy from Barodah.

On the south-western side of the old town stands the antiquated palace of Sivaji. We were shown into an attractive chamber called the Jallah Mandir, the "water pavilion." Surrounded by a variety of beautiful creeping plants and almost encircled with water, it is cooled by quaint little Oriental fountains that splash and spirt upward all day long. This peculiar water-bound chamber is almost fairy-like. But the deity of this place is the huge sword with which the treacherous Sivaji slew his trusting foe, Afzah Khan, the general of Bijapoor. By a strange contradiction, this sword is called Bhawanee, the goddess of love, and the people believe that the sweet goddess has imparted to the old sword a charm which is deadly to the enemies of the Mahrattas.

As we went back through the town we peeped into one or two of the temples. There were in them some curious old idols of heroes rather than gods, but they were as hideous as possible. A little farther on the ground was made lovely with immense numbers of wild flowers, red, yellow, and blue.

From the Star City of the Deccan we went back a few days' journey and crossed the "Nira bridge," one of the fine old Mahratta works, to visit the village and hill-temples of Jijuhre. The village was insignificant enough, but the hill on which stands the temple of Khandoba, the warrior-god of the early Mahrattas, was very striking. It is flat-topped and rises abruptly from the surrounding plain, its entire surface covered with temples, gates, pillars, stone monuments of every conceivable object, and has the appearance of a huge cemetery. If it had not been for the presence of our pundit I doubt if we should have been allowed to visit this once-famous temple.

We went up on foot through an odd mixture of gateways and pillars, all curiously carved, and here and there were stone figures of mythological birds and beasts, abundantly provided with shaindoor, a kind of red paint, and offerings of flowers. The largest temple had an image of Khandoba, a terrific-looking monster. In one of the upper chambers there was a colossal drum that gave sunset warnings and served to call the priests, priestesses, and other attendants to prayers, midnight devotions, or revelries; which latter are held on certain days, or rather nights, of the waxing moon. About two hundred women. all young, many of them mere children, are attached to this temple, which is in every sense one of the relics of the ancient Mahratta usages before the introduction of Brahmanism. Many of these girls were scattered about in groups or were seen reclining at their ease in a semi-nude costume about the aisles of the temples, producing a charming Oriental effect, though one could not help shuddering at the thought of their lives. And, in spite of the doom laid upon them even before they were born, many of them had singularly interesting, pensive faces. One girl who was pouring water into the vessels around the shrine of Khandoba was a picture of grace and adorned with glittering jewels. These strange priestesses of passion live in cells attached to the temples or are scattered in the service of their peculiar divinity around the temples in the neighborhood, but here they are yearly recruited, and here they are formally married as virgins to the idol of Siva or Khandoba, as the case may be. There are here long corridors and intricate arrangement of passages, with little stairs leading up and down and around, where the girls are kept under the surveillance of old women who once were doomed to the same service. How inexplicable is such a life, looking at it from a Christian's point of view! But with these poor devotees the more revenue they bring in for the temple the better their future life, in which they dream of becoming loved wives and mothers of divine sons and daughters in a heaven prepared for them.

We noticed in our ramblings over this curious spot a strange-looking man, naked as the day on which he was born, his hair, long and streaked with gray, falling in masses around his naked shoulders, his hands and feet emaciated, the nails on his fingers and toes looking like huge claws, begrimed with dirt and masses of red paint, sitting alone, muttering all to himself and twirling in his hands an old battered-looking lota, or drinking-vessel, made of some dark metal. This was the mad *gossain*, or devotee, of Jijuhre. When we approached him he started up and took his place on the edge of a crumbling rock.

This poor mad creature was an object of profound veneration and worship, and his story was as pathetic as it was singular. The spot on which he had seated himself had a peculiar interest to him, and he haunted it even in his maddest moments. It was called Dewanee-garh, "the maddening rock," because one of the priestesses of the temple leaped from it and was killed instantly. This girl's name was Krayâhnee. It was said that on her marriage with the god Siva and her installation in the peculiar life of the temple it was found that she had conceived a strong passion for the mad gossain, then a young Mahratta noble named Hotah Bhow. He visited her frequently, and they were always seen together, and, as the noble was rich, the priests humored the girl in her singleness of devotion, for she brought large sums of money to the temple. But after a while Hotah Bhow ceased his visits to the temple, and Krayâhnee was urged to take another lover. She pleaded a respite for one month, which was granted. In the mean time, through a Sudra, a male attendant on the temple, she sent Hotah Bhow a message, assuring him of her undying love and entreating him to aid her in her escape from the temple, saying that if he would do this for her she would willingly serve as a slave in his household.

The Sudra, who was himself enamored of the beautiful priestess, took no pains to deliver the message, but brought back to the poor girl a fabricated answer from Hotah Bhow, advising her to make herself happy where the gods had placed her.

Next morning Krayâhnee was missed, and on the following day her body was found crushed and mangled at the foot of Dewanee-garh. Tying her lota, or sacred vessel for ablutions, to her neck, she had leaped from the rock at dead of night. Months after, Hotah Bhow returned from a pilgrimage to Benares, and on hearing of the sad fate of Krayâhnee became so melancholy that he betook himself to the severest course of asceticism known among the Hindoos, called "Gala Naik." Standing for hours on the spot whence the dancing-girl flung herself headlong, he threw back his head and gazed at the sun, holding in his hand the sole relic of his unhappy love, the battered lota. The priestesses of the temple, pitying his sorrows, took him food and fed him at stated intervals. But at length reason gave way under the severity of his expiation; he forgot his vow to practise "Gala Naik" to the day of his death, and is now found wandering over the hillside or perched on the edge of Dewanee-garh, bereft of even the memory of his sorrows, but still clinging to the battered lota of Krayâhnee, into which the priestesses of the temple pour his daily food and drink.

Weary of our climb and saddened by the recital of this story, we retraced our steps to the "dharrum-sala" of the village, and on the following morning started across the country of the Deccan from the Star City of the ancient Mahrattas for Aurungabâd, the golden city of the great Mohgul Aurungzebe, and thence to the caves of Elora.

CHAPTER XI.

From Satarah, the Star City of the great Mahratta Kings, to Dowlutabâd, the Abode of Fortune, and Aurungabâd, the Golden City of the Mohgul Emperors.—Tombs of Boorhan Ood Deen and Aurungzebe. —Mausoleum of Rhabea Duranee.—Sketch of the Mohgul invasion of India.—Manners, Customs, and Religious Ceremonies of the Mohammedans of Hindostan.

Of all the places in the East, there is none more celebrated in Oriental romance and song than the province which occupies the centre of the great table-land of the Deccan, called the Nizam's Dominion. Here the Mahrattas, Rajpoots, Mohguls, French, and English have struggled for mastery. Here are the ancient Golkunda and Hyderabâd, the Abode of the Lion. In the reign of Mahmood Shah, so great was the renown of the Bahmani * court that the celebrated Persian poet Hafiz determined to visit it. "He embarked at Ormuzd, but the vessel encountering a tempest, the Iranian Horace at once abandoned the voyage and despatched instead an ode to Mahmood as his apology." From that time the songs of Hafiz became the favorite melodies at the Bahmani court.

* So-called from Allahu Deen Hasain Shah Gangu Bahmani, who was the first Mohammedan king of Deccan, 1347 A. D. He was a native of Delhi and servant of one of the most learned Brahman astrologers, who was highly favored by the fierce conqueror Mohammed Tooghlak. Hasain greatly distinguished himself in battle with the imperial troops in storming Dowlutabâd. Finally, the emperor Naisirud Deen resigned to him the crown of Deccan. He very greatly extended his dominions under the advice of his early master the Brahman astrologer, Ganzu Bood, whom he appointed as his prime minister.

In 1401, Firuz Shah, who had succeeded Mahmood in 1397, sent from his kingdom an embassy with magnificent presents to the great conqueror Timoor Lâng (Tamerlane), who conferred on him, in addition to the vast provinces he ruled over, the sovereignty of the kingdoms of Guzerat and Malwah; which proved, however, troublesome acquisitions. It was he who caused that famous observatory (the ruins of which may still be seen on the Dowlutabâd Pass) to be built for his Brahman astronomer. The close of his reign is said to have been disastrous. His armies, bent on conquest, were defeated in a battle with Dèo-Rai-Vijya-Nâggur, and Firuz Shah was not only deposed, but strangled, by his own brother in 1422. The ruthless murderer and brother of Firuz Shah was both a warlike and able monarch. He is known in Indian story as Ahmad Shah Bahmani. In 1432 he built the famous fort of Ahmedabâd at Bidhar, still called after him; and not only restored but beautified that ancient city, which more than two thousand years before had been famed in Sanskrit drama as the capital of the Rajah Bhima Selm, the loves of whose exquisitely chaste and beautiful daughter Damayanti and of Nala, the rajah of Malwah, are sung and acted to this day throughout Hindostan.*

This province has been the most celebrated for the beauty and rare accomplishments of its Bahyadiers. They formed a large part of its population; so much was the profession favored that many of these public dancers have become queens, and sons born to them have become kings and learned men. A beautiful and romantic story is still sung here of a Bahyadier named Aminah. Having attracted the attention of Burhan Nizam Shah, she

* It was translated from the Sanskrit into Persian verse by the poet Faizi of Iran, and acted, with all the Indian appendages of dress and character, at the court of the great Akbar.

sent him word that she loved him, and, in spite of her profession, was worthy to be his wife. Doubting the sincerity of her assertion, Burhan Nizam Shah subjected her secretly, through a friend, to the most painful trials, in every one of which she gave evidence of an innate nobleness of character. Thus, having proved the sincerity of her attachment, he married Aminah, who continued to be his favorite queen and counsellor even after he had espoused (from motives of policy) the princess of Bijapoor.

The appearance of the country of the Nizam's Dominion, however, is not as full of interest as its history. Without forests of any extent, and with but few lakes, it is intersected by innumerable small streams or nullahs* and reservoirs, with occasional hills that rise in curious detached blocks, as if accidentally dropped here and there by some Titans at play.

After many days of a painful journey through wide fields of desolation and gigantic cities now crumbling away, we encamped at a dhurrum-sala† in the ancient city of Bidhar, once a place of great renown and the capital of the Mahratta kings, who seem to have shifted their capitals as the Bedouin does his tent. Attached to the dhurrum-sala were long sheds, places of shelter for the cattle, side by side with that of the human cattle. These had grass and fodder provided for them gratuitously by the Brahmans in the vicinity.

This old Mahratta town contains some very curious stone buildings carved with the figures of Hindoo gods and goddesses. Its chief attraction, however, is the beautiful Bidharee ware. We bought a little box and the bowl of a hookhah, which were very gracefully orna-

* Creeks or water-courses, found full to overflowing in many places during the rainy season, but which often dry up in the hot months.

† A free rest-house for travellers.

mented with silver-work. The metal of which these articles were manufactured is a jet-black compound of copper and tin which is capable of a high polish. The natives here seem happy and independent. We saw some very handsome Hindoo women in the bazaars, but the Mohammedan women were those of the lowest castes.

The difficulties of the road very much increased after leaving Bidhar. We were bumped and battered over a stony road, nor was there anything to be seen but a great wilderness for many miles. When we inquired the distance to the next halting-place our guide, who was very musical, stopped his song and replied, "*Chulla joa oodhur hai*" ("Go along! it is there"). But where we could not make out. Finally, we were obliged to spend the night under a tree in our wagons not far from a great nullah which was thought unsafe to cross after sunset. On the opposite side of us was a large party of men and women, gossains and priests, fellow-travellers, with four wagon-loads of dancing-girls, some of whom were very interesting seen in the dusk. They were a troup of actors and actresses returning from some village theatre to their head-quarters at Oude Gera, a city in this vicinity.

A little after dawn next morning we crossed the nullah, which was by no means as dangerous as represented by our guide. Along the road we saw some beautiful wild flowers and trailing vines, among them a little hardy blossom like the anemone, and of a lovely rose-color. In the afternoon of the next day we crossed the Godaveri, the famous Tyndis of the ancients, rising in the Thull Ghauts and flowing through the length and breadth of the great high plain of the Deccan to pour itself into the Bay of Bengal. We found no difficulty in fording the river at this season, when the rains were over. In some places its banks were high and steep, and here and there were striking views of the country. We met hosts of carts and natives on horses crossing the river at this point. After another long day's journey we took refuge at last at the dhurrum-sala at Aurungabâd. From the verandah of the dhurrum-sala at this truly picturesque Mohammedan city is a most enchanting view—the Dhuna River winding away through the plain; the leafy woods, not very dense, but full of trees noble and stately; the lime-groves in full blossom sweetly scenting the air, while with pertinacious grace the full-blown leaves of many creeping vines droop over the verandah to fan us gently in the evening breeze; in the distance the domes, the tall, graceful minarets, the shining roofs of mosques and palaces of the once-famous city of Arungabâd amid eternally verdant gardens. Gradually the sun sets on the charming scene, but we still linger and gaze; few lights are seen, but now and then a rushlight or the glimmer of a fire prepared for the evening meal.

Twilight is deepening into darkness as we start for a walk, accompanied by pundit. We see in the distance a tall square tower, dark in color and crowned with half-ruined battlements, and behind it, far away, the mighty Dowlutabâd, grim, silent and watchful, against the dusky sky. Some strangely weird-looking figures of priests and fakeers are returning from a mosque adjoining, and here and there a bright star shines softly upon the tombs of the dead Mohammedans buried on the summit of the far-off Piphlaghaut.

Dowlutabâd, "the abode of fortune," with the fickleness of the goddess after whom it was named, fluctuated between the Mohgul conquerors of the Deccan, the Rajpoots and Mahratta kings, for several centuries, till finally it passed into the possession of the East India Company. We obtained permission from the governor of the fort to visit this remarkable fortress, which is built on a rocky hill, an isolated, prodigious block of stone, with a perpendicular scarp of nearly a hundred and fifty feet all round it. The summit is pointed like a cone, and capped with a curious old tower, on which is mounted a heavy brass gun. The only means of ascending the fort of Dowlutabâd is through a narrow passage hewn out of the rock and leading to a large subterranean chamber, whence a gallery, also excavated out of the heart of the hill, leads to the top. After traversing this gallery the road passes by the khilladar's (or governor's) house, a handsome building with an arched verandah. The fortress is protected by a fosse and a circular wall winding round the hill to the very summit; the lowest part of the wall is made to enclose the little native town lying at its base, now deserted and fast crumbling away. The view from the summit is very inspiring; we could see the country around, far and near, though there was a slight haze on the distant horizon.

The revenues of the Soubah, or district of Dowlutabâd, including that of Ahmed Nuggur, is said to have yielded the emperor Aurungzebe the sum of two hundred and fifty-nine laks of rupees. In 1758 this fortress fell for a short time into the hands of the French, but by the recall of M. Bussy it was once more captured by the Mohgul rulers of the Deccan. The Nizam's flag, that once floated so proudly over its summit, is now supplanted by that ever-aggressive standard, the union jack.

Aurungabâd, on the left bank of the Dhuna River, is one of the most disappointing of the old Mohgul cities, and is fast crumbling to decay. It was once the centre of Mohgul power in the Deccan. Aurungzebe removed his capital from Dehli to this spot, whence its name the "Golden Seat," owing to his chair of state being made of pure gold. The town is approached through a gateway which looks, like the rest of the place, old and dilapidated; the streets, however, are broad, and some well paved. The gardens and reservoirs are numerous, but the whole atmosphere of the town is strangely depressing. The groups of grave-looking Mohammedans pirs, or holy men, naked, filthy fakeers, and porters, who parade the streets, make it seem odd and grotesque, but do very little toward enlivening the town itself. It is surrounded by a wall flanked with towers at regular distances. The minarets, mosques, and some of the dwellings are still possessed of much architectual beauty. Among its most famous manufactures are fine kinkaubs, or gold- and silver-wrought silks, and dried fruits, which are sent to Bombay and other parts of India for sale.

The palace of Aurungzebe stands on the south of the Dhuna River, and is only remarkable for its extent. It is full of dark chambers, narrow passages, stained ceilings and floors, that might once have been beautiful, but which now have an unwholsome look of mould and decay.

Having devoted an entire day to Aurungabâd, we rode out on the following morning to Rowzah, "the city or garden of tombs," but most celebrated as the last resting-place of Aurungzebe. The town of Rowzah itself is a charming spot. It stands on the brow of a gentle hill, and the views from every part of it are very fine. There was an air of bustle and activity too among the people, and elaborate culture was everywhere manifest throughout its immediate neighborhood. Temples, mosques, holy places, groves, and gardens for the dead abound here, and the shops seemed well stocked. We had a beefsteak * for lunch, cooked in a Mohammedan "khanadhar," or restau-

* Beef is never exposed for sale in a Hindoo city.

rant. The houses are well built and extremely picturesque with their low projecting balconies. Many of the buildings are furnished with open courtyards in front. Sometimes a high wall encloses, as at Aurungabâd, a group of buildings, the dwelling of some wealthy Mohammedan merchant with his hareem. Groups of well-dressed Musulmans, with here and there a Mahratta or a Hindoo, were passing to and fro exchanging graceful salutations; water-cariers, porters, and venders of fruit and cloth jostled one another in the streets; and from the balconies there peeped out at us now and then coquettish-looking young girls brilliantly attired, with here and there a face that displayed great beauty.

Finally, we came to the famous Mohammedan cemetery. Here we paused a while at the tomb of the great Aurungzebe, which lies near that of a saint called Bhooran Ood Deen. The mausoleum of the latter is more costly, and is held in even greater veneration, than that of the Mohgul emperor. It was covered with a handsome green velvet mantle, lamps were burning within, musicians were beating their drums outside, and pirs, or holy men, were standing around the tomb and reciting prayers for the dead and prostrating themselves at certain intervals.

Outside the walls of the city of Aurungabâd is the object best worth seeing, the tomb of the loving and faithful Rahbea Dhoorane, the favorite wife of Aurungzebe, though, at best, it is a poor copy of the famous Taj-Mahal at Agra. Arriving at the farthest edge of a wide path, the spires of the mausoleum rise before one amid a wide area of rich dark foliage. It stands alone and immediately behind the wall that separates it from the old palace of Aurungzebe. The approach is through a gateway. In front is a canal with a number of fountains at play. At the end of the avenue is the mausoleum itself. The windows are of very exquisite workmanship, reminding one of Rahbea herself. The tomb is quite low and unpretending, lying in the centre of the building, and one has to descend a number of steps to look upon it. It is enclosed by a light and elegant marble screen, fancifully chiselled, looking like lacework. On the tomb itself is laid a covering of scarlet velvet. The minarets at each of the corners are also full of beauty. To the left we pass through a fine Gothic arch gracefully carved, and enter a noble hall supported by fluted pillars and with handsome etchings along the walls and ceilings. It is now used for the assemblies of Mohammedan priests and bishops, who meet here from different parts of the country twice every year to discuss matters bearing chiefly on the religious disputes that arise among themselves.

Above even the last resting-place of the dead queen, and far beyond all the other features of interest in this mausoleum, is a little unique chamber that stands apart, surrounded with fragrant orange and sweet lime trees and clustering blossoms of rare tropical flowers. It is the loveliest retreat that the heart of man could have devised, and is still touched with the lingering romance of Rahbea's love for and power over the proud Aurungzebe; for here he often sought the beautiful queen for purposes of quiet meditation or relaxation from the cares of state, and here, if we may believe all the reports, Rahbea often knelt for hours before her husband pleading for the lives of men and women whom he had doomed to death. Amid all the cruelty, avarice, and bloodshed that stained the life of Aurungzebe, the tender picture which this little chamber conjures up is pure and refreshing.

Mohammedan priests and pirs, or saints, are in constant attendance upon this tomb. Morning services are held here every Monday. Fahtiahs, or prayers, are offered for the dead queen and all other dead souls, portions of the Koran are read or chanted, and lamps are kept burning on especial festal nights. As we were leaving the place a number of Mohammedans entered the tomb to pray, and one of the pirs informed me that certain cures and miracles are yearly effected by the prayers offered up to the dead queen.

We went to see the Friday "prayer-meeting" in the finest mosque of this once-princely Mohammedan city. The Jummah Musjid, as the great mosque is called, is a quiet, unpretending structure. From a distance it is imposing, rather from the insignificance of the buildings in its vicinity than from any architectural claims of its own. But the interior is both simple and grand: the roof is exquisitely arched, and upheld by pillars of elegant design and workmanship. At the extreme end there is a raised platform whence the *moolah* * prays with his face turned toward Mecca, and behind this pulpit were hung heavy kinkaub curtains of native manufacture. The mosque was well filled, and the sight was both solemn and inspiring. More than a thousand men (with a few women sitting veiled and apart), all clad in flowing white robes, brilliant *cumberbunds*, and variegated turbans, rose, knelt, folded their hands and prostrated themselves simultaneously. The earnest voice of the *moolah*, the deep responses of the assembled congregation, their expressions of devotion and self-abasement, were sufficient to bring Christian and pagan into sympathy.

We rode next morning to the gardens and tomb of Shah Safid, "the pure saint." The rose, the jessamine, and the *mohgre* † bloomed here in great profusion; we noticed some beautiful birds hovering among the cypress and other trees, and we passed two splendid reservoirs full

* Mohammedan bishop. † A white rose, scented like a jessamine.

of fish, and enjoyed the quiet of this resting-place of the great friend and spiritual adviser of Aurungzebe. The mausoleum itself is a simple structure, without any architectural adornments. We did not see any of the descendants of this famous Mohammedan saint, but some holy men who did the honors of the gardens showed us all that was worth seeing, and the cemetery was a very bright, cheerful place in the morning sun.

There are four great eras in the history of India—the early dominion of the Brahmans, the Turk and Moslem invasion, then that of the Mohguls, and finally the rise of British sovereignty in Hindostan. Before introducing the reader to the peculiar rites and ceremonies of the Mohammedans of Hindostan, I have thought that the most important events of Mohgul invasion and occupation of India would not be out of place here.

It was about the beginning of the seventh century A. D. that first the Turks, and then the Afghans, obtained by means of their superior military discipline easy conquests over the Rajpoot chieftains. India was at this time in a most prosperous and happy condition, governed chiefly by the Brahmanic system of village communities. Each village was in itself a little republic, providing for and administering its own affairs through officers who were in all respects independent citizens, subject to none but the jurisdiction of the village itself, save in the case of war, when they volunteered to aid the Rajpoots in quelling such disturbances as arose. The Rajpoots, on the other hand, comprised the nobility and soldier-like chivalry of India. Romantic in their attachments, tenacious of their honor, devoted in their attentions to the softer sex,* they

* The practice of female infanticide among the Rajpoots may be traced to the conquest of India by the Turks and Afghans. Too haughty to give his daughter in marriage to a conqueror and enemy,

were ready to engage in deeds of daring and adventure. But, unhappily, they were divided into clans, each under its own chief, as among the Scotch Highlanders, which not infrequently were disturbed by internal feuds. They were easily subdued, one clan after another being dispersed or destroyed, until the greater part of Hindostan fell into the hands of the Moslem conquerors.

The expedition of Sultan Mahmood, undertaken in 1024 A. D., is the one most famed in Indian story. In the fair park-like province of Guzerat stood a wonderful Hindoo temple, none other than the famous temple of Swayan Nath, or "the Self-Existent," as the god was called. This god was worshipped here under the shape of a gigantic man formed of black stone. For his ablutions water was brought from the Ganjas, a thousand miles distant. The priests, devotees, and ascetics of this temple were numbered by hundreds; one thousand elephants belonged to it and were maintained for the service of the god. Stationed about the temple in superb trappings, they added an imposing feature to this shrine on festal occasions; banners of cloth of gold, standards of peacock-feathers gemmed with rare jewels, musical instruments of every kind and shape, with hundreds of hired musicians, formed part of the daily service here. Nor were these all: the dancing-girls attached to the temple were composed of the most beautiful women that India could furnish, and so great was the prestige of this shrine that kings dedicated their most beautiful daughters to enrich its coffers, in addition to the revenues of two thousand villages that were ceded to it by the combined princes of Hindostan.

Sultan Mahmood, who had seated himself on the throne

and unwilling that she should marry an inferior without a large dowry, the Rajpoot father got rid of the difficulties of his position by destroying his female children at the moment of birth.

of Delhi, heard one of the boasts uttered by the priests of this temple, and there and then vowed its destruction, placed himself at the head of his troops, and, marching four hundred miles overland through a barren and almost impassable country, advanced upon the environs of the temple, which were strongly fortified and garrisoned by Rajpoot soldiers. Twice the priests and soldiers of Swayan Nath beat back the Moslems, but in the third onslaught the latter bore down everything before them. In vain the Brahman priests implored them to spare the idol, offering the conqueror large sums of money for its ransom. Mahmood, regardless of their prayers and offers, gave the signal for its destruction. In an instant the huge god of stone was battered to pieces, and out of its hollow sides there rolled an immense treasure, jewels of inconceivable value. The spoils of this temple alone rendered the Mohguls all but invincible in the East. After sacking the temple they bore off in triumph its wondrous gates of sandal-wood inlaid with gold, and at the death of Mahmood, in 1030, these gates adorned the splendid mausoleum erected over his remains. Eight hundred years after they were captured by the English troops and restored to the temple of Swayan Nath by the order of Lord Ellenborough, then governor-general of India.

The Mohammedan capital in India was established at Delhi by Khottub, who made himself master of that city, of which he had been governor, about the year 1215. He was succeeded by Altinash, who, like Khottub, rose to the state of an emperor from the condition of a slave. The capital was now permanently fixed at Delhi, and it was in the reign of this king that the beautiful round tower of Khottub Minar, the highest known column in the world, was built. It is a minaret of fine red granite inlaid with white marble and crowned with a magnificent dome. This

Altinash was succeeded by his daughter Rhezeah, a woman of great natural ability, who administered the affairs of the kingdom with remarkable wisdom. Dressed as a sultan, she gave audience to her nobles and officers and heard and redressed the wrongs of her people. Nevertheless, the authority of these Mohammedan kings over the Rajpoot chiefs was very uncertain, for at every change in the government, which was very frequent, the Hindoo princes attempted to recover their independence. Thus when the Gheiyas Tooklak (or Toghlak) possessed himself of the throne of Delhi, the greater part of India was in a state of revolt.

Ferozee Shah, crowned emperor in 1351, greatly enriched and beautified the city of Delhi, built the great canal through the province of Delhi from the river Jumna to that of Caggar, two hundred miles of which have been reopened by the British government, thus fertilizing a vast tract of country which had long been a great desert. It was after the death of this prince that the Mohgul Timoor Lâng (Tamerlane), who had conquered Persia, captured and destroyed the city of Delhi. Years after Timoor Lâng's death one of his descendants, named Baber, once more established the Mohgul monarchy in India, about the year 1498, when the Portuguese maritime discoveries began to make an important revolution in the commercial world.

Baber was succeeded by the great emperor Homayoun, whose remains are marked by a magnificent tomb near Delhi. Akbar, his son, one of the wisest of the Mohgul rulers, had the prudence to marry a Hindoo princess, the daughter of Baharmal, the rajah of Jeypoor in the province of Rajpootana. He conquered the beautiful kingdom of Cashmere, one of the most enchanting spots in the world. He built the city and famous palace of Fettihpoor-

THE DEWANI-KHAS, DELHI.

Shikri in the province of Agra; his palace of white marble and a magnificent mosque are still to be seen in excellent preservation. It was in the reign of Akbar that Christian missionaries first received a hearing at a Mohammedan court. They were sent to Agra by the bishop of Goa. On Friday evenings it was also the custom of this prince to assemble all the learned men around him for the purpose of holding free discussions, where Mohammedans, Christians, Jews, Brahmans, and Fire-worshippers gave their opinions and discoursed about the most interesting themes of the day without restraint or fear. He also instituted free public schools for Mohammedan and Hindoo children.

Akbar died at Agra in 1605, and over his remains there still stands a splendid mausoleum of vast dimensions. He was succeeded by his son Selim, better known under the title which he assumed of Jehan Ghir, "conqueror of the world." The life and history of this king are the most romantic in the annals of India.

Noor Jehan, "the Dawn of Life," so well known by the name of Noor Mahal, or "the Light of the Palace," was the daughter of a poor Persian adventurer, a noble in his own country, reduced by a series of misfortunes at home, which led him to seek better fortunes in India, accompanied by his wife and little daughter. The distressed condition of the poor father and mother and the beauty of the child attracted the attention of a rich merchant of Candiesh, whose caravan these Persians had been following in order to keep themselves from starving. It was through this merchant's influence that the father of the little Noor Jehan obtained the subordinate position of gatekeeper at the court of Akbar. Noor Jehan, who was in the habit of playing round the palace-gate, attracted the attention of Akbar. Struck with her beauty, he at once introduced the little maiden to his Rajpootanee wife, with whom she became a great favorite, and thus the little Noor Jehan became the playmate and companion of the young prince Selim. A deep attachment sprang up between the children. But at length, when Noor Jehan attained the age of womanhood, her father suddenly withdrew her from the court and consummated a marriage for her with Shere Afkhan, a rich nobleman of Bengal, and thus removed the beautiful girl from her dangerous royal lover Selim. Selim was also married about the same time by Akbar to a foreign princess of Kabool. But the moment his father died, and Selim had ascended the throne under the name and title of Jehan Ghir, he determined to obtain the beautiful Noor Jehan for his wife. With this end in view he wrote to the viceroy of Bengal to seek some pretext to place Shere Afkhan in confinement that he might the more readily succeed in his designs. Shere Afkhan, suspecting some treachery on the part of the viceroy, repaired to his house fully armed, and, as certain hostile steps confirmed his suspicions, he slew the viceroy as he attempted to lay hands on him, but the guards in waiting, hearing the cry of their master, rushed in and despatched Shere Afkhan. That very night the emissaries of Jehan Ghir carried off Noor Jehan to Delhi.

But Noor Jehan, prisoner as she felt herself at the court of her former lover, refused to listen to his proposals of marriage until he should prove himself innocent of her husband's murder. After several years Jehan Ghir satisfied the beautiful widow that he had never intended Shere Afkhan's death, but only his temporary imprisonment in order to obtain her for his queen. Finally, the nuptials of Noor Jehan and Jehan Ghir were celebrated with splendor. The power and influence exercised by this beautiful woman at the Mohammedan court was unparalleled in the history of the Mohguls of India. Her name was associated with that of Jehan Ghir in the palace, in the council, on the throne, in the judgment-hall, and even on the coins of the country. Noor Mahal, or "the Light of the Palace," as she was ever after called, was more or less influenced by the counsels of her father, who was raised to the office of grand vizier, and is acknowledged to have been one of the best and wisest ministers who ever ruled at the court of a Mohammedan king.

Mohabat Khan, a noble in the service of Jehan Ghir, had somehow incurred the displeasure of Noor Mahal, but being a man of great talents he was employed to quell a rebellion entered into by Shah Jehan, the eldest son of Jehan Ghir, to dethrone his father. Having defeated the son and won him over to his cause, Mohabat Khan took the father prisoner. No sooner did Noor Mahal hear of the captivity of her husband than she placed herself at the head of her troops, and, mounted on an elephant, proceeded to give battle to Mohabat Khan and to rescue her husband. She was defeated, and fled to the court of Lahore for safety. But Mohabat, who had resolved to put Noor Mahal to death, extorted from Jehan Ghir a warrant to that effect, and through letters which he caused Jehan Ghir to write he induced the unsuspecting and loving wife to join her husband in captivity. Once in the enemy's camp, she saw that her death was determined upon. Professing herself willing to submit to her fate, she pleaded only a last interview with her husband, which Mohabat granted, but took care to be present himself. On the day appointed for her execution Noor Mahal quietly entered the presence of her unworthy husband and her implacable foe. She stood before them in deep silence, her hands clasped, her veil thrown back, and her beauty shining with an additional lustre through her flowing tears. Jehan Ghir burst into a passion of tears, and, throwing himself at the feet of his captor, pleaded so eloquently for her life that the heart of Mohabat was subdued. He not only granted her life, but, strange to say, became a friend to Noor Mahal, and finally restored her and her husband to the throne of Delhi.

With but few exceptions, however, rebellions, assassinations, treachery, and misrule marked the reigns of all the Mohammedan emperors of India. Upon the death of Aurungzebe, the grandson of Jehan Ghir, the empire of Hindostan was divided by his command between his three sons, which partition led to a series of most disastrous civil wars, and, happily for the country, almost terminated the Moslem power in India.

In 1738 the Persian emperor, Nahdir Shah, took Delhi with little effort. The night of the capture a report was raised that Nahdir Shah had died suddenly, and the populace rose *en masse* and massacred over seven thousand Persian soldiers. On the following day Nahdir Shah gave the fearful command which almost decimated the population of Delhi, after which he reinstated the humbled monarch, Mohammed Shah, on the throne, and returned to Persia, carrying away with him treasure amounting to seventy million pounds sterling and the celebrated peacock throne of Shah Jehan. In 1760 the nominal king of Delhi, Alum Shah, became tributary to the East Indian Company.

The Mohammedans of Hindostan, like those elsewhere, are divided into a number of sects, all more or less acknowledging the apostleship of Mohammed, but differing in their estimate of the inspiration of the Koran and other minor points of doctrine. The Sunnis, for instance, hold that the traditions of the Prophet are of equal authority with the Koran; they therefore venerate the successors of

Mohammed, Abu Bahkr, Omar, Usman, and Ali, as divinely-appointed Khalifahs or teachers; the Arabs, Turks, Afghans, and the Rohillas of India more or less belong to the Sunni sect. These undertake long pilgrimages to Mekka, and are very tenacious on points of doctrine, often putting to death the heterodox of their own religion. The Shiahs, another very powerful sect of Mohammedans, wholly reject the "Sunnahs," or traditions, and with them the four successors of the Prophet. They perform pilgrimages, not to Mecca or Medinah, but to the tomb of Husain at Kaibelah. The Koran is their only guide. The Shiahs are found in the vicinity of Cabool, Oude, and parts of Bundelcund.

The "Hanifi," as another sect of Mohammedans is called, are the disciples of Abu Hanifah, an Arabic theologian of great renown who flourished about the year 80 of the Hejira. He denied predestination as unworthy of a divine and merciful Creator, and declared fate to be nothing more or less than the free will of the individual. He was thrown into prison for his bold utterances, and died there. Years after, Maluk Shah Seljuki erected a splendid mausoleum to his memory in Bagdâd, to which spot his followers in Hindostan make special pilgrimages.

The Shaffids, again, are quite a distinct sect, so called from their leader Shaffid Abu Abdullah, another celebrated Arabic divine. He was born in the city of Gaza in Palestine in the year 150 of the Hejira, but educated in Persia, where he composed most of his works on theology and jurisprudence. Some of his precepts are still taught in the Shaffid Mohammedan schools. This sect is scattered over the province of Najapatam and in the city of Nagpoore.

The Maliki, still another of the Mohammedan denominations, follow the teachings of one Malik Ibn Aus, a man of some learning, but whose works are filled with astrology and mysticism. Many of his followers are to be found among the mendicants and fakeers of Hindostan.

The Hanbhali sect are not very numerous, but are said to be extremely dogmatic in their own belief. They adhere to the precepts of the priest after whom they are called, and deny the divine origin of the Koran, holding only such maxims contained in it as are based on pure morality and monotheism. These comprise the most advanced and enlightened schools of Mohammedans to be found in India to-day.

Last, but not least, are the Suffis, a refined, learned, and mystical sect of Mohammedans. They are divided among themselves on doctrinal points: some are pure rationalists, others materialists, and yet others again pantheists; the latter promulgate theories about the soul that are in form and idea similar to those of the high-caste and educated Brahmans.

Such are the most important sects to be found among the Mohammedans of Hindostan. Their intermixture with the Hindoos has produced a number of minor sects and classes of Musulmans, as well as a very marked change in their manners and customs. The Hindoos seem to have very greatly influenced the Mohammedans. The feeling of caste and defilement and other Hindoo restrictions have gradually assumed more and more importance in the Moslem mind in India. An Indian Mohammedan is hemmed about with endless observances reaching down even to preserving the sanctity of his pots and pans, as with the Brahmans. A Mohammedan will as religiously guard his "lota," or drinking-vessel, from defilement as if he were a high-caste Brahman, and superstition attaches to all his surroundings and habiliments and actions—to his earrings, which are worn as a charm, his sandals, his *topi*, or turban, his beard, and even his toe- and finger-nails, which can only be pared on certain days of the waxing moon. Thus it will be seen that the Mohammedan on Indian soil differs very greatly in his habits and feelings from the Mohammedan of Persia and Arabia. As the early Aryan accommodated himself to the deities and superstitions of the aboriginals, so the Mohammedan has greatly conformed to customs, manners, and superstitions indigenous almost to the soil of India.

This social fusion is especially perceptible in the condition of the women of Hindostan. The Hindoo woman has gradually borrowed the seclusion of the zenana from her aristocratic Mohammedan sister (the hareem and the zenana are but different names for one and the same thing), while the latter in her turn has adopted many of the rules and endless ceremonies of the Hindoos. Thus, for instance, marriage among the Mohammedans must be contracted very early, and solemnized when the youth is eighteen and the maiden thirteen. The courtship is always carried on by some elderly females, who are instructed to find out and report the charms of such young people among whose parents matrimonial connections are deemed desirable. This done, the astrologer, who is very often a Brahman, is consulted; he examines the horoscope of the young couple and decides whether the marriage will be auspicious and when it shall take place, etc. After this comes the betrothal, consisting of no less than six different ceremonies: First, a present of betel-leaves to the relatives of the young girl is given by the future bridegroom; these leaves are often folded in fine gold tissue-paper and stuck with cloves; each clove must be perfect, with the little blossom attached to the end of it. The second is called "sweet solicitations." The young man repairs to the young girl's house with attendants carrying presents, and in returning to his own bears back with him large presents of sweetmeats. This is followed by an important ceremony called "treading the threshold." At dawn the young man stands before the door of the young girl's home, repeats a prayer, and boldly crosses the threshold; here the mother embraces him, ties a colored handkerchief around his neck, puts a gold ring provided for the occasion on his finger, and fills his palms with money—signs of her cordial acceptance of him as a future son. This is followed by a three days' visit to the future bride's home; on each day he partakes of a meal every dish of which is some kind of sweetmeat; on the fourth day he joins the family at their ordinary meal, where the ceremony of sharing the salt takes place. The young woman, closely veiled, is seated by her lover; at the opening of the meal he takes some salt on his platter and transfers a part of it to her plate, and she does the same; this little act renders the marriage contract sacred. The day previous to the wedding is spent in purification, bathing, and anointing of the bride and bridegroom at their respective homes. The ceremonies are much like those of the Brahmans. The person of the young girl is rubbed over with a compound of grain, flour, turmeric, ashes of rose-leaves, and fragrant gums mixed into a paste with sweet oil. This preparation is laid on the person of the young woman, and left to dry for an hour or two, after which she is bathed with seven waters, four hot and three cold. This done, her fingers, toes, tips of her ears, and all the joints of her body are anointed with a mixture of sandal-wood powder, ashes of burnt rose-buds, and sweet oil, after which she is sprinkled with rose-water, and conveyed, all closely veiled, to the mosque, where she repeats seven Kalimahs for herself and her future husband.

On this day a procession in order to exchange wedding-garments from one to the other takes place.

The marriage ceremony is always performed in the evening. I was present at the marriage of the daughter of a moolah (or Mohammedan bishop) named Allih Bashka Deen, and the ceremony derived its chief attraction from the gentle loveliness of the bride and the beauty of her dress. She wore a purple silk petticoat embossed with a rich border of scattered bunches of flowers, each flower formed of various gems, while the leaves and stems were of embroidered gold and silk threads. Her boddice was of the same material as the petticoat; the entire vest was marked with circular rows of pearls and rubies. Her hair was parted in Greek style and confined at the back in a graceful knot bound by a fillet of gold; on her brow rested a beautiful flashing star of diamonds. On her ears, neck, arms, breast, and waist were a profusion of ornaments. Her slippers, adorned with gold and seed pearls, were open at the heels, showing her henna-tinted feet, and curved up in front toward the instep, while from her head flowed a delicate kinkaub scarf woven from gold threads of the finest texture and of a transparent, dazzling, sunbeam-like appearance. This was folded gracefully about her person and veiled her eyes and nose, leaving only her mouth and chin visible.

While the guests, relatives, and friends of the bride were all assembled at the bishop's house the bridegroom had started off to perform what is called the "shaba ghash," or nocturnal visit. Gayly dressed, handsomely mounted, the young Akbar Khanibni Ahbad, attended by his nearest relatives and friends and accompanied by a host of musicians, rode to the mosque at Kirki, where he offered up three distinct prayers—one for the future wife, one for himself, and one for the happiness and success of all his undertakings, especially the one he was about to consummate. This done, he and his friends mounted and approached the house of the bride. The moment the cavalcade of the bridegroom appeared in sight a number of well-dressed young Mohammedans rushed to the gate of the courtyard, and with loud shouts most violently opposed his entrance, whereupon he scattered money in handfuls among them, which was the signal for them to give way. Here the youth dismounted, but was not permitted to walk into the house, for a stalwart-looking man took him up in his arms and attempted to rush in with him; here again he was once more resisted by another party of friends and relatives, till he again scattered a handful of gold coins among them, thus carrying out the Oriental saying: "He lined the path to his love with golden flowers." After this no further opposition was made. The bride and bridegroom, both veiled, the latter with two coverings over his face, took their places in the centre of the room, and every one stood up. The khazi, or judge, then stepped forward, and, having removed the double veil from the bridegroom's face, began the ceremony. The young man repeated after him certain prayers—one deprecating his own merits and attractions in comparison with those of the bride—after which came long repetitions from the Koran treating of fervor, love, and devotion, followed by repetitions of the Mohammedan creed and a general thanksgiving. At this point all the assembly prostrated themselves, the khazi joined the hands of the bride and bridegroom, the latter repeated word for word the marriage-vows, and the whole was concluded with a benediction, after which the bride, still veiled, was carried to the bridegroom's house, and he followed in her train, accompanied with music, beating of drums, and loud shouts of joy from his attendants and followers.

On the birth of a child. if it happens to be a male, all the female attendants utter loud shouts of joy. The mother is kept on very simple diet, and obliged to drink water made hot by a heated horseshoe being plunged into it; this has the power of guarding against internal devils, who are supposed to be very active on such occasions, lying in wait for mother and child. The moolah is then ushered into the chamber: he takes the child in his arms and repeats in his right ear the Mohammedan summons to prayer, and in his left the creed. A fakeer is then introduced: he dips his finger in some honey and puts it into the child's mouth before it has tasted any of its mother's milk, which is to ensure it all the luxuries of life. After these have retired an astrologer casts the horoscope of the child, and there and then predicts its future, which, good or bad, is accepted as fate and without a murmur. Meanwhile, the nearest relatives assemble around the father and dress his hair with blades of grass—a Hindoo observance, grass typifying the fragility of human life and affections—and he in turn makes them presents according to his circumstances.

The naming of the child takes place on the eighth day after birth. If a son, it is named after the father's clan or tribe; if a daughter, after the mother's side of the family. The choice of the child's name depends on the day of its birth and the appearance of the planet under whose influence it is supposed to be born, as much as on the parentage. The mother remains apart from the household till the fortieth day after childbirth; then she is bathed, fumigated, and purified, and so prepared to enter the mosque, where she offers up thanks for her safe deliverance from the perils of childbirth, and either reads or has portions of the Koran read to her, offering a sacrifice of two goats for a son and one for a daughter.

On the same day, in the afternoon, another ceremony is held—that of shaving the hair of the child. A priest and a barber attend to this rite; prayers are offered, water is sprinkled over the head of the child, and the hair shaved off is carried in procession to the water's edge, and then launched on a little raft to float down the river. By this ceremony all evil is guarded from the infancy and childhood of Mohammedan children. Very often sacred locks are left on the top of the heads of Mohammedan children, like those of the Brahmans, and these locks are consecrated to some saint or noble ancestor.

The other ceremony worthy of notice here is that attending the death and burial of the Mohammedans in India. When a Mohammedan is thought to be dying a priest is sent for, who prays before the family, then repairs to the sick chamber, where he exhorts the dying man to attend to the welfare of his soul, and proceeds to read the chapter on future life, rewards, and punishments, and the two most important creeds—faith in God and in Mohammed as his prophet. After death the body is placed on a bier and conveyed with great pomp, beating of drums, wailing of women and near relatives, to the Musulman cemetery, where there are always tanks and utensils for bathing the dead before interment. Here the body is carefully washed seven times, and then perfumed with powdered sandal-wood, camphor, and myrrh. The forehead, hands, knees, and feet of the dead man are especially rubbed; these parts, having touched the earth at moments of prayer, are held more sacred than the rest of the body. The two great toes are then tied together; a shroud or winding-sheet, prepared by the dead man himself, on which he has caused to be written from time to time the most beautiful passages from the Koran, is folded around him very firmly and around each arm. After this the body is replaced on the bier, every one salutes it, and the bearers carry it to the grave. Here all the friends and relatives stand in three rows, and at the head of every row is a priest, who solemnly begins the chant, consisting chiefly of prayers and confessions for the dead. The body is at length lowered into the grave with its face toward Mecca, and each relative, taking a little earth in his hand, repeats the solemn utterance of their Prophet, made in the name of God and his archangel Gabriel: "We created you, O man, out of earth, and we return you to the earth, and we shall raise you up again on the last day," and throws the earth softly on the bier. The grave is then closed, and fatiahs, or prayers for the dead, are offered on the spot at stated seasons throughout the first year.

CHAPTER XII.

The Temples of Ellora, the Holy Place of the Deccan.—Nashik, the Land of the Râmâyanâ.—Sights and Scenes on the Banks of the Godaveri.—Damaun, the most famous of the Indo-Portuguese Towns.

We bade adieu to the old historical city of the great Aurungzebe just as the first streak of sunlight was gilding the conical summit of the fortress of Dowlutabâd, and, wending our way laboriously up the steep Pipla Ghaut, we emerged on the other side on a fertile plain planted with magnificent trees and covered with innumerable mausoleums and tombs, through which our bullocks made straight for the western boundary of the beautiful hill of Rauzah. Here we reached a spot of perfect tranquillity and beauty, but which must have been at some ancient time a scene of intense activity. The present little village of Ellora, consisting of a number of Hindoo dwellings, is almost hidden among groves of fine trees, and is only remarkable because it lies immediately at the foot of a high wall of rock in which the vast cavern-temples of this neighborhood are found and to which it owes its prosperity.

We alighted from our wagons on the verandah of a well-built pagoda; near it was a fine reservoir with flights of broad stone steps leading down to the water's edge. On the bank or upper stonework of this reservoir are a number of artistic little Hindoo temples or shrines, the roofs supported by light delicate pillars, giving an airy and graceful appearance to the whole village. As soon as Govind had gone through his prayers and ablutions we started off, accompanied by a couple of sage-looking Hindoo guides, for the cavern-temples. We followed our guides for some little distance, when they left the highroad and struck a narrow, steep path, and all at once, when we were least expecting it, a sudden turn brought us into the presence of the great "rock-cut temples" that render this spot the holiest of all places in the Deccan. Down went Govind and our guides prostrate on their faces and hands.

The solitude, the quiet stillness of the spot, with the bright morning sun flooding hill and plain and penetrating the depths of these excavations, were impressive. The temple before us was a large open court and deep vaulted chamber, massive and elaborately carved, and chiselled from the heart of the mountain itself, and rising up nearly a hundred feet. There were many other temples in the hillside, with doorways, arches, pillars, windows, galleries, and verandahs, supported by solid stone pillars filled with figures of gods and goddesses, heroes, giants, birds, beasts, and reptiles of every shape—quite enough to baffle the most careful student in anything like a thorough examination of their vast and intricate workmanship.

We went in and out, climbing stone-cut steps up, down, and round about the caves, not knowing which temple to admire most or on which to bestow undivided attention. It would take weeks to explore them thoroughly. There is a very fine cavern-temple dedicated to Pur Sawanath, "the Lord of Purity," the twenty-third of the great saints of the Jains of this era.* An image resembling those

* Pur Sawanath and Mah-vira, the twenty-third and twenty-fourth pontiffs of the present era of the Jains, seem to have superseded all the former saints in sanctity of character. They are described by the Jains

that are seen of Buddha, stone tigers, and elephants bear up the altar on which he is seated; from the middle of the altar there projects a curious wheel on which is carved the Hindoo astronomical table, and a seven-headed serpent is seen over the head of the god.

Another very beautiful excavation, consisting of three temples or compartments, is dedicated to Jaggar-Nath Buddh, or "the Enlightened Lord of the Universe;" these temples are best known, however, by the name of Indra Sabha, or "the assembly of Indra." These caves are two-storied, containing images of Indra—"the darter of the swift blue bolt," as he is called—seated on a royal elephant, with his attendants about him, and of Indranee, his wife, riding on a couchant lion, with her son in her arms and her maids around her. The sacred trees of the Hindoos—*Kalpa Vriksha,* the tree of the ages or of life—are growing out of their heads; on the one overshadowing Indra are carved peacocks, emblematic of royalty, and fruits resembling the rose-apple, sacred to love, grow on

as having thirty-six superhuman attributes of mind and body—beauty of form, fragrance of breath; curling hair, which does not increase in length or decrease in quantity, the same qualities being attached to their beards and nails; a white complexion, exemption from all impurities, hunger, decay, bodily infirmity or disease of any kind. The spiritual attributes are those of justice, truth, faith, love, benevolence, freedom from all anger and all earthly desires, immense power of devotion; hence of working miracles, of making themselves heard at vast distances, speaking intelligibly to men, animals, and gods, of materializing spirits and conversing with them, and the power of scattering war, plague, famine, storms, death, sickness, or evil of any kind by their immediate presence. The heads of these Jain saints are always described as surrounded with a halo of light, whose brightness is greater and more far-reaching than that of the sun. The Brahmans, it is said, with great adroitness, in order to draw to these temples the Jain pilgrims from Guzerat, Bombay, and other parts of India, take care to represent their god Parshurama, an incarnation of Vishnu, to be none other than the Jain saint, Pur Sawanath.

the one sprouting from the head of Indranee. This temple is unrivalled for its beauty of form and sculpture.

The next temple we visited was the Dho Máhal Lenah, "the double palace." It is full of figures and sculptured story celebrating the marriage of the god Siva with Parvatee. It is an excavation of great depth and extent, filled with countless gods and goddesses, among which the figure of Yama, the judge of the dead, commonly called Dhannah, is especially remarkable. Not far from this cavern-temple a lovely mountain-torrent comes leaping down in beautiful cascades. Near a wide pool is a rude cave with a deity in it called Dàvee, who draws multitudes of pilgrims to her shrine yearly because of her reputation for performing miracles.

There is also a temple famous in Indian song and story called Khailahsah, or "highest heaven." The mountain has been penetrated to a great depth and height to make room for this wondrous bit of sculpture. Within an area stands a pagoda almost, if not quite, a hundred feet high. It is entered by a noble portico guarded by huge stone figures of men; towering above it are, cut out of the hill, a music-gallery of the finest workmanship and five large chapels, and above all there is in front a spacious court terminating in three magnificent colonnades: huge columns uphold the music-gallery; stone elephants, looking toward us, heave themselves out of this mass of rock-work, and right in front is a grand figure of the Hindoo goddess Lakshimi being crowned queen of heaven by stone elephants, that have raised themselves on their hind feet to pour water over her head from stone vessels grasped in their trunks.

Everywhere we found fresh objects of wonder, and each new cave seemed the greatest marvel of all. The entire hillside is perforated with chatiyas, monasteries, pagodas, towers, spires, obelisks, galleries. and verandahs, all cut out of the solid rock.* Nothing could be wilder and more fantastic than the effect produced by these excavations, situated as they are amid natural scenes very wild and romantic—waterfalls, ravines, gorges, old gnarled forest trees, and a dense undergrowth of brushwood.

Naturally, freely, unexpectedly, as the tree grows, was the development of early Hindoo art. Everywhere one sees an unrestrained imagination breaking through and overleaping the bounds of judgment, reason, and even that intuitive sense of refinement to which the Hindoo mind is by no means a stranger.

Our journey next was quite an adventurous one. We started straight across the high plain of the Deccan for the Thull Ghauts. In some parts the country is sandy and desolate, and in others well cultivated, but in no way remarkable till we reached the rugged but grandly mountainous country through which our road lay, circuitous and difficult, but wild and beautiful, as far as Nashik, or "the City of the Nose," sacred to the Hindoos for various local traditions, but above all as being the spot whence the Godaveri takes its rise. The real source of this famous river, however, is some eighteen or twenty miles distant, at Thrimbâk. On our road lay a deep and dangerous nullah or creek, which we forded with much difficulty, assisted by a number of natives whom we were obliged to hire from a little village lying half a mile from its banks. Passing this, we saw the Ghauts for the first time, with their fine forests, and here and there a mountain-stream, not yet dried up by the hot summer sun, tumbling down the mountain-sides or flowing over pebbly beds,

* Those who desire to have a detailed account of these caves will find an admirable description of them given by Col. Sykes in the third volume of the *Bombay Asiatic Society's Transactions.*

sometimes gleaming into the sunlight and sometimes hidden in verdure, and anon lying in deep eddying pools at the foot of the Ghauts, that rise up grand and defiant on every side.

With their forests of foliage and rich jungles the Thull Ghauts are a perpetual wonder and mystery to the natives, and the spot on which the handsome city of Nashik stands is a paradise to the Brahmans. Through it the Godaveri, sometimes called the Gunga, flows, spreading gladness and plenty everywhere. Here it was that Rama, with his beautiful wife Sita, spent the first days of their exile near a dark and dreadful forest, out of which issued the beautiful deer in pursuit of which he was obliged to leave Sita, who became an easy prey to his enemy Rawana. Here Lakshman, the brother of Rama, cut off the nose of the giantess Sarp Naki, the snake-nosed sister of Rawana, from which event the city itself is named.

There is doubtless an historical basis to all these local traditions, for Nashik is a place of great antiquity, and is mentioned by Ptolemy by the name which it bears to-day. This land was no doubt at one time debatable ground between the advancing Aryan tribes and the aboriginal settlers. Here the Buddhists took refuge from the persecutions of the orthodox Brahmans, excavating the temples and caves that abound in this region.

Nashik is now a Brahman city in the fullest sense of the word. Brahmanic power, influence, culture, and tradition are felt everywhere. Govind, our pundit, was in his best humor. It seems he had long desired to make a pilgrimage to this sacred spot, and here he was without any actual expense to himself and at the right moment. Nashik is said to have a population of from twenty-five to thirty thousand inhabitants, chiefly Brahmans of great wealth and famed for their religious sanctity of character.

At the jatras, or tribe-meetings, a great concourse of Brahmans, Hindoos, Rajpoots, and Mahrattas from all parts of India pour into this city, and our visit happened at this time, for the pilgrims were arriving from all parts of the Eastern world. Most of the streets are, like those usually found in Oriental cities, narrow, ill-drained, and badly paved, but there are some that are well kept, and a fine broad thoroughfare leads almost, but not quite, through the centre of the city to the banks of the Godaveri. The lofty houses of the Brahmans, many of which are three stories high and almost palatial in appearance, were thrown open to the strangers. Pilgrims thronged the streets and were encamped along the roadside in tents in the open air or under the shade of huge trees. Highways lead everywhere down to the river, whose sanctity may be conceived from the vast numbers and characteristics of the temples that line its banks and dot the islands and rocks in the river-bed, nearly all built of a hard black rock capable of high polish, and some in the purest style of Hindoo architecture.

As we were detained here a couple of days, being obliged to purchase a fresh pair of trotting bullocks in order to prosecute the rest of our journey, we determined to stay over and see the celebration of the *Holi*, one of the most curious festivals among the Hindoos. We took up our abode in the travellers' bungalow, some little distance from the native city, and looking out upon the English burying-ground. It is a charming spot, with a wild tangle of trees forming a sort of garden around it.

The native town of Nashik seems to be divided into three parts, the handsome and well-built portion being occupied by the wealthy Brahmans, *vakeels*, or lawyers, and *gurus*, or priests. The second division, which bears marks of great age and is not very sightly, is inhabited by merchants and traders in grain and other articles of Indian commerce. The bazaars are remarkably well stocked with shawls brought from Cashmere, silks and kinkaubs from Aurungabâd, *gowrakoo*, a native manufacture of tobacco and used for smoking, and *jaggery*, a dark-brown sugar from Bombay. In the jewellers' shops we saw some very pretty specimens of gold and silver ornaments, such as are worn by Hindoo women. The vegetable and fruit markets here are very fine. Among the fruits large trays of beautiful flowers were disposed, of which the rose of Nashik seemed to me the finest I had seen in India. Sheep, goats, and cows wander about the streets of the bazaar unmolested. Indeed, I saw cows putting their heads into the open grain-bags exposed on the shop-windows of the *bunyas* or grain-dealers, and have a good feed, for there was no one to hinder them.

One day, as we were wandering about the streets of Nashik, we strayed into an open court, and thence through an arched entrance, into a large hall, where we suddenly came upon a company of men weaving a peculiar and beautiful Oriental silk. The loom was of the old-fashioned Indian type, set into the ground; the upper thread was of a pale-gold color, and the lower of the most exquisite blue, and the fabric after it was woven had a little knot of yellow left on the surface, which gave it the appearance in one light of being woven of gold threads, and in another light of pale blue. A number of women were seated close by preparing the silk thread for the weavers by means of a very rude spinning-wheel.

From the bazaars we set off to visit some of the most artistic temples that embellish the banks of the Godaveri. There are five structures here to-day in great repute: the temples of Maha Dèo, or the high god, Siva, Parvati, Indra, and *Jaggar Nath*, commonly called Juggernaut.

Each of these temples has a large number of laymen, priests, and priestesses, or dancing-girls, attached to them. The dancing-girls were seen everywhere in the temples, on the banks of the river, and in the booths erected here and there, performing their various dances for the amusement of the pilgrims, and some of these girls were of the finest type that I have seen in any part of India.

We went into the temple of Maha Dèo, which contains some very rich and bold carvings. A figure of a god was seated on a stone altar, and all over the shrine were scattered flowers, oil, and red paint, or "shaindoor." At the door of this temple we saw seated a very old woman, who, they told me, was once a famous beauty and a priestess of this temple. She sat there muttering idly to herself and basking in the sunlight. Age had very forcibly set its seal upon her. Her skin was drawn into the most complicated network of wrinkles, her arms were almost devoid of flesh, and her limbs were as feeble and tottering as those of an infant just attempting to walk; but her eyes, large, dark, and piercing, still retained a great deal of their original beauty. The people, however, regarded her as one inspired, and the women attached to the temple had a tender care for her, taking her into an adjoining chamber every night to sleep, bringing her out to her accustomed place every morning, and feeding her at regular intervals.

On the banks of the Godaveri is shown a spot where women without number have become suttees, or, as they called them here, Sadhwees, or "pure ones." At a very gentle curve of the river are the cremation-grounds of the Hindoos, and here the ashes of men burned at a distance are brought and scattered in the holy stream, which is thought to have its source in the heart of the great Maha Dèo himself.

Next morning, when we issued into the streets of Nashik once more, the scene that presented itself to our astonished gaze was that of a vast multitude gone mad. Crowds of women dressed in fantastic attire, especially in white- and yellow-spotted muslin sarees, men in curious garbs, boys dressed like sprites or wholly nude and besmeared with yellow paint, fakeers, gossains, ascetics, Hindoos, and Brahmans, were seen in the streets shouting, laughing, throwing red paint about; rude jests were being passed; women were addressed in obscene or ribald language; persons blindfolded in the streets were left to grope their way until they removed the bandage from their eyes, friends sent on bootless errands, etc. In fact, it was a complete saturnalia of the rudest and most grotesque description. It was the festival of the *Holi*,* held in honor of Krishna's sportive character on the night of the full moon in the month of February.

That evening we went out on the banks of the Godaveri to see the termination of the festival, and it is simply impossible to describe the wild enthusiasm of this vast concourse of people. The banks of the river, the steps of the numberless temples, the courts within courts, the shrines, the altars, the great halls and music-galleries with forests of carved pillars, were closely packed with countless throngs of white-robed priests, half-naked gossains, or sparkling dancing-girls, while thousands of men, women, and children lined the banks of the Godaveri, eager and enthusiastic participants in the gay, bewildering scene. As we stood gazing at the strange spectacle we heard the wild, discordant sounds of various musical instruments, the shrill blast of innumerable conch-shells, and the deafening beat of the tom-toms, whereupon huge fires began

* A most popular Hindoo festival held all over Hindostan in honor of Krishna.

to blaze almost simultaneously from shore to shore at regular distances, and everywhere round them groups of strangely dressed boys performed weird circular dances, holding each other's hands and going around them; then, suddenly letting loose, they darted and leaped round and round one another and round the fire at the same time. This dance is ostensibly performed to commemorate the dance of the god Krishna with the seven gowpiahs, or milkmaids, but there is scarcely a doubt that this festival originally meant to typify the revolution of the planets round the sun.

The light from these blazing fires streaming out upon the moonlit river, the wild discordant music, the hilarious shouts, the frantic dancers, the sparkle of the dancing-girls, the white-robed figures of the countless multitude, now flashing in sight in the glare of the firelight, and anon vanishing in the deep shadows beyond, the piles of black temples, the great trees with their arms bending down to the river or stretching toward the clear sky,—all combined to render the last night of the festival of the Holi at Nashik a most weird and singularly fantastic sight.

From the first to the last day of our visit here there was nowhere perceptible the least trace of European influence on the people or in the city. The people and the city were just what they might have been in the days when Ptolemy wrote about the latter, purely and wholly Hindoo, and full of a Brahmanic atmosphere of religious mysticism —a civilization quite different from anything we had ever witnessed.

There are a number of curious excavations in this neighborhood, about five miles from the town, in the side of a hill that overhangs the highway from Bombay. The hill as well as these cavern-temples is called Pandulená. We rode out on fine horses hired from a native stable close to the bazaar. The ride out was delightful, the views of the country at once grand and beautiful, but the excavations were much less interesting than had been reported to us by Govind, and in no way comparable to the wondrous structures of Ellora. There is one cave here, however, that has a superior finish. The roof is finely arched; the dogaba, or memorial structure, stands at the end and is well executed. Another cave with idols of seated figures has a flat roof, and is not very interesting, save that near it is carved in a niche a huge figure of Buddha. The chief idol here is called Rajah Dhanna—*i. e.* "judge of the dead"—and is held most sacred by the pilgrims, who were now beginning to arrive here in strong numbers. The odors of the stuff with which the filthy gossains rub themselves and their altogether disgusting appearance sent us hastily back to our quiet lodge, and early next morning we bade adieu for ever to Nashik.

From Nashik to Trimbak, eighteen or twenty miles, the country is one of unrivalled beauty. Trimbak is a very sacred spot, where the Godaveri really takes its rise, and is wholly given up to the Hindoo and Brahman pilgrims, who were pouring into the place from all the country round. It is filled by a class of priests whose sole duty it is to instruct pilgrims in the right way to worship and to receive the gifts bestowed on the temples. The houses of these priests adjoin the temples; they lodge the pilgrims without any charge, but each person generally leaves at the temple a gift which exceeds the cost of his stay. We had no time to examine the temples here, for we spent only a night at Trimbak, and started next morning, traversing circuitous roads, crossing some small nullahs, and by dint of travelling all day and night reached the next important halting-place, which was no other than Damaun, a famous old Portuguese town.

The town of Damaun, with its ramparts, gateways, and bastions, is picturesquely situated. There is on one side of it a fine old fortress baptized after a Christian saint and called the "Castle of St. Hieronymus," and on the other a deep, navigable river which still bears the favorite Hindoo name of Gunga. The country all round Damaun is well cultivated. The tara palm, the castor oil, the babool, or *Acacia arabica*,* were seen in the gardens and plantations. But the interior of the Portuguese town struck me as gloomy and exceedingly filthy, and, though it was full of people—Mohammedans, Hindoos, and Christians, with even Jews and Parsees—it lacked that air of sprightliness and vivacity so noticeable in a purely Hindoo population. It was neither one thing nor the other—not wholly pagan, and only partially Christian. The Roman Catholic chapel here was once a grand mosque.

Through the kind introduction of a Portuguese friend we were most cordially received in the home of a venerable native Portuguese named Johnna Castello. The household consisted of himself and the families of two married sons; one of the ladies was indisposed, but the other, Donna Caterina, did the honors of hostess in a simple and unpretending manner. Our pundit had an outhouse placed at his disposal. The establishment did not boast of many rooms, and those in which we were lodged were rough and poorly built of wood. Our meals consisted of rice and curry, fish, *kabobs*,† kid and fowl pillau, with a variety of fine fruits and vegetables. Our meals were served apart and in European style, but the quantity

* A genus of leguminous trees and shrubs, usually with thorns and pinnate leaves, and of an airy and elegant appearance. It is found in all the tropical parts of both the Old World and the New, and also in Australia and Polynesia. A few species only are found in temperate climates.

† Small pieces of meat seasoned and roasted on a skewer.

of onion and garlic with which almost every dish was seasoned helped much toward shortening our stay here. Besides which, it seemed to me that everything was pickled, from the pork (of which the native Portuguese are very fond) to the young bamboo-shoots. At every fresh course some half a dozen hot, biting pickles were handed around.

My womanly curiosity led me into the kitchen of this very well-to-do Portuguese family. It was in keeping with the rest of the place. It was a low wooden structure, black with smoke and age; a long range of open fire-places, made of brick and mortar, ran along on one side; on these earthen *chatties*, or earthen pots, were boiling away, some covered and others uncovered; but hanging from the roof above these pots were long lines of blackened cobwebs that looked as if they had remained undisturbed for a hundred years. The servants were all men, native Christians, and were overlooking the cooking or attending to various culinary duties. They were filthy beyond measure, and so was every nook and corner of the kitchen. The native Portuguese in this old-fashioned city of Damaun struck me as peculiarly uninteresting in their manners and appearance. We saw them in the streets, seated on the verandahs or doorsteps of their houses, chattering or laughing or quarrelling with their neighbors in shrill, harsh tones and with ungraceful gestures. In some aspects Oriental Christianity seems even more degrading than the worst form of paganism.

In the afternoon of the same day, as we were walking about the town, we passed a wedding-procession on its way to the Roman Catholic church, which served in some slight degree to soften the unfavorable impression produced by the people and the town. It was a gaudy sight. Sheets were spread along the street leading to the steps of the chapel; flowers, chiefly the oleander, the rose, and the *mohgre,** were scattered all over these sheets by dark-skinned Portuguese girls dressed in long white trousers and old-fashioned pink frocks. Presently the church-bells began to tinkle merrily, and a company of dark-hued damsels issued in full sight, dressed in tinsel and gold, with long white muslin veils, almost like the Hindoo sarees, bound round their persons. The bride was closely veiled from head to foot in something that looked like the *purdah* † worn by Mohammedan women. We could not see her, but I pleased myself with imagining that she was young and beautiful. Close to her were two young women bearing lighted torches, and in the foremost rank were two Portuguese priests, who led the way to the chapel (once a mosque), each bearing a silver-mounted crucifix. The bridegroom brought up the rear dressed as an English general, with a dark-blue embroidered frock-coat, golden epaulettes, scarlet pantaloons, sword, and a cocked hat with feathers, accompanied by at least twelve other native gentlemen similarly attired; but many of these grand-looking officers were barefooted. This grotesque procession rushed into the chapel in unseemly haste, and we followed. There was nothing very remarkable in the exterior of this chapel. But within, the principal altar was very richly adorned with gilt images of Christ, the Virgin, and saints, with handsome candlesticks and a great deal of gold and tinsel. There seemed to be but few seats. Before the marriage ceremony began the bride dropped her purdah, or veil, and, to my surprise, I found that she was both ugly and old, and about to be married to the young fellow in the general's cos-

* A white flower very much like a double jessamine, with much the same fragrance.

† A veil that covers the whole person.

tume, who certainly looked young enough to be her son. She was a rich old widow, which explained the matter. We did not wait to see the ceremony, as our stay here was limited to two days, and this was our last one in Damaun.

After nightfall, as I looked out upon this strange, semi-Christian, semi-pagan city, old and weather-stained, poorly lighted, and upon that river named after a Hindoo goddess flowing by so sluggishly, but which, after the rainy season, often becomes a cruel foe to the peasant and cultivator, I felt somehow that it was one of the most dismal places in the world, in spite of its peculiar advantages of a rich soil and sea-views. Next morning, through the kind offices of our host, who assisted us in procuring a comfortable berth on board a native craft called a patemar,* we found ourselves sailing before a fine breeze, bound straight for Surat, one of the most ancient and well-known seaports of Western India.

* A patemar is a coasting vessel, built generally in Bombay. It has prow and stern alike, double planked—a handsome craft of about two hundred tons burden, with two masts and great wide lateen sails.

CHAPTER XIII.

The Taptee River.—Surat and its Environs.—The Borahs and Kholees of Guzerat.—Baroda, the Capital of the Guicowars.—Fakeers, or Relic-Carriers, of Baroda.—Cambay.—Mount Aboo.—Jain Temples on Mount Aboo, etc.

THE views along the Western Ghauts and the coast are very grand. We soon lost sight of all their varied beauty, and in a couple of days entered the splendid river Taptee, which flows broad and deep immediately under the walls of the city of Surat.

Almost at the mouth of the Taptee stands a lovely little island; opposite to this is a little town called Domus, a quaint, homelike-looking place, where Europeans spend the hot months. The river flows for miles through a richly-cultivated suburb of gardens, plantations, and beautiful houses, till it reaches the city, which is walled with bastions at certain points, but the walls and towers are fast crumbling away. At one extremity stands the famous old castle of Surat, about three hundred years old, looking older and more stained with time and age than even the fortress of Damaun.

Surat has a double wall and twice twelve gates, inner and outer, communicating with one another. But its history is even more varied and complicated than its "world-protecting" walls and wooden-leaved gates. It is written in the ruins found everywhere in the gardens, palaces of the nawabs, rajahs, and peishwas, as well as in the factories of the Dutch, French, Portuguese, and English, most of which are now transformed into hospitals, lunatic asylums, hotels for European travellers, or pleasure-houses and grounds for wealthy natives.

Here are also grand English and Dutch cemeteries, where many noted English and Dutch lie magnificently entombed in stately mausoleums, in order to impress the Oriental mind, which is always disposed to attach a certain kind of sanctity to piles of brick, mortar, and stone, whether priest, prophet, or knave lie interred beneath.

We tried to visit the "Pinjrapoore," or hospital for sick animals, here; it seems to be arranged much on the same plan as that in Bombay, but this place was too filthy to enter, and in that respect much inferior. Attached to it are large granaries, where all the damaged grain of the bazaars is piled up for the use of the sick animals in the hospital; and this it is which has rendered this place a perfect pest-house of insects and vermin of all kinds.

Fire-temples and towers of silence are numerous here, as Surat has a large Parsee community, who have been established in this region ever since the eighth century. The most curious and interesting people in this part of the world are the Borahs, the Jains, and Buniahs.

The Borahs are divided into two classes, the traders and the cultivators. They are Hindoos converted to Mohammedanism; they form the most active and industrious cultivators of the soil, as well as cotton- and cloth-merchants. Their dress, manners, and language are the same as those of the Hindoos. Cotton is the chief staple. The Borahs occupy an entire street in Surat, and it is especially distinguished as being the cleanest in the native town. Their houses are spacious and well built, with fine open balconies. Their women are well treated. They support here a number of Mohammedan priests, a bishop—have a fine mosque wherein to worship, and one of the best colleges in this part of the country, where the Borah youths receive a thorough commercial education.

The Buniahs are almost identical with the Borahs in their trading and commercial qualifications. They are the great grain-merchants here and everywhere. They are also divided into three classes—the cultivators, the wholesale merchant, and the petty retailer, who travels from village to village with his grain-bags on his shoulders. The Buniahs, however, are Hindoos in religion as well as by birth.

The Jains, of whom mention has already been made, are seen in great numbers in the streets and bazaars. Their dress is a long white robe descending in full folds from the shoulders to the feet, and over the shoulders is thrown another long loose piece of white cloth; the head and beard are closely shaven. But the most striking peculiarity is a bit of white cloth of fine texture which they wear over the mouth to prevent them from destroying, by inhaling into their lungs, the minutest insect life. They are always found with a little broom in their hands, no matter where they go, so as to sweep the ground before seating themselves, with the same end in view—the preservation of all insect life; for this purpose they walk very slowly with their eyes cast on the ground. To destroy life, even unintentionally, is the inexpiable sin, and a Jain will not drink any water until he has strained it, nor will he take any meal or drink of any kind after sunset, lest he should happen to devour some living thing. The Jains have some fine temples in this city.

Surat was long in the possession of the Mohgul emperors. In 1842 the last nawab died, and it passed into the hands of the East India Company. It is still a great trading city; the surtee rassum, or manufactured silk of Surat, is very beautiful; the gold and silver ornaments sold in the bazaars are unique and of fine workmanship. Surat is also famous for the weaving of many varieties of cotton cloths; these are usually woven in small chequered patterns with bright and elegant borders. Potteries are not only numerous, but some pottery of very fine form and quality is sold in the bazaars and is said to be of home manufacture.

The last day we spent in Surat was passed in driving through the suburbs in a native wagon drawn by a fine pair of humpbacked white bullocks (zebus), who carried us rapidly over the ground. We alighted at the palace of the last nawab, called at once the "gift of God" and the "seat of oppression." Of its being the former there is no trace, but the shadow of the latter name seems still to fall upon the partially deserted place. Apart from the collection of Persian and Arabic manuscripts to be seen in a room adjoining the palace of the nawab, there is nothing to interest the curious visitor. With the removal of the Moslem flag that once waved so proudly over the citadel of Surat the glory of the Mohgul conquerors departed.

The Mohgul quarter of the city is gradually falling into decay; ruin and desolation mark the spot where many a noble pile of Moslem dwellings once stood. The very name of the Mohguls is almost a thing of the past, save that in household song and story their deeds will ever cast behind them a dark and terrible shadow.

We left Surat, or rather *Soo Rashtra*, "the pleasant country," seated in a dhuince, a native wagon on two wheels with a cloth canopy overhead, and drawn by a pair of large, handsome humped oxen, with a Bheel guide, the pundit, and two servants. We had traversed a large extent of country, halted under trees by the roadside and at mean little dhurrum-salas, without fear or molestation of any kind, with but few detentions, and only one accident to our wagon, which was repaired almost at once by applying to the headman of a village near by, who not only sent us a blacksmith, but came out to see the work done himself. The plan adopted in our travels through the Deccan we carried out in our entire journeyings through Guzerat and back—*i. e.* to send the pundit to the governor of the town or to the headman of the village to ask escort and guide for the place itself as well as to the next station; and in no instance were these unfaithful to the trust reposed in them. When they quitted us at the appointed station we generally made them a small present, which brought down upon us showers of blessings and unqualified praise. I did not doubt, however, that our good-fortune in this respect was owing to the dignified bearing and sanctified presence of our Brahman pundit. For the first few miles from Surat to Ratanpoore, "the Jewel City," the road was deep and heavy, and our wagon dragged slowly along, but it was not long before we came out on a magnificent park-like country, which is the characteristic of almost the whole vast province lying west of the Deccan. It was delightful to hear our Bheel guide singing in his deep sonorous voice as he trotted on by our side, in which music he was joined occasionally by our driver. One of his songs was intended to gratify European hearts and ears (with the "inam," or present, in prospect, I suppose), the chorus of which was as follows:

"Bur, bur, nashanee oorta hai,
Ingraje Bhadhar ki,
Mar lia rah Tipoo Sultan,
Wo kaya lurta, hârâm ki."

("Behold proud England's flag unfurl
And wave on every height.
Beaten low lies Tippoo Sultan;
With England who dare fight?")

This chorus was kept up with great animation until we reached the Jewel City, which is named after the extensive carnelian-mines in its neighborhood. Our measure of sleep at the miserable halting-place was stinted, for we started at dawn to visit the mines, situated some distance from the village along the slope of a picturesque hill. The road was literally covered with discarded pieces of carnelian. The mines were neither high nor deep. The entire face of the hill is perforated with galleries or pits that run in every direction. The gems are found imbedded in a slimy black clay holding numerous organic remains. In some parts the pits are carried down thirty feet before the peculiar deposit in which the carnelian abounds is reached. It is also found in many other places here still unknown to Europeans, as the natives keep the secret, as far as it is possible, to themselves and even from one another. It was interesting to see the men working at the mines. They were very poorly clad, with only a *langoutee*, or waist-cloth, round them, and each division was superintended by a number of better-dressed men called *sirdhars*, or "head lords." The stones are collected in great quantities, then tried by means of another sharp stone prepared for the purpose. If they chip easily they are discarded, but if they have a firm, compact texture and a deep-black color, they are selected, cleaned, and exposed on strips of rough straw mattings to the sun's rays for the space of a year or more, since the longer they are thus exposed the brighter the color and polish after baking. The process of baking these stones is both curious and original. The rough stones are piled in small heaps on the ground, which is slightly hollowed out to receive them. Small earthen pots with holes in them are placed over each pile; then a quantity of goat- or sheep-ordure is heaped up on each pot; it is then kindled and allowed to smoulder all night. On the following morning the stones are carefully examined, and if they have acquired the deep bright tint peculiar to the carnelian known to commerce, they are ready for the jeweller's polish; if not, they are once more subjected to the fire. The shops in Baroda, Cambay, and Ahmedabâd have great varieties of these stones for sale; for they are not only carved into rings, beads, bangles, boxes, vases, bowls, and mouth-pieces for pipes, but idols for the Jain, Hindoo, and Buddhist temples are also fashioned out of them.

Our journey from Ratanpoore to Baroda was through a very beautiful country, and, though it is said to be infested with Kholee and Bheel robbers, we passed through it without the least molestation. At one point of the road not far from Baroda we espied a thick wood above which towered the slender spires of some Hindoo temples. The moment these were seen our pundit, driver, and Bheel escort craved permission to retire for *puja*, or worship, for a few moments. The oxen were fastened to the branch of a tree by the road-side, and we alighted and walked about until our pious attendants had finished their devotions to the goddess Bhawanee, enshrined even here as the favorite of the reigning Mahratta kings.

Baroda, or Varodah, "the good water country," is now the capital of the Guicowars, which name means, literally, "owner of heads of cattle." It is the quaintest, the most densely populated, and independent city in this province.

The first Guicowar, a peasant by the name of Pullahji, was employed as a domestic in the service of the Peishwa Baji Roa. He soon raised himself by means of his extraordinary military talents to the rank of a commanding officer of the Peishwa's troops. Shortly after, having won over the army, he declared his independence and established himself on the throne of the Peishwas in Guzerat.

Having sprung from the hardy Khumbis, or cultivators of the soil, he was justly proud of his race, and assumed the ancient title of Guicowar. Whenever opportunity offered, Pullahji, bent on conquest, invaded the Peishwa's territories, carrying pillage and disorder through the richest provinces of Nagpoor Rajpootana. His successors, however, have been obliged to employ the aid of the British troops to hold their own in these provinces, which are at best but partly subjugated.

We crossed an old Hindoo bridge of curious structure consisting of arches placed one over the other, and spanning an impetuous but extraordinarily beautiful river still bearing the polished Sanskrit name of *Vishwamitra*, or "the friendly preserver." It flows strong and swift for many miles through a deep rocky channel. Its banks are singularly striking in some parts, rising on either side from fifty to sixty feet. Its waters, instead of appearing friendly, seemed dark and turbulent, not unlike the barbaric city which stretched along its banks. Temples, mosques, tombs, mausoleums, and dark, sombre-looking fortresses are seen everywhere; great flights of stone steps lead to the fast-flowing river, and all day long these are crowded with men and women washing, bathing, or filling their water-jars. The suburbs of Baroda extend for miles, and in the most densely crowded part of the capital the streets are narrow and crooked, the houses mostly of wood, but built with a view of architectural effect. Some are almost like pretty Swiss châlets, and others not unlike Italian villas. At the cross-roads and in various parts of the streets and lanes are seen queer little temples with the oddest of gods and goddesses enshrined in them—deities of the woods, fountains, streams, and even of the streets—and over these fluttered the gay-colored flags of the Guicowar. As for the inhabitants of Baroda, as seen in the streets, verandahs, and shops, they are quite characteristic. Specimens of every Eastern nationality may be seen here, and, what is more, in the martial atmosphere of the place they seemed more like freebooters, murderers, and warriors than like the simple citizens of a great agricultural district such as Guzerat presents outside of her cities and towns.

The city proper, or rather the citadel, is walled. It is entered by huge gateways guarded by soldiers, and made even more imposing by the lofty round towers that crown it on either side. It is divided into four portions, three of which are occupied by the nobility of the court of Guzerat, and the other by the palaces and buildings of the Guicowar himself. The antechamber of the palace is a huge stone structure supporting a many-storied wooden balcony, from the centre of which rises a lofty pyramidal clock-tower painted in various colors and looking fantastic beyond description. Here we saw the Guicowar going to worship at some temple; he was preceded by a number of led horses and elephants splendidly caparisoned; then came his standard borne on a great elephant, followed by the Guicowar himself. After him came men on foot in scarlet dresses, and more elephants. The elephants here are trained for riding, hunting, war, and even as executioners and combatants.

The English station is very picturesquely situated, and is purely European in appearance. The contrast is all the more striking after seeing the citadel of the Guicowar. It is on the north bank of the river Vishwamitra, and not far from the great highway are the British residency and travellers' bungalow, where we were most comfortably lodged.

One of the most ancient and curious temples to be seen here is situated at the west end of the suburbs of Baroda. It is called Ghai Dawale, "the cow temple." The front is imposing. A portico with granite pillars admits you

THE WALLS OF THE CITY OF BARODA.

into a series of vaulted chambers, and there are numberless idols of gods and goddesses enshrined in niches, with offerings of flowers before them and red paint sprinkled over their persons. A great many corridors lead to other chambers, cells, vaults, and mysterious retreats that have sprung up round it owing to the vast number of priestesses called Páthars attached to it. Another feature of Baroda are the magnificent *bowries*, or wells, that are found here; some are in themselves most exquisite pieces of architecture, and may be called temples built over reservoirs. The entrance to these well-temples are by five or more pavilions; thence a flight of stone steps leads to a second dome, which is arched, and under the outer dome, which is in its turn supported by lofty pillars and is pyramidal, then more steps and more pillars, until the level of the water is reached, which is again covered by a last and beautiful dome supported by innumerable short pillars. The largest of these wells in Baroda is called *Nou Laki*, or "Nine Laks," from its having cost that amount in building. It was erected by Suleiman, the governor of Baroda in A. H. (Mohammedan) 807. The water is very delicious, and here people from all parts of the country assemble to drink—mendicant Brahmans, gossains for alms, and fakeer carriers of relics to trade. The latter is not a mendicant, but a religious trader, whose chief claim to sanctity consists in the marks he wears on his brow and nose. These men go from place to place carrying their curious relics in curtained baskets slung across their shoulders; their shirts and cumberbunds are filled with balls, beads, and pins made from the wood of the *toolie** and other sacred trees. They have beads of sandal and other woods strung into necklaces, bracelets,

* A native name for a tree which is found in great abundance in this part of India, and held very sacred.

armlets, and anklets, mud figures of gods and goddesses made of the sacred clay of the Ganges, the Godaveri, and the Brahmapootra, precious bones of saints and prophets carved into amulets, and any quantity of yellow threads as a preservative against the evil eye. Women and children flock round these relic-carriers, and in return for grain, cloth, silver, and gold they will fasten a small yellow thread, a bead, an amulet, or a precious bit of some dead saint's bone—these, however, they part with only for gold or silver—around their wrists, arms, neck, and feet, to preserve the wearer not only from the evil eye, which is much dreaded in the East, but from all diseases and from sudden death.

Once more in our native wagon, with a fresh guide and escort we started for Cambay, the Khambayat of the ancients. We passed through a luxuriant country, for Guzerat is indeed the garden of the East. The thriving villages enclosed with great hedges of prickly pear; the pretty little wooden houses of moderate size, all built on the same plan, with farms, or cotton-plantations, or fruit-orchards of mangoes, tamarinds, etc., attached to them; the two-storied houses of the priest, the village schoolmaster, and the headman, with their high verdant hedges shutting off the house from curious eyes and separating it from its neighbors,—this all makes up a pretty picture. In the centre of these Guzerat villages there is generally a Hindoo temple, and a space fenced or hedged in where all the villagers assemble for prayers, celebration of holidays, and other festival gatherings.

The Guzerati women are handsome, well-formed, and remarkably industrious; many of them do all their weaving and spinning at home. Their chief food consists of eggs, fowls, milk, cream, and cheese: some of the Guzerat Brahmans will eat fowl and even game. The men are well-formed, athletic, and of fairer complexion than the natives of Southern India.

Cambay is a city of great antiquity and well known to early European travellers. In 1543, Queen Elizabeth of England sent a mission to Khambayat, with instructions to proceed thence to China. The Hindoos state that on the site of Cambay stood twelve hundred and eighty years ago an ancient Brahman city—according to Forbes, the Camanes of Ptolemy. It derives its present name, however, from a copper pillar, called "Khamb," dedicating it to the presiding deity of the place, the earth-goddess Dèvi; the date on this pillar is a little before the eleventh century of our era. Cambay has an air of extreme sluggishness and rapid decay, and one cannot fail to see its changeful history in its numerous foundations. Everywhere are remnants of many cities and many kinds and styles of architecture, built one above the other.

The travellers' bungalow here comprises the upper stories of a spacious stone building, once the English factory. It overlooks the entire city, which is built on an eminence, with its old walls perforated with holes for musketry, its fifty-two towers and ten gates guarded by soldiers, and also looks out upon the great Gulf of Cambay, than which I know nothing more formidable in nature. At low tide for miles out one sees only a vast plain, moist, strewn with shells, and intersected here and there with deep hollows and shifting sandbanks; but when the tide changes, and long before the waters appear in sight, are heard tremendous sounds, crash after crash, thunder after thunder, of the advancing tide, which comes in leaping like a huge monster, thirty to forty feet high, and breaks with terrific violence against the shore, carrying everything before it. Ships and native vessels anchor at a point some miles down the gulf, where the tides are less strong.

Cambay has witnessed many a dreadful scene of carnage by the Mohguls, Hindoos, Persians, and Rajpoots. The only objects of real interest here are subterranean Jain temples; they are situated in the Parsee district. The exterior, or rather upper part, of the temple would be insignificant but for the imposing statue of Parswanath, sculptured in white marble, surrounded by a host of smaller images, many of which are jewelled and are sold as household deities. Our guide pointed to us a queer narrow opening at the side which led by means of steep steps to the underground temples which the Jains, like the early Christians, built for purposes of midnight assembly and worship in order to escape the persecution of the Mohammedan conquerors of Guzerat.

Emerging from one of the gates of Cambay, we wended our way through ruins which are scattered all about the neighborhood. Now a broad paved pathway, now crumbling tombs, anon ancient structures, a broken archway, a cluster of roofless pillars, or, again, dilapidated temples, mark the sites where stood rich and quaint habitations, temples, or pavilions of the ancient Hindoos. The richness and luxuriance of nature seems to have vanished also from these ruinous suburbs, and our road was no longer beautiful, but lay through a deep sandy plain until we entered the ancient capital of the great sultans, Ahâmâdabâd or Ahmedabâd, one of the unrivalled cities of the East.

The travellers' bungalow is a pleasant place, and everything in the way of living is as cheap and good as one could possibly desire. We engaged a very intelligent guide, who spoke Hindostanee well, to take us to the places best worth seeing.

Our first drive was to Mirzapoor to see the Ranee-Ki-Musjid, or "the Queen's Mosque," an enchanting spot.

The moment we alighted in front of it a very old fakeer, with a multitude of necklaces round his neck, came out to greet us, and for a rupee showed us about the place. The mosque and mausoleum here are both beautiful marble structures, erected to the memory of a princess, Rupavati. Her tomb, which is richly ornamented, is of a mixture of Moslem and Hindoo style of architecture. The dome is magnificently fretted, and pillars standing at each tower form a graceful colonnade around the tomb. But perhaps the chief and peculiar beauty was the situation of these partially ruined monuments, amid a wild tangle of fruit and other trees where birds, squirrels, and monkeys find a pleasant home. The second mosque and tomb are not far off, dedicated to the memory of a Mohammedan queen called Ranee Sipra-Ki-Musjid, "the Queen Sipra's Mosque," one of the favorite wives of Ahmed Shah, the founder of the city. These are exquisite buildings too, and in the finest Saracenic style; the pillars and minarets have an air of wonderful loftiness and beauty.

The Kanch Ki-Musjid, or "Glass Mosque," and the Jummah-Musjid, are both remarkably beautiful structures. The Glass Mosque, so called from the whiteness and purity of the marble of which parts of it was built, has a graceful dome after the Turkish style, terminating in a crescent. The Jummah-Musjid is in the vicinity of the great street, "Manik Chouk," which contains the chief bazaars and markets of Ahmedabâd. It is an oblong building, with a fine open courtyard containing a reservoir for washing the feet of the worshipper before entering the precincts of the temple. The light elegant domes of this building are supported by graceful pillars, and its open arches, minarets, and façades are most exquisitely ornamented.

The grand royal cemetery of Sarkhej lies several miles

from the city of Ahmedabâd—a wondrous ruin, the ancient summer residence of Ahmed Shah. To approach it one is obliged to cross a fine pebbly stream fordable at points, called the *Saber-Muttee,* properly *Safer Muttee,* "pure sand." The road leading to these vast ruined structures of palaces, hareems, mosques, tombs, and gardens is still paved in some parts.

We were admitted by a saintly custodian, who became affable the moment silver coins were dropped into his half-open palm. Gury Baksh, or "the bestower of virtue," the spiritual adviser of Ahmed Shah, lies interred here beneath a splendid monument which attracts crowds of pilgrims annually. The tomb and mosque were completed by Khouttub-ood-din, the grandson of Ahmed Shah. The city is founded on the site of a very ancient and populous Hindoo town dedicated to and called after the goddess Ashawhalla, and is built out of the materials of one or more Hindoo cities which Ahmed Shah sacked and plundered, carrying away the stones, pillars, and monuments bit by bit.

Ahmedabâd was given up to the East India Company in 1818, and has been held by it ever since. It is impossible to do anything like justice to the beauties and attractions of this magnificent Mohammedan city. It abounds in stately monuments, mosques, mausoleums, palaces, great reservoirs, and gardens, in a more or less ruinous condition, but which show a high degree of civilization and point to a period when the Mohgul occupation of India was at its highest prosperity.

Leaving Ahmedabâd, we started for Mount Aboo, a place very little known, but one of the most beautiful spots in the world. The magnificent province of Guzerat is separated from Marwar on the north-east by a range of mountains in which are Mount Aboo and a beautiful

Jain Temple.

mountain-lake called Aboogoosh. Passing through Desa, a military station for European troops, and across the Bhanas River, our road lay for many weary days through patches of jungle more or less dense until we found ourselves at the pretty little Marwar village of Andara, which lies at the foot of Mount Aboo. There is a good path from the village to the summit of the mount, and here a beautiful lake, called after the saint "Aboo," who is said to have excavated the basin in which it lies with his nails, and it is therefore called Nakhi Taloa, "Nail Lake." It is an exquisitely shaded bit of water, and in its vicinity are found wonderful Jain temples built of pure white marble. Not far from this spot is the sanitarium for travellers, where we took up our abode, barracks for convalescent European soldiers, and a quiet, unpretending little Protestant church.

The most important of the cavern-temples in the neighborhood are the Tij Phal and the Veinahl Sah. One is dedicated to a Jain saint, Vrishab-Deva. It stands alone in a square court, and all around it are little cells with deities enshrined in them. A number of strange-looking priests worship here, making offerings of saffron, lamps fed with ghee, and incense in small brass pots. One priest deliberately asked us for some *brandy*, and, as we had none to give him, proposed instantly to go back with us if we would give him some, because he suffered from pains in his stomach.

The temple dedicated to Parswanath, the great Jain teacher and saint, is an exquisite bit of architecture built of the purest white marble. From one of the vaulted roofs is suspended a cluster of flowers resembling the half-blown lotus, sculptured out of the rock; its cup and petals are so beautifully carved that they are almost as delicate and transparent as the flower itself. Everywhere the flowers, fruits, birds, and animals indicate that the artists must have taken their models from nature. There is also a fine Rajpoot fortress here. The dog-rose, a beautiful Indian flower called *seotee*, the pomegranate, the wild grape, the apricot, are among the indigenous products of Mount Aboo. The mango tree also abounds here, the white and yellow jessamine, the balsam, and the golden champa, which is sacred to the gods; but the rarest and most beautiful of all the plants is a parasite called by the natives *ambathri*, with lovely blue and white flowers, creeping, entwining, and blossoming around the largest forest trees.

It was a beautiful morning on which we returned to Andara. It was not without deep regret that we bade adieu to this charming mountain-region and the Jain temples enshrined within its heart. We turned again and again to take a last look at the bas-reliefs and the ornaments wrought here with such grace and delicacy of design as to become the despair of our more impetuous artists, before we could make up our minds to quit those extraordinarily beautiful monuments for ever.

CHAPTER XIV.

Calcutta, the City of the Black Venus, Kali.—The River Hoogley.—Cremation-Towers.—Chowringee, the Fashionable Suburb of Calcutta.—The Black Hole.—Battles of Plassey and Assaye.—The Brahmo-Somaj.—Temple of Kali.—Feast of Juggurnath.—Benares and the Taj Mahal.

AFTER eight or nine days' steaming from the fair and picturesque island of Bombay our captain announced that we were about to enter the Hoogley, a river made famous in Indian song and story as "the strong arm of the beautiful goddess Gunga, the compassionate daughter of the proud Himâlayas," but which is in reality a great muddy estuary. The burning sun poured down upon its heavy waters as they loomed out of the distant plain and rolled sluggishly toward the sea, every wave seeming to bear on its troubled brow an impress of the dark history of the land through which it has flowed for centuries.

Late in the same evening the pilot-boat came out to meet us, and not long after we cast anchor at a place called Saugor, where there is a lighthouse. I remember distinctly the oppressive night we passed here, owing no doubt to the combined impurities rising out of the turbid waves and the fetid odors of the adjoining land. Early next morning we were again in motion, sailing up the dusky Hoogley. Its low, muddy banks were dotted with wretched-looking mud huts, relieved only by the ever-graceful palm trees that waved above them. What a contrast this river was to the clear, limpid, and joyous Krishna, the high-banked and proudly isolated Godaveri, the genial, broad-breasted Taptee, and the grand, impetuous Vishwamitra of Western India!

Another day was nearly gone before we reached our moorings. We cast anchor once more amid a dense forest of masts, funnels, and native craft in the harbor of Calcutta. We were met at the Champhool Ghaut, or landing-place, by kind friends. Ascending a magnificent flight of stone steps and passing under a great archway, we hurried into a European carriage, and were driven rapidly from the strange conflicting mass of humanity that always abounds at a great seaport, but especially at the seaports of all the British settlements in India.

The house of our friends here was in many respects furnished like a European dwelling, and one might almost fancy himself in an English home but for the pillared halls; the spacious chambers, with long punkahs or fans suspended from the ceilings, some of which are kept going night and day; the dark, silent barefooted domestics, robed in pure white, who are seen gliding noiselessly to and fro, which lend a powerful magic charm, a flavor of the Arabian Nights, to the interior of even the most ordinary of British homes in the East.

Calcutta, the capital of British India, still bears the name of the black goddess Kali, who is supposed to spread pestilence, famine, and death over the land of which she is the presiding deity whenever her altars are neglected and her thirst for vengeance unappeased. Unhealthy as the spot is, it was rendered infinitely more so by the innumerable corpses that were until within a few years cast upon the waters of the Hoogley: the poverty-stricken inhabitants of the land, unable to pay the expenses of a funeral by cremation, committed their dead to these waters in the belief that its mystic current would purify them from

Native Crafts or Patemars.

all taint of sin. This, however, has been prohibited by the British authorities. Huge cremation-towers now receive all bodies cast upon its waters, whence the never-dying flames are seen constantly ascending, dark and lurid, toward the tranquil blue sky.

The town of Calcutta lies on the eastern bank of the Hoogley, which is the eastern arm of the old Ganges, and held almost as sacred as that river; the natives daily repair in great numbers to its banks to offer up prayers and praises. Here also, amid the din and noise and hurry of native craft, trading vessels, and all manner of river commerce, may be seen at any hour of the day or night the sick and dying of the Hindoo population stretched on the edge of the river's banks, half immersed in the sacred stream, their faces turned to the sky, convulsed or calm, breathing their lives away.

At high water the Hoogley is nearly a mile broad in front of the town, and is very pleasant to look upon. Fine ships and steamers of all nations and countries lie here within sight and sound; picturesque-looking craft of every kind are seen gliding swiftly hither and thither. But at low water the scene suddenly changes; the river becomes a shrunken and muddy ghost of itself, with filthy borders, whence myriad floating particles of miasma are wafted on the air to the poor humanity who are doomed to live and labor in its vicinity.

After passing the triumphal archway you emerge on a spacious open area called the Meidân, or plain; here all the principal roads part and meet, and here on either side one sees a grand display of really stately architecture. This is the handsome and fashionable suburb of Chowringee, and in every respect worthy of being called, as it is, "the City of Palaces." The houses are all European, three and four stories high, some detached, others connected by handsome terraces or open sunny balconies, many with shady verandahs, high carriage-porches supported by stately pillars, while not a few are rendered still more attractive and home-like with gay flower-gardens and fine forest and fruit trees, which latter are not as fine as those found in the gardens of Bombay, owing to the destructive influence of the periodical cyclones that sweep over the valley of the Ganges.

Our first drive was through this the European part of the city, which extends about five miles along the river. A noble and much-frequented esplanade divides the town from Fort William. On one side stands the new Government-house, said to have been erected by the marquis of Wellesley. It is a noble pile, an Ionic structure on a simple rustic basement. A flight of stone steps leads to the north entrance. The south part of the building is ornamented with a circular colonnade surmounted with a lofty dome. There are spacious corridors at each of the four corners, with circular passages leading to the private apartments of the family. This princely building contains magnificent chambers, some of which are richly decorated and filled with valuable portraits of the great viceroys of India. Near the Government-house stand the Town-hall, Treasury, and High Court; opposite is Fort William, commenced by Clive soon after the famous battle of Plassey in 1775, the most systematically-constructed fortress in India. It is said to have cost the East India Company the immense sum of one million pounds sterling. In shape it is an irregular octagon, with bombproof quarters for a garrison of no less than ten thousand men and with room for six hundred pieces of cannon. Toward the front it presents a regular massive appearance, and is not unlike most European fortifications, but on the side overlooking the river it is strikingly varied and picturesque, owing to the extremely irregular and broken character of the structure. It was designed to bear upon objects that might approach the town on either side of the river, and is eminently effective in warding off danger. Immediately beyond the fort the fine steeple of the cathedral is seen rising pure and high above the surrounding foliage. There is also here a palatial residence for an Anglican bishop, and in 1844 the Rev. H. Heber was the first Christian divine appointed to this see, with a salary of five thousand pounds per annum.

Here in this spot is found the secret of the marvellous success of that small band of intelligent Englishmen who first set out for India under the name and protection of trade. Here only a few years after their arrival they laid aside their intention of simple traders; here they mounted their guns, enrolled armed bands of natives to assist them in their new position, made laws, punished evil-doers, rewarded the industrious and such as made no opposition to their pretensions; and here from one step to another they finally became the legislators and rulers of the land. The city of Calcutta does not date farther back than the famous battle of Plassey. The old fortified English factory was erected on a low marshy plain in the middle of a few straggling native villages, bordered on three sides by dense jungles infested with tigers. At that time it had a garrison of only three hundred men; nevertheless, that insignificant English stronghold became in a short time the depository of all the rich merchandise of the Gangetic valley, which excited the cupidity of many of the rajahs. In 1756, Nawab Surajah Dowlah attacked it with an immense army, and after a desperate resistance from the English merchants and soldiers of the fort he finally succeeded in capturing it. Then followed the famous Black Hole tragedy, which Macaulay has so graphically described: "One hundred and forty-six persons were thrust into a dungeon twenty feet square; driven into this cell at the point of the sword, the door was shut ruthlessly upon them. When they realized the horrors of their position they strove to burst the door. They offered large bribes to the jailers, but all in vain. The nawab was asleep, and none dared to awaken him. At length the unhappy sufferers went mad with despair. They trampled each other down, fought for the places at the windows, fought for the pittance of water with which the cruel mercy of the murderers mocked their agonies, raved, prayed, blasphemed, implored the guards to fire among them. The jailers in the mean time held lights to the bars and shouted with laughter at the frantic struggles of their victims. At length the tumult died away in low gaspings and moanings. The day broke. The nawab had slept off his debauch, and permitted the doors to be opened. But it was some time before the soldiers could make a lane for the survivors by piling up on each side the heaps of corpses on which the burning climate had already begun to do its loathsome work. When at length a passage was made, twenty-three ghastly figures, such as their own mothers would not have known, staggered one by one out of the charnel-house. A pit was instantly dug. The dead bodies, one hundred and twenty-three in number, were flung into it promiscuously and covered up." Such was the terrible nature of the affair of the Black Hole. But the day of retribution was not far distant.

In order to understand the position of the East India Company at this time we must go back a few years. The jealousy that had sprung up between the French and English trading companies broke out into open hostilities at the moment of the declaration of war by Louis XV. in 1744. The English were the first to receive reinforcements from home. Four English vessels, having previously captured three richly-laden French vessels on their voyage from China, appeared off the coast of Coromandel in July, 1745. Dupleix, the governor at Pondicherry, apprehensive that, owing to the incomplete state of the fortifications and the insufficient garrison, the place would be taken, prevailed on the nawab Anwar Ou Deen to threaten to revenge upon the English at Madras any injury that the squadron should inflict upon the French possessions within the limits of his government. The Madras officials, intimidated by the authoritative language of the nawab, took immediate measures to prevent the English fleet from attacking Pondicherry. The English squadron, in obedience to the orders received, confined their hostile operations to the sea.

In the following year an indecisive action took place between the English squadron and a French fleet under the command of La Bourdonnais; after which the latter, having reinforced himself at Pondicherry, proceeded to attack the English at Madras. The town was bombarded for several days; a few of the inhabitants were killed by an explosion of a bombshell. The English, knowing that the nawab, with all his countless forces, was on the side of the French, capitulated, on which the assailants entered the town and took it without the loss of a single life.

Robert Clive, then only a writer in the East India Company's service, was among the persons who agreed to submit to La Bourdonnais, on the express condition that the settlement should be restored on easy and honorable terms. At the time when Madras had reverted to the English, Clive had already exchanged the pen for the sword, and had risen to the rank of a colonel in the East India Company's service. On hearing of the atrocity of the Black Hole the English at Madras immediately despatched a naval and military forçe, the one under Admiral Watson, and the other under Colonel Clive, to punish the nawab and protect the English at Bengal.

The bravery and "duplicity" of Clive, who believed in the adage, "similia similibus curantur," enabled him to succeed beyond the most sanguine expectations. Victory was followed by victory, and at length, at the battle of Plassey, Clive at the head of three thousand men, of whom less than one-third were English, and in the course of a single hour's conflict, routed the entire army of Surajah Dowlah, consisting of fifty-five thousand armed men. Surajah Dowlah vanquished and deposed, his prime minister, Meer Jaffer, was appointed in the place of the master, whom he had not only deserted, but betrayed, and thus Meer Jaffer became at once the subject and tool of the English.

The directors of the East India Company, on receiving the news of Clive's success, appointed him governor of their possessions in Bengal, and in 1760 Clive was raised to the peerage with an income of forty thousand pounds a year.

Warren Hastings was the next Englishman who from the position of a clerk in an office at Calcutta rose to be the governor-general of British India.

The kingdom of Mysore, whose lofty table-lands are swept by the cool breezes of the Indian Ocean, has always been inhabited by a more hardy and manly race than that which occupied the lower plains of Hindostan. Hyder Alee, an illiterate common soldier, impelled by a daring spirit of adventure, seized this kingdom of Mysore and seated himself on the throne of Seringapatam. The next step taken by this daring adventurer was even more startling. In the month of June, 1780, and when in his eightieth year, he led an immense army into the Carnatic, carrying slaughter and destruction wherever he appeared. Two small English armies, headed by Colonel Baillie and Sir Hector Munro, tried in vain to check his course; they were not only overwhelemed, but compelled to retreat, and it seemed as if the British empire in Southern India trembled on the very verge of destruction. It was this critical juncture that brought out the great genius of Warren Hastings. He at once took upon himself the supreme direction of affairs, superseded the incapable council at Madras, and without loss of time despatched the brave veteran Sir Eyre Coote with a small but resolute force to the assistance of the English at Madras. At once the forces of Hyder Alee were checked, siege after siege was raised, until at length the English and Mohammedan armies met on the plains of Cuddalore, whence, after a desperate fight, the latter was driven in wild and disorderly confusion. Hyder Alee died two years after this defeat, bequeathing to his son, the famous Tippoo Saihib, his throne and his hatred of English domination.

Very shortly after Warren Hastings, impeached by the House of Commons, resigned his office as governor-general of India. Then followed that famous trial which not only extended over seven years, but, when dismissed from the bar of the House of Lords, left Warren Hastings a ruined statesman and an insolvent debtor. The East India Company, however, came to his aid with an annuity of £4000 a year, and a loan, half of which was converted into a gift, of £50,000.

During the administration of the next governor-general, Lord Cornwallis, the implacable Tippoo Saihib suffered a signal defeat. Sir John Shore followed Lord Cornwallis, and was succeeded by the earl of Mornington, the elder brother of the "Iron Duke." He no sooner arrived in India than his attention was called to the intrigues of the

French with Tippoo Saihib, who were planning, with the assistance of fresh European troops, to drive the English out of Hindostan. The treachery of Tippoo was anticipated by a declaration of war. On the 5th of March, 1798, a British army, commanded by General Harris, with the aid of several native powers, entered the territory of Mysore, stormed the city of Seringapatam, overthrew the dynasty of Tippoo Sultan, and annexed that magnificent province to the British dominions.

The British had no sooner gained possession of the lofty table-lands of the Mysore than a new and more formidable enemy, the warlike and predatory tribes who inhabited the table-land of the Deccan, opposed their further progress. The most renowned of these kings, the rajahs of Berar, Scindia, and Holkar, formed the famous northern confederacy under the leadership of a still more powerful chief, the Peishwa, whose government was at Poonah, the capital of the Deccan. The British were soon plunged into an extensive war with these wild and fierce northmen. On the 4th of September, 1803, the fort of Alleghur was taken by storm, and on the 11th of the same month General Lake met twenty thousand of these intrepid warriors, headed by able French officers, and defeated them, capturing Delhi, one of the most ancient capitals of Hindostan and the seat of the intolerant and luxurious Mohgul emperors. Triumph followed triumph; Agra, Ahmednuggur, and the golden city of Aurungabâd surrendered.

At length the united powers of Scindia and the rajah of Nagpoor made one more desperate attempt to oppose the English power in the Deccan. The armies of the Mahratta kings were marshalled at the small village of Assaye to meet the British troops. On ascending the rising ground to reconnoitre the enemy's forces, the English commander, who was no other than General Wellesley, perceived a vast host extending in a line along the opposite bank of the Kelnah River near its junction with the Jewah. Their right consisted entirely of cavalry, and their left was formed of infantry trained and disciplined by De Boigne, with over one hundred pieces of cannon, which rested on the fortified village of Assaye. These were completely overthrown by Wellesley with a force not exceeding eight thousand men, and of whom not more than fifteen hundred were English.

The power of the Mahratta kings, once shaken at Assaye, was at length completely humbled on the plains of Argaum. They were compelled to sue for peace, which was only granted them at the expense of enormous territory. From this time British influence became paramount through the whole of Northern Hindostan, and these were the last and most famous of General Wellesley's conquests in India. He returned to England in 1805 to win for himself greater fame than even that which he achieved on Indian soil.

Magnificent as is the city of Calcutta architecturally, it was considered at one time one of the most unhealthy of spots. The entire country is flat; here and there are extensive muddy lakes, breeding under a tropical sun malaria and all manner of diseases; a line of dank, tangled forests still stretch across the land, and is not very distant from the town. In former times this jungle was the abode of innumerable wild beasts, and it is even now infested with jackals, who immediately after nightfall howl in sudden accord, uttering the most demon-like yells. These local disadvantages have been partially removed. The streets have been well and carefully drained; many of the stagnant, muddy pools have not only been filled up, but converted into blooming gardens; and the magnificent Botanical Garden with which Mr. Hooker has enriched

Calcutta is said by good judges to be the finest in the world. Nevertheless, the air is still impregnated to a certain extent with the impure exhalations arising from the low jungles in the vicinity of this city, called the Sunderbunds.

From the palaces of the conquering Anglo-Indians the drive to the "Black Town," as the native portion of the city is still called, is enough to discourage the most enthusiastic of Christians in the world. This quarter of Calcutta stretches for some miles toward the north, presenting at once a sad contrast to the stately and grand portion occupied by the English. The transition is all the more marked because of the architectural pretensions of the one and the rude mud habitations of the other. Here reside at least three-fourths of the entire population of Calcutta. The streets are more or less narrow, filthy, unpaved, and unswept. The houses are built principally of mud, bamboo, or other coarse woods, swarming with an excess of population. Within this wretched vicinity are found no less than twenty entire bazaars extending from one end of the "Black Town" to the other, well stocked with goods from all parts of the world, rare and valuable products of the Indian loom, shawls and paintings from Cashmere, kinkaubs from Benares, teas and silks from China, spices, pearls, and precious stones from Ceylon, rupees from Pegù, coffee from Java and Arabia, nutmegs from Singapore; in fact, everything that the wide world has ever produced is displayed in shops that are nothing but miserably patched mud or bamboo dwellings. Through these native bazaars the teeming population seemed to flow and gurgle unchanged through all changes of governors, constitutions, and rulers—the same to-day, in type, character, feeling, religion, and occupation, as it was before the beginning of the earliest known history. Here, assembled from the four winds of the heaven, were all the elements of an unspeakably motley crowd—nut-brown, graceful Hindoo maidens tripping daintily with rows of water-jars nicely balanced on their heads; dark-hued young Hindoo men, all clean and washed, robed in pure white, laughing, talking, or loitering around; handsomely-dressed baboos—as the native gentlemen of Bengal are called—in Oriental costumes, but with European stockings and shoes, sauntering carelessly along; dancing-girls brilliantly attired; common street-women jewelled and bedizened with innumerable trinkets and in their distinctive garb; bheesties with water-skins on their backs; Borahs, brokers, Brahmans, Musulmans, sepoys, fakeers, and gossains, in their peculiar costumes, shouting in manifold tongues and various dialects; and, above all, there may be seen strolling jugglers, snake-charmers, and fortune-tellers plying their curious arts and completing the picture of an Oriental bazaar.

In some of the streets a small stream of water, a rivulet of the sacred Ganges, flows bright and clear through artificial channels. Many of the native shops open on it, and all day long hosts of men, women, and children may be seen seated beside it, busy or idle, but always grateful for this truly precious gift of the gods.

Calcutta boasts of a Sanskrit college of high repute, a Mohammedan, and an Anglo-Indian college, supported by the English government. The College of Fort William, founded by the marquis of Wellesley, is chiefly used by Englishmen, who, having been partially educated at the College of Haylesbury, England, are instructed here in the Oriental languages and other branches of study necessary for their respective professions and callings in India.

The government system of native education was established on the foundation of the Hindoo schools already in existence. These schools are divided into two classes or grades, the upper and lower schools. In the upper, by means of Sanskrit, the peculiar philosophy, literature, and religion of the Hindoos are taught; the lower schools are to be found in every village, and may be numbered by tens of thousands; in these the teaching varies and is more or less dependent on the ability of the persons—*i. e.* Brahmans—who are employed to teach. Most of these village teachers are induced for about six pounds per annum to attend a normal school for a year; after having passed the required examination they are invited to take charge of some village school.

There are eight great centres of education in British India, and each is wholly independent of the others. These are the three great presidencies of Bengal, Madras, and Bombay, Scindh, the North-western Provinces, Oude, the Central Provinces, and British Burmah. Each of these has its own special director of public instruction, with a staff of inspecting officers. Among the institutions that are wholly supported by the government may be classed the village school, in which the vernacular of the district is taught with a few other studies; the zillah, or district school, in which the higher classes are often educated in English and prepared for the universities; the talook schools, which also are preparatory schools; colleges with European professors, in which a thorough English education is imparted to the students, as are now found in the chief cities of Benares, Delhi, Agra, Lahore, Poonah, Madras, and Calcutta; and the Elphinstone College at Bombay. Normal schools, technical colleges for medicine, engineering, and surgery, mission and other private schools abound, besides which there are thousands of purely native schools scattered throughout the vast territory of

India, still existing under the old Brahmanic village system of education.

Native female education is hardly begun by the government, and the task is very difficult, owing to the peculiar social restraints still imposed on the better class of Asiatic women. The Parsee female schools in Bombay are said to be the best supported and the most efficient in this respect. About twenty-five years ago Mr. Bethune opened in the city of Calcutta a school for native women. It was liberally supported by Lord Dalhousie, and since his death by the state.* This was the beginning of a movement which has found great favor not only in Bengal, but in the Northwestern Provinces and the Punjaub. There are now in Bengal two normal schools for teachers and two hundred and forty-four schools for girls, with 4844 pupils. There are no fewer than six hundred and fifty schools in the Punjaub, with an aggregate of 20,534 pupils. These elementary schools in the Punjaub, Lahore, and Umritsur are superintended solely by native gentlemen. In addition to these the zenana mission-work, carried on so successfully by American and European missionary ladies, is slowly but surely preparing hundreds of women and children for a day that may ripen into better things; like a grain of mustard-seed once cast into the right soil, it will stretch out strong boughs to the four corners of the earth for the birds to lodge under.

Another school of religious thought, already mentioned, called the Brahmo-Somaj, "assembled in the name of God," is even more closely allied with the dawning freedom and emancipation of the Hindoos from the priestcraft and spiritual tyranny of the Brahman hierarchy. From this new school of religious thought a large party of about five thousand souls seceded some few years ago. They chose for their leader the able and astute philosopher, the late

Keshub Chunder Sen, one of the most talented and spiritual men among the Hindoos of to-day. This association has a church in Calcutta, where the members meet once a week or oftener for the purposes of meditation and worship.

Various means of improvement are now open to the British subjects of India. The English residents in Calcutta, Madras, and Bombay are among the most kind and liberal people in the world. Quite independent of the government establishments, they privately support a vast number of charitable institutions, and there is no end of societies for religious and other educational objects; and although the changes effected in the religious and social condition of the majority of the peoples since the occupation of India by the British are hardly perceptible, nevertheless some very important steps have been taken toward ensuring the good of the people at large, especially in the prohibition of sutteeism, infanticide, the terrific sacrifice of life that at one time characterized the festival of the god Juggernath, not to speak of the tortures of maddened fanatics and self-condemned ascetics, the horrible practices of the Thugs and that of the Meriahs of Orissa. All these savage practices are more or less repressed by the constant and vigilant operation of protective laws instituted by the British rulers.

Before leaving Calcutta we paid a visit to the Khali Ghaut, and alighted before a great hall with a towering but ungainly roof above it. This was the famous temple of the black goddess Kali. There was something more entangled, enchanted, and demon-like about this building and its interior than any other that I had ever entered in India. It was the festival of Juggernath. A number of white-robed priests were preparing to place the grim goddess in a car and to lead her forth to grace the festival. The temple consisted of a vast number of low pillars; it was dimly lighted, and, although light was flooding the earth everywhere in great splendor, it was not allowed to enter here, but it worked its way hither and thither and quivered dubiously in unearthly tints on the face of the black goddess dimly visible in the distance. A more hideous and repulsive image can hardly be conceived by the heart of man than this veritable female fiend after whom the city of Calcutta is still named.

No one seemed to object to our entering the temple, so we walked down the dim aisles and stood face to face with the grim and terrible Kali. It would be impossible to give utterance to the sense of horror that crept over me as I looked at this strange, enigmatic deity of the Bengalees. The black face was surmounted by long hair which had the appearance of innumerable serpents; a red tongue protruded from the hideous mouth; the expression of the eyes was strange and fierce, almost to madness; she was furnished with four arms, in one of which she grasped a knife and in the other the head of a man; in another pair of hands higher up she held a lotos and the *chakra*, or the wheel. Round her neck hung the skulls of murdered victims, and she stood on the body of a prostrate man, who is represented trumpeting forth her praises even while she is in the act of crushing him to death.

The pundit explained to us the meaning of this horrible figure; no further text was needed. This grim idol is to the Hindoos a fearful warning against sensuality. The lotos in the upper hand, which is the emblem of purity, and the wheel of retribution, are transformed in the lower hands into a knife and a bleeding human head. She puts out her tongue derisively, and crushes her victim—all indicating, as plainly as our Bible, "The wages of sin is death." Human sacrifices were offered to her at no very remote period, but now, by order of the British government, the sacrifices to her are limited to goats and kids, which are offered to her every morning.

As we were standing and looking at this strange idol, a number of barefooted priests came through a narrow court, entered the temple, and took their places beside the shrine. Two men very handsomely dressed approached from an opposite direction bearing a fine goat, which was tied by the feet, and laid it at the foot of the altar. Then one of the priests took from the altar a vase containing some red paint mixed with oil, with which he touched the forehead, fore feet, and breast of the goat; he then sprinkled some consecrated water on it. This done, a low-caste man stepped up, took the poor palpitating beast, inserted its head into a curiously-fashioned guillotine, secured it there by means of a wooden pin, and then dealt it one blow; the head was severed, and was presented to the officiating priests, and the executioner carried away the body. Such offerings are made by both men and women as an atonement for personal offences. Thus the wrath of the black goddess of Calcutta is supposed to be appeased. Goats are also sacrificed to her by Hindoo women when they have had bad dreams or when they anticipate any calamity, in order to avert the coming evil.

On the next day was the procession of Juggernath. A wilder and more incongruous scene I never witnessed. We spent several hours in watching the procession, which, issuing from the native town, traverses a large circuit round the principal thoroughfares, pauses at the bank of the river, and then retires to the country-seat of the idol, some few miles from the temple. The idol is made of wood, is about six feet high, with a grim human countenance—very unlike the carvings of Krishna to be found in other parts of India—painted blue, and seated in a lofty chariot borne aloft on sixteen high wheels. It was

IDOLS IN THE TEMPLE OF JUGGERNATH.

drawn by long ropes held by thousands of enthusiastic men, women, and children, who often bribe the priests for the privilege of conducting the god to his country-house. A number of priests and gayly-dressed priestesses, standing on the platform of the chariot, chanted the praises of the "lord of life," while the people shouted, screamed, and clapped their hands amid the wild beating of drums and din of hundreds of native musical instruments. The air was heavy with the incense offered to the idol, while nature around seemed to be steeped in repose, myriads of bees murmured softly their idyllic hum among the wayside flowers, doves were seen nestling together among the shady leaves of huge pepul trees, and around the cool recesses of huge tanks and reservoirs numbers of peacocks sat or strutted quietly about, unfurling their glories to the noonday sun. More puzzling than even the festival of Juggernath is the curious state of things still existing in British India, for side by side with the Church of the Brahmo-Somaj, the advanced thought and intelligence of the educated baboos and other highly philosophic and cultivated natives of Bengal, are the temples of the goddess Kali and the strange festival of Juggernath.

With regard to European influence, it must be admitted that it is hardly, if at all, felt by the majority of the native population. The viceroy and the great English grandees are separated from the natives for whose interests they are there by law and custom which nothing can overcome, and the officials around whom the whole Indian empire revolves are often ignorant of the Indian languages, races, religious and social prejudices, and mode of life of the hundreds of provinces that lie within the railways, while those beyond are to them, as the wilds of Africa, an undiscovered country. I have often heard gentlemen of great intelligence in other respects speak of the people of India with profound contempt, classing in one indistinguishable mass Brahmans, Hindoos, Parsees, Mohammedans, Arabians, Persians, Armenians, Turks, Jews, and other races too numerous to mention.

Our next visit was to Benares, the far-famed ecclesiastical metropolis of Hindostan. We rested full two hours just outside this sacred spot to enable our pundit to perform the prescribed observances before entering this holy of holies. When he appeared before us he was bathed, shaved, anointed, and clothed in pure white, and even to his sandals he was a new man. He kept his eyes half closed, so that his thoughts should not be tempted to stray from the object of his deep contemplation. Presently we were joined by a crowd of pilgrims who passed into the city, some prostrating themselves full length as they drew near. In the morning light Benares presented a most imposing appearance: the buildings are lofty and mostly in the Hindoo style of architecture, stretching for several miles along the edge of the Ganges, from which ascends a long line of stone steps. Next morning we visited several of the Hindoo temples, especially the temple of the monkeys, which was one of the most ludicrous I have ever witnessed. A number of tame monkeys played about the temple even while the most solemn services were being performed within. The large area for the cremation of dead bodies sent hither from all parts of Hindostan was the most astonishing thing I have ever seen, and the huge funeral pyres ever burning here produced on my mind an ever-memorable effect. We were glad to turn our steps from the revolting sights and scenes of the cremation-ground to a beautiful mosque which stands as a symbol of Moslem power in the very heart of this Brahmanic city, towering up above the surrounding buildings on the site of a once magnificent Hindoo temple which was torn

THE WINDOW OF MÂN MUNDER, BENARES.

down, by the order of Aurungzebe, to give place to the present graceful structure. We remained for an hour or more within the walls of this mosque, and came away charmed with the glistening mosaics, the capitals of the columns, the vaults, ceilings, and arches, and the thousand and one mysterious optical illusions of light and shade caused by the wonderous architecture of the Moslems. Our next visit was to the Hindoo Sanskrit College, the most famous institution of learning in Hindostan, and well worth seeing. The students often assemble here at sunrise, and even after sunset, to continue their studies, and in no part of India do I remember meeting so many noble-looking young Hindoos as were assembled in these halls on the morning of our visit.

From Benares we made a long and tedious dâhk-journey—*i. e.* by changing horses at different stations—to Agra, in the upper plains of India. The country we passed through was beautiful. The picturesque native villages of immemorial antiquity, their names, their fields, their hereditary offices and occupations, have come down to them out of a dim past and through countless generations, and everywhere we saw fields of millet and wheat, the flaming poppy, and the tall luscious sugar-cane plantations; cream-colored, dreamy-looking oxen moving sleepily about in the fields or drawing water from the wells and tanks; men, women, and children basking under the shade of huge trees or bathing languidly in the cool tanks, giving one the feeling of passing through dreamland.

The great sight of sights at Agra, as every one now knows, is the famous Taj-Mahal, and hither we repaired the morning after our arrival; and I must confess, though I had heard of it and read the many elaborate descriptions of it, I had no idea of its matchless beauty till I stood under its roof surrounded by its pillars and walls. It would take pages to describe the wonderful outlines of the windows, the ornaments of the walls, arches, domes, and minarets, or even the exquisite carvings and arabesques of a single frieze; so that I will not attempt here what has already been so often done. The impression left on the mind is very deep and solemn. When I first caught sight of the Taj through the noble gateway at the entrance to the grounds, I experienced feelings of mingled awe and wonder, which increased in proportion as we examined it more closely. Even the enormous platform on which the Taj stands is of white marble, inlaid with precious stones, and all the lower parts outside of the building are also most elaborately and tastefully carved. The dome is perfect in its proportions of pure white marble, with an exquisite minaret of gold. In the centre is the tomb of Noor Mahal, also called by her proper name, Mamtaz Mahal, the favorite wife and queen of Shah Jehan, built to her memory two centuries ago. Above the tomb is a mass of the most delicate inlaid work, and the screen-like wall which surrounds it is entirely composed of leaves and all sorts of flowers containing innumerable precious stones. The echoes of our voices produced the most wonderful reverberations, impossible to imagine or adequately describe. We visited the Taj also by moonlight, and found it a hundred-fold more enchanting. The gardens in which it stands are purely Oriental, and recalled to my mind many passages from the old Persian poets. There are lovely white marble fountains and tanks and promenades with inviting seats here and there for rest, while a profusion of fragrant flowers, shrubs, and the dark silent cypresses which stand like muffled mourners around the monument add a pathetic beauty to the lovely spot.

Having seen the Taj, there was nothing left to do but to return to the "Aviary" on Malabar Hill.

And now, as I close these brief sketches of life and travel in India, the romance, antiquity, the song, and story still stir the memory with the powerful enchantment of a land where all nature seems to lie dreaming in its glory of perpetual sunshine, warmth, and color.

THE END.